ADVANCE PRAISE FOR

Growing up on Facebook

"*Growing up on Facebook* is an insightful analysis of how the pioneers of social media live, curate and contest Facebook. This book exposes their engagement with networked publics, involving curated acts of presence and absence, connection and disconnection to archive the changing shape of young adulthood. With young people's reflections at the centre of their analysis, Brady Robards and Siân Lincoln's book sets new agendas for the study of social media and new questions for those interested in young people's lives."
—Johanna Wyn, Redmond Barry Distinguished Emeritus Professor, Youth Research Centre, The University of Melbourne

"Unlike generations which grew up *with* TV, radio, and movies, to grow up *on* Facebook means that one's life is sustained and somewhat enabled by a medium. This engaging book reveals what happens to human development as it is enveloped in the architecture of platforms. Brady Robards and Siân Lincoln offer remarkable insights on life, love and maintaining a sense of self while growing up, on Facebook and off."
—Zizi Papacharissi, Professor and Head of Communication, University of Illinois at Chicago

"A deeply nuanced look at the impacts of popular social media technologies. In a media environment dominated by breaking news and hot takes, *Growing up on Facebook* takes a serious examination of the longer-term effects of social media, looking at how young people's identities and relationships are constructed through and with the platform. Drawing from cutting-edge media theory and rich empirical data, the stories told by Brady Robards and Siân Lincoln reveal how we grapple with a platform that archives our most personal digital interactions."
—Alice E. Marwick, Assistant Professor, Department of Communication & Principal Researcher, Center for Information, Technology and Public Life, University of North Carolina, Chapel Hill

"How would it feel to be faced with your Facebook Timeline? By asking young people to reflect on their past and present selves, whether shown on or, significantly, often hidden from the platform, Brady Robards and Siân Lincoln insightfully peel back the contextual subtleties of identity work in the digital age."
—Sonia Livingstone, Professor of Social Psychology, Department of Media and Communications, London School of Economics and Political Science

Growing up on Facebook

Steve Jones
General Editor

Vol. 109

———————

The Digital Formations series is part of the Peter Lang Media and Communication list.
Every volume is peer reviewed and meets the highest
quality standards for content and production.

———————

PETER LANG
New York • Bern • Berlin
Brussels • Vienna • Oxford • Warsaw

Brady Robards and Siân Lincoln

Growing up on Facebook

PETER LANG
New York • Bern • Berlin
Brussels • Vienna • Oxford • Warsaw

Library of Congress Cataloging-in-Publication Data

Names: Robards, Brady, author. | Lincoln, Siân, author.
Title: Growing up on facebook / Brady Robards and Siân Lincoln.
Description: New York: Peter Lang, 2020.
Series: Digital formations, vol. 109 | ISSN 1526-3169
Includes bibliographical references and index.
Identifiers: LCCN 2019040516 | ISBN 978-1-4331-4275-8 (hardback: alk. paper)
ISBN 978-1-4331-4274-1 (paperback: alk. paper) | ISBN 978-1-4331-4276-5 (ebook pdf)
ISBN 978-1-4331-4277-2 (epub) | ISBN 978-1-4331-4278-9 (mobi)
Subjects: LCSH: Facebook (Electronic resource) | Social media—Social
aspects. | Internet and youth. | Youth—Social conditions.
Classification: LCC HM743.F33 R64 2020 | DDC 004.67/80835—dc23
LC record available at https://lccn.loc.gov/2019040516
DOI 10.3726/b16323

Bibliographic information published by **Die Deutsche Nationalbibliothek**.
Die Deutsche Nationalbibliothek lists this publication in the "Deutsche
Nationalbibliografie"; detailed bibliographic data are available
on the Internet at http://dnb.d-nb.de/.

The paper in this book meets the guidelines for permanence and durability
of the Committee on Production Guidelines for Book Longevity
of the Council of Library Resources.

© 2020 Peter Lang Publishing, Inc., New York
29 Broadway, 18th floor, New York, NY 10006
www.peterlang.com

All rights reserved.
Reprint or reproduction, even partially, in all forms such as microfilm,
xerography, microfiche, microcard, and offset strictly prohibited.

Printed in the United States of America

Contents

Acknowledgements	vii
Chapter One: Introduction	1
Chapter Two: Is Facebook Still Cool? Was It Ever?	13
Chapter Three: Sites and Spaces of Growing Up: Blurring the Digital and Physical	27
Chapter Four: Scrolling Back through Facebook Timelines: Making Sense of Digital Traces	51
Chapter Five: Shaping and Performing Professional Identities: From Education to Employment	77
Chapter Six: Love, and Making It 'Facebook Official'	101
Chapter Seven: Mediating Family Life	125
Chapter Eight: Documenting Leisure: Partying, Travel, Music, and Hanging Out	147
Chapter Nine: Disconnections, Absences, Conclusions	169
About the Authors	189
Index	191

Acknowledgements

Like all books, this book was only made possible by the efforts and contributions of more people than can be named on the front cover.

First and foremost, we would like to thank our participants. We spoke to 41 young people in Australia and the UK over the course of the project. Their words and insights have given this project substance and life, as they navigated nostalgia, embarrassment, and a few awkward moments as they scrolled back through their Facebook Timelines with us.

In the latter stages of the project, we were assisted by two colleagues—Benjamin Pinkard in Australia and Jane Harris in the UK—who worked with us to help with recruitment and to conduct a portion of the interviews. Thank you Ben and Jane. We acknowledge the University of Tasmania and Liverpool John Moores University for funding the initial data collection and some writing time and to our colleagues at these institutions for their support.

Brady would like to acknowledge Professor Andy Bennett, who supervised Brady's PhD, where some of the initial ideas and approaches later developed in the Facebook Timelines project were born. We are also both indebted to Andy for introducing the two of us, and starting us on this research partnership and friendship.

We thank and acknowledge our various academic communities who contributed to the intellectual development of the work by listening, asking questions, and pointing us in productive directions as we shared findings from the project along the way. We especially acknowledge the delegates at conferences hosted by the Association of Internet Researchers (AoIR), the Australian Sociological Association (TASA), and the Digital Intimacies symposia, where earlier manifestations of the ideas and findings in this book were presented. In particular, we want to acknowledge Paul Byron, Crystal Abidin, Kath Albury, Paul Hodkinson, Jean Burgess, Ben Light, Stefanie Duguay, Son Vivienne, Brendan Churchill, Ashleigh Watson, and Emma Kirby. The foundations of this book were borne out of a special issue of *New Media & Society* published in 2014 called '10 years of Facebook'. We got to work with a number of outstanding scholars when doing this issue and we thank them all for stellar contributions.

Finally, we are greatly indebted to the staff at Peter Lang. We thank our initial Acquisitions Editor Kathryn Harrison and then Erika Hendrix who guided us through the latter stages of the book. We are also greatly indebted to the Digital Formations Series Editor Steve Jones for supporting the idea and providing feedback as we went. Both Erika and Steve were obscenely patient with us as we asked for more extensions than we care to admit. Thank you!

Parts of Chapter Six 'Love, and making it "Facebook Official"' appeared in the form of a journal article published in *Social Media + Society* in 2016, volume 2, issue 4, under the title 'Making It "Facebook Official": Reflecting on Romantic Relationships Through Sustained Facebook Use'. We thank the editors and anonymous reviewers for their help in shaping the ideas in this chapter.

Brady dedicates this book to Luke Newman—his Facebook stalking powers are unmatched.

Siân dedicates this book to Yannis Tzioumakis & Roman Tzioumakis—with so much love.

CHAPTER ONE

Introduction

Brady is sitting across from Sarah, ready to interview her in her kitchen in a regional town in Tasmania, an island state off the south coast of Australia. The interview is about Facebook use over time among people in their twenties (Sarah is 28), but before it even begins, Brady and Sarah are talking about Sarah's home and her family. Sarah's dog jumps up on Brady, and they start talking about when Sarah first got the dog. Sarah instinctively and unprompted reaches for her phone, and scrolls back through her Facebook Timeline, to find and show Brady photos of the dog as a puppy. It is a gesture that is organic, in the moment, a reflex, but Sarah's instinctive reaching for Facebook as a memory prompt, and the performative act of showing, work as the perfect illustration for a key finding in our research: that Facebook has come to serve as not just an archive of digital traces of life, of stories of growing up, but also as a prompt for deeper and shared memory-work.

As part of the same research project, on the other side of the world, in Liverpool, a city in North West England, Siân sits in a cafe with Charlotte (20). As they scroll back through her Facebook Timeline together, Charlotte comes across a photo from a night out, taken and posted a couple of years ago when she was in her late teens. It is the first time she has seen the photo since it was posted, and while looking at it again brings back good memories it also presents questions around how this photo represents her now. In this moment, Charlotte is confronted by a younger version of herself, that has been traced onto Facebook and recorded by default into her now longitudinal social media history. Seeing the photo prompts her to consider its meaning as she embarks on her professional, career-focused future. Will this photo of her drinking and having a good time with friends look bad to a future employer? Or does it represent someone capable of having a good time and leading a balanced life? Should the photo remain on her Timeline or should it be deleted? Charlotte's reflections are thoughtful amidst many other reactions our participants in this book have to scrolling back through their digitally mediated personal histories with us: fond reflection, nostalgia, sadness, excitement, embarrassment, and ambivalence. What is it like to have 'grown up' in the era of social media?

When Mark Zuckerberg and Harvard classmates Eduado Saverin, Andrew McCollum, Dustin Moskovitz and Chris Hughes developed a website called thefacebook.com for fellow students to 'rate' and 'score' each other, little did they know that it would evolve into a platform and enormous corporation that would have a radical impact on how people connect, communicate, and indeed remember. A decade and a half on, Facebook continues to dominate the social media landscape, not just as a single platform but as a growing 'polymedia' (Madianou & Miller 2013) ecosystem of platforms including Instagram and WhatsApp. As of March 2019, Facebook claimed to have 1.56 billion daily active users and 2.38 billion monthly users (Facebook.com 2019). The site has changed the ways we communicate with each other and share information, it has challenged how we conceive of our identities, and broken down some traditional barriers of public and private lives in unprecedented ways. Facebook is in many ways pervasive, but at the same time is highly contested, with wide-reaching implications for privacy (Fuchs 2017), the flow of news and information, politics, power, and is embroiled in controversies that erode public trust.

As Facebook has grown and as users of the platform have 'grown up' alongside it, this book sets out to understand the sustained use of a social network site in the context of a broader and increasingly complex social media landscape. *Growing up on Facebook* draws on the experiences of 41 young people living in the United Kingdom and Australia who have grown up using Facebook, and other social media platforms that have emerged around it, documenting and sharing their lives: from the mundane and everyday, through to critical moments and key transitions. For our participants, their teenage years and early twenties have been marked out by use of and time spent on social media. By scrolling back with them through their own social media histories, we have come to learn much about the social media practices of young people, as well as the extent to which Facebook and other platforms play a role in their everyday lives and identities. Our research reveals how memories and personal histories are mediated through the site and the complex terrains of disclosure that young people navigate by being in networked publics, with different platforms involving different social, cultural and political contexts. We bring together a broad and growing body of research on social media with our own empirical work. Analysis of our research data has presented the following key questions that we aim to address in this book:

- What do young people's disclosure practices (what and how people say things on social media) look like and how have they changed over time? Related to this, what are their friending strategies and impression management processes, and how have these changed over time?
- What are the longer term implications of using a social media platform like Facebook in the context of memory and remembering?
- What are the implications for the ways users conceptualise privacy after reflecting on their longitudinal digital traces, through the Facebook Timeline?
- What is visible, and what is invisible on Facebook? Are the critical, fateful, and traumatic moments obscured or conspicuously absent on Facebook? What is left unsaid, or later erased?
- What are the challenges associated with 'growing up' on Facebook? What are the opportunities, the possibilities?

These questions have emerged from our *Facebook Timelines* project, a three-year study with 41 participants in their twenties who had been using Facebook for more than five years at the time of our interviews (see Chapter Four for a more detailed methodology). In 2014, we co-edited a special issue of the journal *New Media and Society* entitled '10 years of Facebook', to mark the tenth year of Facebook and to reflect critically on the social impact of the platform. The issue brought together a number of international scholars working on a variety of different aspects of Facebook, including how teenagers negotiate context in networked publics (Marwick & boyd 2014), the mobilisation of social capital on Facebook (Ellison, Gray, Lampe & Fiore 2014), Facebook use in urban India and associated gender dynamics (Kumar 2014), use among lesbian, gay, bisexual, transgender, and queer (referred to forthwith as LGBTQ+) people (Taylor, Falconer & Snowden 2014), Facebook's 'mobile career' (Goggin 2014), Facebook as a location-based social media platform (Wilken 2014), along with disuse and disconnection from Facebook (Light & Cassidy 2014), and more. This research inspired us to undertake our own study to specifically examine the *sustained* use of Facebook among young people over time. Working on this special issue confirmed to us that despite discourses of flight from the site (which we explore in Chapter Two), Facebook was still very much dominating the social media terrain and that much more could still be expected from the site; it was deeply embedded in users' lives and was likely to be for some time. Of course, since we started the project in 2014, much has changed for Facebook, and we begin to trace some of these controversies around public trust and changing attitudes towards Facebook in this book.

By 2014 it was evident that Facebook itself was curating its own 'growing up' narrative through a variety of design developments that capitalised on the longitudinal use of the platform, harnessing the way Facebook users had come to rely on it as a contact list, a photo album, and a personal record of life, bound up in nostalgia. For example, in 2011 Facebook moved from the profile to Timeline configuration, wherein disclosures from past years were much more readily accessed simply by clicking a year rather than having to load previous pages and scroll back with some effort (see Tufekci 2008 for an early consideration of social media disclosure practices). This change in the accessibility of past content 'tidied up' profiles on the one hand, but also led to concerns about how easily past disclosures could now be resurfaced and accessed. Prior to the Timeline iteration of the profile, posts from years prior were difficult to access, and would require a significant amount of 'digging' (scroll down, load more, scroll down, load more), which gave users a level of protection. The shift to the Timeline configuration allowed posts from the early years to be quickly resurfaced. This development was a not so subtle nod to Facebook's broader marketing strategies that aside from narratives of sharing and connectivity, Facebook was now capitalising on nostalgia and memory.

This trend continued through several other features. In 2012, Facebook rolled out the 'Year in Review' to algorithmically highlight certain posts, new friends, and images posted that year to summarise a year on Facebook back to users, but also to serve as a point of reflection and remembering. What this feature also emphasised was yet another year a user had spent on the site and the continued significance of it as a platform of connectivity. In 2014, to mark the site's tenth year, Facebook introduced the 'Look Back Video'. As with the year in review function, the look back videos algorithmically curated key disclosures—images, status updates, friendships—based on number of likes, comments, and so on, and then set a highlight reel of these disclosures to emotive music (for a longer description and analysis, see Robards 2014). Again, commonalities can be drawn between looking over old photo albums or scrapbooks, but the difference here is that these videos were not entirely created by the users themselves. Look back videos were co-constructed by friends (through tags) but also developers at Facebook, who craft the algorithms that do the curating. This 'co-constructed' performance of identity is a theme we will revisit throughout this book. Spiridonov and Bandaru (2014), engineers at Facebook, reported that 200 million users watched their look back videos (around half of all users at the time), and more than 50% of those that watched them shared these videos back to their networks.

More recently, Facebook introduced the 'Friendversary' whereby users 'celebrate' anniversaries with Facebook friends. However, not all friendships are celebrated, as Cassini Davies (2015) argues. As with the features outlined above, the Friendversary videos are created through algorithmic calculations based on likes, shares and comments that determine 'which of your online friendships are worthy of an anniversary' (Cassini Davies 2015). This presents some intriguing questions for us, on how Facebook *reads* friendship, and in turn how users incorporate Facebook's prompts (such as the friendversary) into their own memory-work and how they relate to their friends.

Perhaps most explicitly, Facebook's 'On This Day'/'Memories' function—which has now also been integrated into Instagram—highlights posts made on this day in years gone by. After the popularity of the third party application Timehop, Facebook rolled out the 'On This Day' function in 2015 to capitalise on the longitudinal use of the platform (Constine 2015). This function invites users to resurface previous disclosures, either by re-sharing old photos or posts to their own Timeline, or to send them to friends privately by Messenger. Taken together, all of these developments point to the ways in which Facebook has sought to capitalise on the sustained, longitudinal use of the platform, and our project was designed to study this very process.

Our *Facebook Timelines* project, which this book reports on, engages with the contextual circumstances of Facebook use and interrogates how relationships and identities are mediated through the site and with what consequences. According to Cassini Davies, one of the developers of the Friendversary feature described it as a way of capturing 'meaningful shared histories'. However, how meaning is interpreted into those histories is of significant interest to us when we consider the growing up narratives of young people on the site that are essentially mediated representations—and eventually memories—of growing up experiences as told by users and their friends. But how do these experiences connect to what happens in other realms off the site? In what ways do they become meaningful and in what sense? As we will demonstrate in this book, 'meaningful' disclosures are not always constructed within Zuckerberg's vision of the site as a platform of connectivity and friendship. Indeed, much of our data revealed how meanings of the same data could differ, leading to drama, break ups, and disconnection.

The Facebook Timelines Project

The Facebook Timelines project was designed to capture the many complexities that emerge from Facebook use over a sustained period of time. We were particularly interested in working with young people who were in their twenties in the mid-2010s, because they were the first generation to be able to truly say that have 'grown up' on Facebook. Born between the mid 80s to mid 90s, many in this group had a social media history as users of sites such as Friendster, Bebo and MySpace that predates Facebook (Robards 2010). In this respect, we are working with young people who 'pioneered' social media use, and from whom we can learn much about the role and significance of social media in everyday lives, cultures, and practices.

We employed a combination of in-depth qualitative interviewing and a method that we have termed the 'social media scroll back' (Robards & Lincoln 2017) which involved scrolling back with our participants through their Facebook Timelines. This allowed us to gain insights into how Facebook is embedded into the everyday experiences of young people from ordinary everyday activities like going out, hanging out with friends, and being with family, through to key critical moments and rites of passage, such as voting for the first time, graduating from high school, entering into (and exiting) first relationships, traveling alone for the first time, and entering into employment careers.

We placed our participants very much at the centre of our project, and we framed our participants as 'co-analysts' of their own digital traces. This methodology enabled us to understand the individual contexts in which disclosures were made. For many of our participants, Facebook has become a digital archive for experiences of transition (towards 'adulthood') and rites of passage, co-constructed and shared in 'networked publics' (boyd 2010). Enrolling our participants as co-analysts of their own digital traces meant they played an active role during the interviews in interpreting, explaining, and providing context for the disclosures we were looking at together. As we discuss in Chapter Three, we were not interested in analysing Facebook profiles in the abstract, without our participants being present (and indeed this would present some challenging ethical issues) nor do we draw data directly from Facebook profiles themselves. Rather, we were interested in the context that surrounds users' disclosures, particularly the context of growing up, and thus our participants were in the 'driving seat' throughout the process, navigating their way through their own digital traces. The data presented throughout this book, especially Chapters Five to Nine, draws on the discussions we had with participants as they scrolled back through their Timelines which allowed us not only to observe the text (Facebook) but also to observe the reactions of our participants as they confronted disclosures that in many cases they had not seen for a number of years. In order for us to understand the extent to which Facebook is embedded into the lives of its users, it was important for us to be able to understand the different types of 'labour' (Fuchs 2017) undertaken by our participants in their use of Facebook. For example, the 'backstage work'—to borrow from Goffman (1959)—that goes on before announcing a romantic relationship and making it

'Facebook Official' (Robards & Lincoln 2016; see Chapter Six) or the work that goes into re-kindling a friendship after an argument or falling out has occurred as a result of a post being 'taken out of context' (to use danah boyd's (2008) words). Our methodology has enabled us to understand the frameworks within which disclosures occur.

While we have published some of the findings from the Facebook Timelines project in shorter forms, for instance examining Facebook profiles as manifestations of Giddens' (1991) 'reflexive project of the self' (Lincoln & Robards 2017), and the mediation of romantic relationships on Facebook (Robards & Lincoln 2016), and the 'scroll back' method we used in this study (Robards & Lincoln 2017), this is the first time we have brought these findings together in long form. The book length has allowed us to explore fully the findings from this study, contextualised in a broad literature and through interview data that cover a range of arenas of young people's lives.

Outline of This Book

This book falls within a vibrant and rapidly-growing literature on Facebook and social media use more generally. We engage with much of this literature throughout the book, but with specific overviews in Chapters Two and Three. In Chapter Four we provide a more detailed summary of our approach in the *Facebook Timelines* project, before moving on to four substantive chapters examining what we describe as four 'arenas' of growing up: employment and education (Chapter Five), love and relationships (Chapter Six), family (Chapter Seven) and leisure (Chapter Eight). In Chapter Nine, we examine practices of disconnection, and also what was left unsaid in the substantive chapters.

As we note above, this study is among the first to explore the sustained use of social media by the first generation who have grown up using social media, documenting many aspects of their teenage years on it. This book is particularly concerned with the 'everyday' contexts within which Facebook is used and the extent to which everyday experiences, lives, and cultures play out in networked publics. In doing this we also contribute to a body of literature that explores everyday cultural practices in different contexts and indeed builds on our respective research backgrounds in youth culture and private space (Lincoln 2012) and in the formation and presentation of young people's identities on social media (Robards 2010, 2012). In exploring these everyday practices through qualitative research, the complexities of the minutiae are borne out and have informed the structure of this book. Below we describe each chapter in further detail, to help guide your reading of the book.

In the next chapter, Chapter Two, we ask: is Facebook still cool? Was it ever? This chapter is a response to suggestions of a dramatic flight from Facebook, and the argument that it is no longer relevant in studying young people's social media use or lives. Certainly, as we note in Chapter Two, a range of platforms have emerged around Facebook such that more young people are spending time on Instagram or Snapchat or TikTok or YouTube, and we take an explicitly 'polymedia' (Madianou & Miller 2013) approach in thinking through where Facebook sits in a constellation of social media platforms. However, as our research has revealed, Facebook is still very much at the centre of this social media landscape, and provides a useful prism to understand longitudinal social media use.

In Chapter Three—'Sites and spaces of growing Up: Blurring the digital and the physical'—we outline the broader context of the research, situating Facebook as a mediated site of everyday life and 'growing up' narratives. Whereas in previous scholarship around the internet, there has been a division between the 'online' and 'offline', we take a more contemporary approach, following key scholars (Marwick & boyd 2014; Vitak 2012; Duguay 2016) that point to the blurring and collapsing of previously imagined neat divisions between online and offline. Instead, we think about distinctions and blurring between digital and physical spaces. This chapter also situates Facebook use within a historical context, reflecting on changes in the way young people interact and socialise in digital social spaces. From Friendster and MySpace through to Snapchat and Instagram, we build on our understanding of the broader polymedia environment established in Chapter Two. In Chapter Three we also set up a range of key concepts and frameworks that we build on throughout the book, such as Giddens' (1991) reflexive project of self, Goffman's (1959) dramaturgical framework relating to the presentation of self, Livingstone's (2008) work on social media literacies, strategies of control (Hodkinson & Lincoln 2008; Lincoln & Robards 2017), and spatial metaphors of space, place and belonging used to make sense of young people's uses of social media (Hogan 2010; Day Good 2012; Lincoln 2012).

In Chapter Four—'Scrolling back through Facebook Timelines: making sense of digital traces'—we introduce the research design and methodology of the Facebook Timelines project, in which we explored sustained use (five or more years) of Facebook among young people (n = 41) in their twenties. As we will explain, by focusing on this group, we sought to uncover how 'growing up' stories have been told and archived, and how disclosure practices (what people say and share on social media) change over time. We question how we can understand the digital trace inscribed through the Facebook Timeline as a longitudinal narrative text. We introduce the notion of scrolling back through Facebook with our participants as co-analysts of their own digital traces as a productive way for better understanding how young people's lives are increasingly mediated and recorded in digital social spaces.

In Chapter Five—'Shaping and performing professional identities, from education to employment'—we explore the first of four significant arenas of life for our participants: the transition from education to employment. For our participants, many of whom were making crucial decisions about their futures, education and employment were recurrent themes as they reflected back on their Facebook Timelines. In this respect, our participants engaged in a process of self editing to better align their current aspirations with digital traces of their past selves. We argue that processes of reflexive ordering of narratives around employment represent a digital manifestation of what Giddens (1991) described as the reflexive project of self. Our participants described being told to prepare for potential employers searching for them online, producing anxieties around personal identities and pursuits colliding with professionals contexts. This led to participants engaging in a 'tidying' or 'cleaning' of their profiles in light of aspirations to project what they have internalised as appropriate professional identities. In this sense, Facebook Timelines serve not only to communicate a sense of self to others, but also act as texts of personal reflection and of growing up, subject to ongoing revision.

In Chapter Six—'Love, and making it "Facebook Official"'—we explore the second significant arena of life for our participants: romantic relationships. Going Facebook Official—changing your relationship status to 'in a relationship' and tagging your partner—has become a socially and culturally significant marker of progression in making romantic relationships visible and formalised. However, going Facebook Official can also be a contested process, fraught with drama and with repercussions associated with naming relationships in semi-public spaces. In drawing on our empirical work with participants, we discuss a range of different practices that our participants engaged in as they navigated romantic relationships on Facebook. We finish with a critique of the ways in which Facebook might work to produce normative relationship traces, privileging neat linearity, monogamy, and obfuscating (perhaps usefully, perhaps not) the messy complexity of romantic relationships.

In Chapter Seven—'Mediating Family Life'—we consider how Facebook has been taken up by all ages, and how the site has become more embedded into everyday life, becoming a space for family dynamics and connectivity. In this, our third empirical chapter, we consider the impact of wider inter-generational adoption of Facebook, which highlights mismatched conventions around disclosure practices, and how this produces context collapse, tension, and drama. Our data offer insights into both positive experiences of Facebook's role in mediating family life, but also points of trauma and disagreement in familial relations both on and off the site. Here, we return to concepts established earlier in the book around context collapse and social media literacies, examining how young people are inducted into Facebook often under the guidance of parents, friends, and older siblings. In scrolling back with our participants through their Facebook Timelines, complex and contested family lives were revealed, pointing not only to how families are mediated on Facebook, but also to the ways in which Facebook offers co-constructed narratives of family histories. In this sense, we consider what is often left unsaid on Facebook, whereby family dynamics inform how disclosures are made (or not).

In Chapter Eight—'Documenting leisure: travel, partying, and hanging out'—we discuss a fourth and final arena of life: leisure. Facebook serves as a crucial site for organising, recording, and later reflecting on a wide range of leisure pursuits. Our discussion encompasses alcohol consumption and nights out on the town, travel, and cultural pursuits like attending music festivals. We explain how documenting a night out on the town, for instance, is complicated by 'pedagogies of regret' (Brown & Gregg 2012) as young people are taught to reflect critically on how images and stories involving alcohol and other drugs might compromise future professional identities, bringing us full circle to our first empirical chapter, Chapter Five, on education and employment. We also contest the division between leisure and work in this chapter, pointing towards forms of labour that may be unpaid but also aspirational, with the potential to lead towards paid work in the future. Many creative occupations fall into this category (music, design, photography, videography, and so on), but so too have entire career trajectories emerged around the management of social media profiles, and the rise of social media influencers.

Finally, in Chapter Nine—'Disconnections, absences and conclusions'—we bring together the threads of the book and look outwardly to future challenges for Facebook and social media more broadly. If, as we have suggested throughout the book, Facebook has become an important archive of memory and experiences, to what standards should we hold it when it comes to privacy and how our data are used? In this chapter we examine practices of *dis*-connection, following Light's (2014; Light & Cassidy 2014) call for more attention to be paid to the ways in which people disconnect on and through social media. We look at instances of 'social media abstinence', discourses of restraint, and periods of account deactivation among our participants. In this chapter we also turn to two areas of current and future research that are important but that we have not attended to closely in the book directly: political engagement and mental health. We finish with some reflections on declining public trust in social media and what this means for Facebook as an archive of personal histories.

References

boyd, d. (2008). *Taken out of context: American teen sociality in networked publics*. University of California, Berkeley, PhD Thesis.

boyd, d. (2010). Social network sites as networked publics: Affordances, dynamics, and implications. In Zizi Papacharissi (Ed.), *A Networked self: Identity, community, and culture on social network sites*. New York: Routledge, pp. 39–58.

Brown, R., & Gregg, M. (2012). The pedagogy of regret: Facebook, binge drinking and young women. *Continuum*, *26*(3), 357–369.

Cassani Davies, L. The unexpected charm of Facebook's friendship anniversaries in The Atlantic, 11th November 2015 https://www.theatlantic.com/technology/archive/2015/11/the-virtue-of-the-facebook-friend-anniversary/415272/. Accessed March 7, 2017.

Constine, J. (2015). 'Facebook's Timehop Clone "On This Day" Shows You Your Posts From Years Ago', TechCrunch, https://techcrunch.com/2015/03/24/facehop/. Accessed August 8, 2019.

Day Good, K. (2012). From scrapbook to Facebook: A history of personal media assemblage and archives. *New Media & Society*, *15*(4), 557–573.

Duguay, S. (2016). "He has a way gayer Facebook than I do": Investigating sexual identity disclosure and context collapse on a social networking site. *New Media & Society*, *18*(6), 891–907.

Ellison, N. B., Gray, R., Lampe, C., & Fiore, A. T. (2014). Social capital and resource requests on Facebook. *New Media & Society*, *16*(7), 1104–1121.

Facebook.com, 'Company Info', https://newsroom.fb.com/company-info/. Accessed July 22, 2019.

Fuchs, C. (2017). *Social media: A critical introduction*. London: Sage.

Giddens, A. (1991). *Modernity and Self identity: Self and society in the late modern age*. Stanford: Stanford University Press.

Goffman, E. (1959). *The presentation of self in everyday life*. London: Penguin.

Goggin, G. (2014). Facebook's mobile career. *New Media & Society*, *16*(7), 1068–1086.

Hodkinson, P., & Lincoln, S. (2008). Online journals as virtual bedrooms?: Young people, identity and personal space. *YOUNG: Nordic Journal of Youth Research*, *16*(1), 27–46.

Hogan, B. (2010). The presentation of self in the age of social media: Distinguishing performances and exhibitions online. *Bulletin of Science, Technology & Society*, *30*(6), 377–386.

Kumar, N. (2014). Facebook for self-empowerment? A study of Facebook adoption in urban India. *New Media & Society*, *16*(7), 1122–1137.

Light, B. (2014). *Disconnecting with social networking sites*. Basingstoke: Palgrave Macmillan.

Light, B., & Cassidy, E. (2014). Strategies for the suspension and prevention of connection: Rendering disconnection as socioeconomic lubricant with Facebook. *New Media & Society*, *16*(7), 1169–1184.

Lincoln, S. (2012). *Youth culture and private space*. Basingstoke: Palgrave Macmillan.

Lincoln, S., & Robards, B. (2017). Editing the project of the self: Sustained Facebook use and growing up online. *Journal of Youth Studies, 20*(4), 518–531.

Livingstone, S. (2008). Taking risky opportunities in youthful content creation: Teenagers' use of social networking sites for intimacy, privacy and self expression. *New Media & Society 10*(3), 393–411.

Madianou, M., & Miller, D. (2013). Polymedia: Towards a new theory of digital media in interpersonal communication. *International Journal of Cultural Studies, 16*(2), 169–187.

Marwick, A. E., & boyd, d. (2014). Networked privacy: How teenagers negotiate context in social media. *New Media & Society, 16*(7), 1051–1067.

Robards, B. (2010). Randoms in my bedroom: Negotiating privacy and unsolicited contact on social network sites. *Prism, 7*(3), 1–12.

Robards, B. (2012). Leaving MySpace, joining Facebook: 'Growing up' on social network sites. *Continuum, 26*(3), 385–398.

Robards, B. (2014). Digital traces of the persona through ten years of Facebook. *M/C Journal, 17*(3), 1–6.

Robards, B., & Lincoln, S. (2016). Making it "Facebook official": Reflecting on romantic relationships through sustained Facebook use. *Social Media + Society, 2*(4), 2056305116672890.

Robards, B., & Lincoln, S. (2017). Uncovering longitudinal life narratives: Scrolling back on Facebook. *Qualitative Research, 17*(6), 715–730.

Spiridonov, A., & Bandaru, K. (2014) 'Looking back on "Look Back" videos', Facebook Engineering Blog, https://engineering.fb.com/core-data/looking-back-on-look-back-videos/. Accessed August 22, 2019.

Taylor, Y., Falconer, E., & Snowdon, R. (2014). Queer youth, Facebook and faith: Facebook methodologies and online identities. *New Media & Society, 16*(7), 1138–1153.

Tufekci, Z. (2008). Can you see me now? Audience and disclosure regulation in online social network sites. *Bulletin of Science, Technology & Society, 28*(1), 20–36.

Vitak, J. (2012). The impact of context collapse and privacy on social network site disclosures. *Journal of Broadcasting & Electronic Media, 56*(4), 451–470.

Wilken, R. (2014). Places nearby: Facebook as a location-based social media platform. *New Media & Society, 16*(7), 1087–1103.

CHAPTER TWO

Is Facebook Still Cool? Was It Ever?

Do people still use Facebook? Is it past it? Is it still cool with the kids? Yes, probably not, and no!

In 2018, Pew Internet Research—based on a survey of teens in the US—announced that Facebook was 'no longer the most popular online platform among teens' (Anderson & Jiang 2018). Many commentators used this as evidence of the platform's inevitable decline—if it's no longer being used by young people, surely it is doomed to fail. They likened the results to the decline of MySpace, and pointed to how quickly MySpace went 'south', reading Pew's survey results as evidence that 'teens don't think Facebook is worth their time any more' (Novak 2018). Others suggested teens were abandoning Facebook in 'dramatic numbers', even going as far as to suggest these results pointed to an 'existential threat' to Facebook (Solon 2018).

This narrative of a 'flight from Facebook' is not new. In 2013, Daniel Miller was already arguing that Facebook was 'so uncool', based on ethnographic work with teens in eight different countries from the UK to India and Brazil. Cannarella and Spechler (2014) went one step further to construct an epidemiological model of social networks to predict the decline of Facebook based on the decline of MySpace, as if the two platforms were the same.

And yet, despite all these discourses of flight and decline, Facebook is still central to the wider social media landscape, and arguably central to everyday understandings of the internet itself. Facebook invented modern understandings of 'social media', and continues to reinvent itself through redesigns and acquisitions (most notably, Instagram and WhatsApp). While the Pew data is interesting, it remains to be seen whether or not the teens of 2018 later go on to use Facebook more actively as they get older. From a more critical data privacy perspective, suggesting that Instagram has usurped Facebook among teens is also somewhat of a misnomer, as Facebook owns Instagram and therefore the two are interconnected.

To fully understand disuse, the very idea of 'Facebook use' also needs to be unpacked. Many of our own participants (who we introduce in later chapters) talked about 'not really using Facebook anymore', but then went on to talk about how Facebook was still very much part of their daily routine: scrolling through their Facebook newsfeeds in the morning, using Facebook Messenger to chat with friends (individually and in group chats), hanging out in closed groups, setting up study groups and organising group assignments, planning social lives, parties, concerts, and reading reviews of bars and restaurants. When they said they were 'not really using Facebook anymore', they meant they were not *posting* as much as they used to on their Timelines—not uploading as many pictures or making explicit status updates.

But certainly, they were still *using* the platform, just not in the ways they had previously, or in ways that involved explicit, visible disclosures to their own networks. They may take 'Facebook vacations' when they temporarily disable their profiles for a set period of time or simply choose to take time away from it (see Chapter Nine), but for our participants at least their profiles and Facebook more broadly holds too much data for them to completely abandon them. For our participants, Facebook is a rich archive of images, texts, links and contacts ('friends') that they will undoubtedly dip into again; it is a phone book, contacts list, photo album, even video diary of their lives. Additionally, as their parents and families adopted Facebook, and as Facebook became 'uncool' (largely because of its widespread adoption by older generations), their use changed, and so did the perception of Facebook itself (see Chapter Seven). Importantly for our work—and for this book—changes in use are explicitly linked to 'growing up' and developing a more 'mature', nuanced social media literacy.

In a blog written by a self-described 'actual teen' in 2015, Andrew Watts explains this ambivalence quite neatly:

> It's dead to us. Facebook is something we all got in middle school because it was cool but now is seen as an awkward family dinner party we can't really leave. It's weird and can even be annoying to have Facebook at times. That being said, if you don't have Facebook, that's even more weird and annoying.

This 'ambivalence' (Robards & Vromen 2015) towards Facebook helps to explain our argument that Facebook still occupies a central place in a social media landscape, perhaps even among teens who say they don't use it. The oscillation between Facebook being 'dead' and at the same time central to social life is paradoxical, bound up in judgements about taste and reputation alongside Facebook's enduring narratives of connection, community, and its capacity to archive lives. In academic research on the topic, the ambivalence around Facebook has been explained through a consideration of 'context collapse'.

Context Collapse

Part of developing a sense of identity comes in the form of building and rehearsing a biographical narrative that we communicate to others (Giddens 1991: 54). As Goffman (1959) would say, different 'regions' (or locations, stages, places) call for different versions of that autobiography. In a workplace context, we might introduce ourselves to new colleagues with some reference to our department or location or projects. On a first date, we might share our hobbies, and talk about favourite films or novels. When catching up with someone we haven't seen for many years, we might reconnect by quickly filling in major events or even telling stories about mutual friends from years gone by. In digital spaces, when we write the 'about me' section of a LinkedIn profile or a dating app or a Twitter biography, this can be more challenging, because we are not always sure who might be reading—the form of words may be rehearsed repeatedly before being posted. All of these 'recitals' of this biographical narrative hinge on what is appropriate in those spaces for the people we are with, or to continue with Goffman's (1959) dramaturgical framework, what is appropriate on those stages for those audiences. We will consider Goffman's dramaturgical framework in further detail in the following chapter as we critically engage with his ideas in our analysis of 'growing up' narratives on the Facebook Timeline. Moreover, Goffman's dramaturgical framework provides a useful model through which to understand the use of Facebook by our participants within the wider context of their lives. The framework enables us to take account of the multiple platforms (across digital and physical spaces) upon which they are performing identity and to make sense of the different contexts of performance. It helps us to see how participants' lives are mediated across different platforms and how the boundaries between them are built, navigated, managed, or collapsed down by users.

Marwick and boyd (2011: 115) have pointed out that 'the need for variable self-presentation is complicated by increasingly mainstream social media technologies that collapse multiple contexts and bring together commonly distinct audiences'. What is an 'appropriate' presentation of self in one context (like in a bar with friends or playing *Cards Against Humanity*) might be completely inappropriate in another context (like in a church or at a job interview). In physical spaces, we have boundaries like walls and doors and distance to mediate these different regions. Goffman (1959) spoke of the significance of these physical boundaries, giving the vivid example of the kitchen door in a restaurant. Seemingly just a partition between 'front of house' and the 'backstage' kitchen, this door is highly significant in relation to performance. For a waiter working 'front of house', they are expected to 'perform' professionally, inline with the restaurant's reputation and ethos, caring for customers and ensuring a pleasant dining experience. As they push the door into the kitchen, this facade can change, with the waiter engaging in banter with kitchen staff, maybe venting about difficult customers, only to regain their professional poise as they re-enter the restaurant. In this example, the physical boundaries provide guidance and structure on social etiquette and expectations, even if front and back stage may momentarily merge (for example as the kitchen door opens and the chef is shouting, overheard by customers).

In digital spaces like Facebook, however, we can potentially be interacting with a range of different groups of people in a single space: friends from high school that we haven't seen for years, past lovers, potential employers, family, and close friends. This context collapse creates an awkward 'performative context', where it can be challenging to determine what an 'authentic' (Marwick and boyd 2011: 124) presentation of self might look like. This is one source of the ambivalence young people feel towards Facebook, captured in the Andrew Watts 'dead but must have' paradox.

Vitak (2012) suggests that context collapse also has its uses, and is perhaps a key feature of some social media platforms. Having many different contacts and friends in one place—such as on Facebook—can make it easy to widely disseminate important news quickly. For example, announcing the birth of a child or organising a rally. On the other hand, Vitak observes (aligning with Marwick and boyd 2011), context collapse on social media also 'makes it more difficult for individuals to vary self-presentation by audience' (Vitak 2012: 465). As a potential solution to this, Vitak points to some of Facebook's more granular sharing features, whereby users can post certain disclosures to specific 'Friends Lists'. For example, if you wanted to share a photo of your child only with family, you might set up a Friends List that only included family members. To put a call out to see if anyone wanted to join you for a music festival, you may have a Friends List that contains only your closest friends. In these ways, users are able to reinscribe boundaries around collapsed contexts. Vitak found that although using these features did require a greater investment of time, they tended to produce more 'honest ... intimate ... and sincere' (2012: 466) disclosures from users. In the years since Vitak's study, closed groups and group IM (Instant Messenger) chats have come to serve a similar although sometimes more narrow and deliberate function.

Duguay (2014) interviewed young lesbian, gay, bisexual, trans, and queer (LGBTQ) young people (n = 27) to study context collapse. She found that her participants engaged in a range of strategies for managing context on Facebook, including ambiguity. Duguay's conceptualisation of ambiguity aligns with boyd and Marwick's (2011) notion of 'social steganography', where social media users hide messages in plain sight. For instance, Duguay describes her participants William and Talan who were not out as gay to their families, but had posts on their Facebook Timelines that hinted at their sexuality. For William, a photoshopped picture of him marrying the lead singer of a boy band, and for Talan, a photo of him in drag. For friends who knew William and Talan, the messages here were clear, but for family members who did not know they were gay, the message was more ambiguous. In this way, context collapse is managed through social processes of distance and familiarity to control cultural messages.

Duguay (2014) also found some participants using the more nuanced sharing and privacy settings that Vitak (2012) studied. For instance, one of Duguay's participants, Kyle, explained that 'If I stop talking to someone, they'll slowly go down in privacy settings', suggesting a hierarchy of access based on frequency of contact. Kyle went on to explain that 'eventually, if I think that there's no point in me having them on Facebook, they go' (Duguay 2014: 902). There is a lot of effort involved in this kind of management of privacy, however, and as Duguay observes, many of her other participants were 'frustrated by Facebook's labyrinth of privacy settings' (2014: 902). The effort involved in managing context in Kyle's example, points to the stark differences between presenting one's self in physical spaces where the default mode of utterance is ephemeral, versus digital spaces where the default is persistent. Although, with the rise of ephemeral social media such as Snapchat and Instagram stories, this paradigm is shifting again.

Of course, users of social media have become accustomed to this context collapse over the years as social media has entered into the domain of everyday life, and as people have developed conventions for being in digital social spaces, with young people often in the 'vanguard' (Livingstone 2008: 394) of forging those conventions: who to friend, what to post, how to respond, and how to represent one's self. Context collapse is precisely one of the explanations as to why Facebook is no longer considered 'cool', and why its uptake among teenagers in particular appears to be dropping off (Anderson & Jiang 2018). As we discuss further in Chapter Seven, our own participants explain how being friends on Facebook with parents and older relatives can create uncomfortable tensions or at the very least shape the disclosures they make on Facebook. At the same time, however, we also have participants that relish the familial connections Facebook affords, even if that 'imagined audience' limits what they might otherwise post.

To find ways around this experience of context collapse, social media users have diversified the platforms they use. While Facebook might continue to be a central platform, used for a range of functions (including closed groups, messaging, events, product and service reviews, etc.) other platforms have emerged around it: Snapchat, Instagram, Tumblr, Twitter, Reddit, and dating apps like Tinder, Grindr, Her, and so on. This diversification of platforms is described by Madianou and Miller (2012: 170) as 'polymedia', a term which captures 'an emerging environment of communicative opportunities'. Madianou and Miller argue that taking a polymedia approach—attending to 'new media as an environment of affordances' (2012: 170)—allows researchers to look beyond individual platforms to instead consider the 'social and emotional consequences of choosing between those different media' (2012: 170).

In a book called 'Growing up on Facebook', we might appear to be taking a decidedly 'mono-media' approach. While we are focussing on Facebook, and as we will explain the Facebook Timeline became our primary focus during interviews, it also became clear to us over the course of our study that Facebook does not sit alone in a social media landscape. Indeed, it is much more productively understood as part of a wider social media ecology. The obvious examples are Facebook's 2012 one billion dollar acquisition of Instagram, and its 2014 19 billion dollar acquisition of WhatsApp. Indeed, our participants talk about boundary work between Facebook and Instagram, and explain how they often cross-post from Instagram to Facebook, or how they might screenshot a Snapchat message and then post that to Facebook. The more nuanced examples of polymedia, however, are in how our participants talk about moving across platforms based on their affordances and contexts (or in Goffman's dramaturgical framework, 'audiences').

For example, a connection between two people might begin on a hook-up app like Grindr. The conversation might move on to Snapchat to get around the wider visibility and presence that being 'online' affords on Grindr. These two people might meet in-person, and then become friends on Facebook. Facebook reveals a historical perspective—a longitudinal narrative of digital traces that we explore in this book—that Snapchat does not have. The pair may also follow each other on Instagram, and regularly watch each others' daily stories. In this example, each form of digital media affords a different set of connections and contexts. While our focus in this book is on Facebook, we acknowledge—and don't shy away from—the broader, more nuanced and complex polymedia landscape Facebook sits within.

Indeed, the polymedia approach helps us understand experiences of ambivalence towards Facebook that our participants describe. That said, it is also important to note that this book captures a very specific—and unprecedented—critical moment in time, that is, the first time that we have ever been able to talk about the significance of a single social network site and long term use of it for young people. As we will explore in more detail in Chapter Four, one of the reasons we chose to work with young people in their twenties was because they had joined the site in their early teens. For a significant proportion of them, this meant they had joined Facebook in its very early days. In this context, *graduation from one site to another* was the norm with other versions of social network sites such as MySpace being tossed by the wayside rather than being used *in conjunction with* Facebook: one site replaced another for the majority of our participants (Robards 2012). As we explain later on in this book, participants' stories of these 'graduations' and transitions from one site to another, who then eventually build a 'suite' of social network sites as more become available, also provides a history of social media and its embeddedness in everyday life, as told through the narratives of young people in the 'vanguard' (Livingstone 2008) of these developments. In this respect, a focus on this one social network site is vital.

This brings us part of the way to understanding whether Facebook is 'cool' or not. Our discussion above suggests that no, it is not, often because of context collapse and polymedia affordances. However, a more historical framing is perhaps useful here to understand the cultural shifts around Facebook, particularly reflecting upon Facebook's in-site developments, for example, the move from the profile to the Timeline, look back videos, friendversaries, and so on. As we argue, these developments do not really draw explicitly on 'narratives of cool' but rather necessity. So what might be going on here? To what extent was this actually clever marketing that worked with themes of 'connection' and 'community', then later 'archiving of the self' and the preservation of life narratives? In order to answer these questions, we need to look back 15 years to Facebook's beginnings.

Dorm Rooms and In-Groups

The history of Facebook from an in-house social networking site for Harvard University students to a global phenomenon is well-versed, but a brief look back at its origins and rapid ascent provides an important historical framing when considering its case as a 'site of cool'. 'The Facebook' as it was originally called, was based on the paper profiles that students and staff would fill in at the start of the academic year taking a traditional 'freshman' practice online. As reported in *The*

Guardian 'within 24 hours, 1,200 Harvard students had signed up, and after one month, over half of the graduate population had a profile'. This rapid uptake clearly signifies something 'cool', which undoubtedly was linked to the unprecedented access that students had through the site to other student profiles. Within the same year, the network was rolled out eventually to all US universities. This happened hierarchically with the roll out taking place first in Boston, then to other Ivy League Universities, then all universities in the US, arguably an implicitly cool, yet prestige-ladened approach to the roll out. The site was renamed Facebook.com in 2005 while the site continued to be rolled out to US high schools then into UK universities before becoming accessible 'to anyone with an email address'. Since then, uptake has been phenomenal with 2.27 billion active users as of the third quarter of 2018 (www.statista.com). As we argue above, stories of flight from Facebook are common and have been for some time, yet official figures show that despite varying degrees of use that we also evidence in this book, Facebook is still very much embedded into everyday lives and it is this "embeddedness" that is particularly interesting to us as we consider the extent to which Facebook is—or ever was—cool.

Narratives of "cool"?

In February 2016 Facebook celebrated its thirteenth birthday. In a post made on the day, founder and CEO Mark Zuckerberg set out his vision for the future of the site using words such as friendship, connect, communities, safety, information; clearly reflecting the ethos of Facebook while emphasising that the site is at the heart of connecting people in everyday life. The post begins:

> Today is Facebook's 13th birthday.
>
> We take this moment to reflect on friendship and bringing people together. The world needs more of that right now.
>
> Lately I've been reflecting on how we can do more to bring people together. We've mostly focused on connecting you with friends and family so far. Friendship is one of the greatest sources of meaning and happiness in our lives. But there is more we must build to help people come together. (Zuckerberg, Facebook post, Saturday 4th February, 2017).

Zuckerberg's promise to do more to 'help people come together' brings forth the core philosophy of the site which is ostensibly about connecting people; bringing people from across the globe into one place. As can be noted in the very early history of Facebook, the site has always claimed to be about connection and this has remained the core of its business ever since.

When talking about their initial motivation to sign up to Facebook, the majority of our participants described it as being 'the cool thing to do' and 'what everyone else was doing at the time'. Like many popular fads and trends, Facebook became *the* place to be, while alongside this, we consistently heard stories of participants 'graduating' to the site (from MySpace, for instance) in conjunction with key transitions such as going to high school or starting university. In this respect, joining Facebook offered our participants a marker of their maturing lives and moves towards being a young person well-established in their teens.

In the early days of Facebook it was undoubtedly cool: it was new, novel, there was a real buzz around it and people were signing up for Facebook profiles at unprecedented levels: the site had 12 million active users in December 2006, 58 million active users by December 2007 and 360 million active users by December 2008 (www.newsroom.fb.com). While other social network sites such as Bebo and MySpace existed and had enjoyed some popularity and success, the social media landscape looked very different to how it looked a decade later. As one of the few social network sites in existence—and as a site doing things a little differently to its predecessors—Facebook was novel and exciting in a number of ways. It promoted 'connection' as being at the heart of the Facebook community, and moreover, connecting with existing networks of people. This was rather different from previous social media, such as Friendster and MySpace, that were about making social connections visible; performing social capital. The 'connection' approach adopted by Facebook was undoubtedly attractive for potential young users who, like our participants, were also embarking on a significant life change when moving to high school and beyond. Facebook offered them an opportunity to stay in touch with friends and peers who may have moved to another school, while enabling them to connect with new friends in different schools and workplaces.

Facebook offered a platform through which interactions and socialising with friends could be continued outside of the classroom or lecture hall via the message feature, writing on friends' walls, or using functions such as 'poking' other users. Unlike MySpace, the interface was fairly generic but slick. The move to Facebook marked a visual shift away from the teenage bedroom-like aesthetic of MySpace, representing a more mature confident image of self. The content that Facebook could handle, in terms of uploading and displaying larger albums of photos, was also enabled by improved technologies and connections such as the move from dial-up to high-speed connections. It was more interesting than chatting on MSN and ICQ because you could share details about yourself including your favourite films, books, music, your political beliefs, relationship status and sexual orientation.

You could 'become a fan' of different groups, celebrities, and movements. Much like MySpace you could 'add' friends but the emphasis was much more on being friends with people you already knew and managing a 'real' profile, using real names. The move to commonly using real names on the internet was a significant shift caused by Facebook. In this way, it could be described as cool because it was promoting an authentic self (at least in essence) and presenting the idea of a social network site as an *extension* of the existing you rather than another version of it, a theme underlined in Zuckerberg's emphatic comments that you have one identity and to have more 'lacks integrity' (Kirkpatrick 2011, p.198) which we explore later in the book.

Facebook as a company has been very proactive in capitalising on the ways in which users engage with the site but we would argue that the notion of 'cool' (or uncool) relates more to how the site has been *used* rather than how the site has been *developed*. We can take four key developments on Facebook to consider how narratives of connection are favored over narratives of cool, namely the Timeline (2011), Year in Review (2012) the Look Back videos (2014) and Friends Day videos (2017). A focus on the 'sustained', 'longitudinal' use of Facebook has become central to the company's own operating model, reflecting how the site was never simply a 'fad'. In 2011, the 'Timeline' iteration of the Facebook profile was introduced, a feature that neatly archives all available posts by year visibly representing a chronological de-compartmentalising of users lives year on year. In 2012, Facebook introduced the 'year in review' feature that enabled users to create a series of 'highlights' from the previous year based on the number of 'likes' determining the most popular posts, images, videos and so on. In 2014 and in line with their tenth birthday celebrations, Facebook developed the 'look back video' a feature that enabled users to take a nostalgic look back over the last decade of their lives as articulated on Facebook.

The Friends Day videos produced by Facebook to celebrate their birthday similarly continued this discourse. The personalised videos, much like the Lookback videos created for Facebook's tenth birthday were generated algorithmically drawing on the number of comments and likes on past disclosures, and on predicting who your 'closest friends' are on Facebook. The video that appeared at the top of every users' newsfeed in the days leading up to the birthday, could be edited before being shared with friends. In addition to the video, a button on the bottom of Facebook Messenger enabled users to share images and GIFs that centred around the theme of friendship that they could then send in a personal message to their friends as a symbol of their appreciation for them. Taken together, these functions clearly promote Zuckerberg's vision for the future: that connection and friendship are key to modern, civic society. However, as Light (2014) argues 'although Mark

Zuckerberg publicly advocates particular social network site (SNS) ideals (such as connectivity), there is no guarantee that these will always come into being or unfold in the ways they were expected to' (1172).

If narratives of cool are not explicitly embedded in site development as a way to advertise, then where do these narratives of cool play out? We would argue that they are primarily found in use, and therefore we briefly turn our attention to how narratives of 'cool' have shifted for users, and especially for our participants before developing some of these themes in our later empirical chapters.

In the Facebook Timelines project we were interested in working with young people in their twenties because they would have been in their early teens when they first joined the site. As the site has grown, so too have our participants, and much like the teenagers using it, Facebook was also finding its feet during this time. The teenage years signal a period of change marked by physical, emotional, psychological changes, embarking upon major transitions such as undertaking important exams, entering into the world of work, leaving home, beginning sexual relationships and so on. Although, we should note, as many scholars have, that these transitions are often by no means linear (see for example: Furlong & Cartmel 1997; Furlong 2009; MacDonald & Marsh 2005; MacDonald 2011, 2016; Woodman 2012; Woodman 2013: 429; Woodman & Wyn 2015). It Is a period when young people shift from being dependant on their parents to becoming more independent, even challenging what they have been taught by adults up to this point.

Was It Ever Cool?

We started this chapter with three questions: Do people still use Facebook? Is it past it? Is it still cool with the kids? Respectively, our answers are: Yes, probably not, and no! As a site offering users a way to connect that people had never experienced before inevitably gave Facebook a 'cool' status in the early years. It rapidly became the place to be, there was a thrill in being able to track down old friends and connect with new ones, to share feelings and thoughts, to profile the self on one's own terms, and to share a personal life narrative. Facebook's rapid growth is testament to its popularity, and as we mention above at this point Facebook had very little competition once the critical mass of users moved off MySpace. Facebook of course, was not just picked up by a young demographic. While indeed registered users were below 24 years old in the main at the outset, it gradually expanded to being adopted by every age group. We discuss the data around this expansion in more detail in Chapter Seven. As we have outlined here, this led to an inevitable clash of contexts, with young people feeling surveilled by parents, aunts and uncles, even grandparents. This suggests that Facebook was a cool site for our participants in the early days of engaging with friends, but the increased presence of family members using the site has shifted Facebook's status to 'cool once'.

Being cool, being seen, finding one's own boundaries with privacy, contemplating futures, negotiating family and friends are all critical parts of youth and growing up. This book provides an insight into how this has played out for our own young participants, through the lens of Facebook. Indeed, their own navigations of 'cool' can be mapped on to Facebook's own evolution and growth, as we will explore.

References

Anderson, M., & Jiang, J. (2018). 'Teens, Social Media & Technology 2018', *Pew Internet Research*, available online: http://www.pewinternet.org/2018/05/31/teens-social-media-technology-2018/.Accessed July 26, 2018.

Cannarella, J., & Spechler, J. A. (2014). Epidemiological modeling of online social network dynamics. arXiv preprint arXiv:1401.4208.

Duguay, S. (2014). "He has a way gayer Facebook than I do": Investigating sexual identity disclosure and context collapse on a social networking site. *New Media & Society*, *18*(6), 891–907. http://doi.org/10.1177/1461444814549930.

Furlong, A. (2009). *Handbook of youth and young adulthood: New perspectives and agendas.* London: Routledge.

Furlong, A., & Cartmel, F. (1997). Risk and uncertainty in youth transition. *YOUNG: Nordic Journal of Youth Research*, *5*(1), 3–20.

Giddens, A. (1991). *Modernity and self identity: Self and society in the late modern age.* Cambridge: Polity Press.

Goffman, E. (1959). *The presentation of self in everyday life.* London: Penguin.

Kirkpatrick, D. (2011). *The Facebook effect: The inside story of the company that is connecting the world.* New York: Simon and Schuster.

Light, B. (2014). *Disconnecting with social networking sites.* Basingstoke: Palgrave Macmillan.

Livingstone, S. (2008). Taking risky opportunities in youthful content creation: Teenagers' use of social networking sites for intimacy, privacy and self-expression. *New Media & Society*, *10*(3), 393–411.

MacDonald, R. (2011). Youth transitions, unemployment and underemployment: Plus ca change, plus c'est meme chose? *Journal of Sociology*, *47*(4), 427–444.

MacDonald, R. (2016). Precarious work: The growing precarite of youth. In A. Furlong (Ed.), *Routledge handbook of youth and young adulthood.* London: Routledge.

MacDonald, R., & Marsh, J. (2005). *Disconnected youth? Growing up in Britain's poor neighbourhoods.* Basingstoke: Palgrave Macmillan.

Madianou, M., & Miller, D. (2012). Polymedia: Towards a new theory of digital media in interpersonal communication. *International Journal of Cultural Studies*, *16*(2), 169–187. http://doi.org/10.1177/1367877912452486.

Marwick, A. E., & boyd, d. (2011). I tweet honestly, I tweet passionately: Twitter users, context collapse, and the imagined audience. *New Media & Society*, *13*(1), 114–133. http://doi.org/10.1177/1461444810365313.

Miller, D. (2013). 'Facebook's so uncool, but it's morphing into a different beast'. *The Conversation*, available online: https://theconversation.com/facebooks-so-uncool-but-its-morphing-into-a-different-beast-21548. Accessed July 26, 2018.

Novak, M. (2018). Facebook officially less popular with American teens than Instagram and Snapchat. *Gizmodo*, available online: https://www.gizmodo.com.au/2018/06/facebook-officially-less-popular-with-american-teens-than-instagram-and-snapchat/. Accessed July 26, 2018.

Robards, B. (2012). Leaving MySpace, joining Facebook: "Growing up" on social network sites. *Continuum*, *26*(3), 385–398. http://doi.org/10.1080/10304312.2012.665836.

Robards, B., & Vromen, A. (2015). Logging out? Why young people love to hate Facebook. *The Conversation*, available online: https://theconversation.com/logging-out-why-young-people-love-to-hate-facebook/. Accessed August 29, 2019.

Solon, O. (2018). Teens are abandoning Facebook in dramatic numbers, study finds. *The Guardian*, available online: https://www.theguardian.com/technology/2018/jun/01/facebook-teens-leaving-instagram-snapchat-study-user-numbers. Accessed July 26, 2018.

Vitak, J. (2012). The impact of context collapse and privacy on social network site disclosures. *Journal of Broadcasting & Electronic Media*, *56*(4), 451–470. http://doi.org/10.1080/08838151.2012.732140

Watts, A. (2015). A teenager's view on social media, *Medium*, https://medium.com/backchannel/a-teenagers-view-on-social-media-1df945c09ac6. Accessed September 3, 2019.

Woodman, D. (2012). Life out of synch: How new patterns of further education and the rise of precarious employment are reshaping young people's relationships. *Sociology*, *46*(6), 1074–1090.

Woodman, D. (2013). Young people's friendships in the context of non-standard work patterns. *The Economic and Labour Relations Review*, *24*(3), 416–432.

Woodman, D., & Wyn, J. (2015). *Youth and generation: Rethinking change and inequality in the lives of young people*. London: Sage.

CHAPTER THREE

Sites and Spaces of Growing Up: Blurring the Digital and Physical

> Young people have always devoted attention to the presentation of self. Friendships have always been made, displayed and broken. Strangers—unknown, weird or frightening—have always hovered on the edge of the group, and often, adult onlookers have been puzzled by youthful peer practices. Yet the recent explosion in online social networking sites such as MySpace, Facebook, Bebo and others has attracted considerable interest from the academy, policymakers, parents and young people themselves, the repeated claim being that something new is taking place. What, then, is distinctive about the youthful construction of self and peer relations, now that this is mediated increasingly by social networking sites?
>
> (Livingstone 2008: 394)

Writing more than a decade ago, many of Livingstone's observations and questions are still applicable and insightful at the time of our own writing. In discussing the rise of social network sites, led by a 'vanguard' of the young, Livingstone reflects here upon the importance of identity-work for young people. She describes this 'explosion' in the popularity of social network sites as being bound up in a devotion young people exhibit towards presenting themselves. In Buckingham's terms, the identity-work going on in these spaces is being done by young people 'as social actors in their own right, as "beings," and not simply as "becomings"' (Buckingham 2008: 19). Crucially, for us in this book, this 'youthful construction of self' (Livingstone 2008: 394) is a key part of growing up. *Growing up on Facebook*, then, is about how identities are constructed—or more accurately, co-constructed. The question we paused on in the quote above from Livingstone is a question that many researchers over the last decade (and longer, before Livingstone posed the question in this way) have worked to answer, and indeed a question that has been part of our own project.

In the last chapter, we started to examine the work of other researchers including Marwick and boyd (2011), Vitak (2012), Madianou and Miller (2012), and Duguay (2014). Before we embark more fully on the data and stories from our own study in the following chapter, in this chapter we want to continue with the threads from the previous chapter to provide an overview of the work done to date to answer this question about how young people construct self and peer relations through social media. We also want to go back even further, to set up the framework of identity that underpins subsequent chapters.

Online, Offline, and Digital Dualisms

Rather than setting out to locate a particular distinction between the forms of identity construction and performance that occur 'online' and those that occur 'offline', like many scholars working in this area, we have found it more useful to understand these forms of sociality, these modes of being, as so deeply interrelated that it is possible to envisage a position from which no such distinction exists. When people speak of 'talking to' friends today, they might mean in-person over coffee, by Skype while they are folding laundry, 'on the phone' while walking the dog, by SMS text message during a long meeting, in text layered over unflattering selfies exchanged on Snapchat, or in a group chat on Facebook late at night. The physical and digital are enmeshed in each of these examples, with various experiences of co-presence shared between a range of actors.

In places where internet access and social media use is ubiquitous, many young people now grow up in these enmeshed contexts, where digital and physical are blurred. So to say someone 'went online' to do something, to talk to someone, to find information, is becoming (if it isn't already) somewhat anachronistic. The title of this very book is indeed a nod to that anachronism.

The online/offline distinction, most problematically, is also the root cause of what Jurgensen calls 'digital dualism' (2011). 'Digital dualists', Jurgensen suggests, 'believe that the digital world is "virtual" and the physical world "real" (2011, para. 2). This dualism minimises and even disregards the meaningful and very *real* effects of digitally mediated connection: from a 'tap' on Grindr indicating someone on the app finds you hot, to reassuring daily check-ins a child might send their parents on

Facebook while on their first trip abroad, through to the overwhelming sense of joy one might experience at seeing the first photos a long term friend posts of their new baby on Instagram, or the heartbreak one might experience after receiving an email relaying the news of the death of an old colleague. All of these examples point to the very real and powerfully affective implications of digital connection, that we might see on screens and hear through speakers, but that we experience physiologically, in our bodies.

Jurgensen goes on to explain that one of the clearest examples of digital dualism resides in a dominant discourse that 'the problem with social media is that people are trading the rich, physical and real nature of face-to-face contact for the digital, virtual and trivial quality of Facebook' (2011, para. 6). This discourse is evident in a range of articles and guides in the popular press, intended to help people engage in a social media detox or to connect with 'real friends', but this dualism is also present in more academic writing, including Sherry Turkle's (2011) book *Alone Together*, and Evgeny Morozov's *The Net Delusion* (2011).

We seek to embrace the blurring of the digital and physical. To do this though, we must also interrogate the ways in which digital spaces raise new opportunities and challenges for young people whose experiences of growing up are mediated through digital platforms. Or, if not altogether *new* opportunities and challenges, at least reconfigured permutations of existing ones. One example that we will explore further in Chapter Five, is reputation, and in particular how reputation and professional identity might be managed in the context of employment and careers. Maintaining a sense of reputation—a story about one's self—is important, especially when it comes to finding work. Digital traces, such as photos, status updates, comments, and so on, are often persistent by default, sharable, 'screenshotable', and easily recontextualised. This has contributed to a powerful moral panic around the risks of sexting, for instance, that intersect with discussions of reputation, experienced especially unevenly for young women when it comes to reputational harm, slut shaming, and impact on future employment and relationships (Hasinoff 2015; Dobson & Ringrose 2015). As a counterpoint to this, there are also opportunities afforded by digital media, such as how Instagram might be used as a professional portfolio of work for a creative artist who can demonstrate appeal to an employer through a large following (on internet celebrity and microcelebrity, see Abidin & Brown 2018) or how people might leverage professional networks on a site like LinkedIn (van Dijck 2013).

We will return to these tensions between opportunities and challenges associated with 'growing up on Facebook' throughout the book. In the following sections we map out our approach to impression management, self-presentation, and identity; themes that are foundational and that we develop further in forthcoming chapters using our research data.

Impression Management and the Presentation of Self

Growing up, and telling the story of growing up, involves 'impression management'. That is, shaping how other people perceive you. We do this through the clothes we wear, the way we speak, the culture we consume, the people we spend time with, and in the last few decades, the ways we use the internet. As one of the first scholars to study social network sites in detail, boyd (2007) observed that 'by early 2006, many considered participation on the key social network site, MySpace, essential to being seen as *cool* at school' (emphasis original, 2007: 1). As we discussed in the previous chapter, much has changed in more than a decade since MySpace was the social media platform of choice, but the presentation of self in digital spaces continues to be an important element of modern impression management.

To understand impression management and how young people enact and make visible 'growing up stories' in digital spaces, it is important to understand impression management and processes around self presentation from a broader perspective. The conceptual work done by others around impression maintenance, symbolic control, and the idealised presentation of self can often be carried over to the identity-work being done 'on the internet'. Despite the focus on new forms of identity mediation in the digital era, identities and belongings have always been mediated: by bodies, by language, by social structures, by culture. The 'explosion' of investment in social network sites, flagged by Livingstone in the opening quote, is also at the core of what this book works to document and frame as a new medium in which identities and systems of belonging can be reflexively articulated, made visible, and acted upon.

In the remainder of this chapter, we seek to develop a framework for identity that can be translated to the forms of sociality that take place on social media. In achieving this goal, this chapter is divided into three sections. First, we develop an understanding of identity as 'always-already' mediated and situated. We also consider the role social network sites play in disturbing or reconfiguring this process of mediation, thus advancing the argument that the emerging practices of identity performance online require ongoing revision and study. Second, we consider how Goffman's (1959) dramaturgical framework may be appropriated as a useful platform from which the presentation of self in everyday life can (and, as we argue, should) be extended to online forms of self-presentation, with some important caveats (Hogan 2010). These forms of identity are, as we have already begun to argue, an increasingly important part of the everyday lives of many individuals, especially young people in the 'vanguard' of developing social practices in these spaces. In the later chapters in the book, we explore particular arenas of life (education, employment, love, family, and leisure) that contribute to the stories around growing up made visible (or not) on Facebook.

What Is Identity?

> In common sense language, identification is constructed on the back of a recognition of some common origin or shared characteristics with another person or group, or with an ideal.
>
> (Hall 1996: 2)

> People mark their identities by symbols of difference.
>
> (Woodward 2000: 33)

> One thinks of identity ... [in order] to place oneself among the evident variety of behavioural styles and patterns.
>
> (Bauman 1996: 19)

These quotes illustrate three key characteristics fundamental to our approach to identity: acknowledging similarity and sameness ('I am the same as that person'); observing difference ('I am different from that person'); and positioning oneself within 'systems' of belonging (whether as subcultures, lifestyles, tribes, movements, or collective identities—'I belong to that group'). These three characteristics of identity allow individuals to negotiate with other identities and to construct their own in an ongoing, open-ended 'project of the self'.

Growing up, navigating 'youth', 'becoming' an adult, arriving at the promised land of adulthood, is all about identity. Learning who we are, where we fit, and what to think, practicing what we will do, and testing relationships. Of course, as Wyn and White (1997) demonstrate, there is no official arrival point at 'adulthood', and indeed contemporary experiences of youth are more non-linear and delayed and precarious than ever before.

Merleau-Ponty speaks of the cultural world as an instrument that we have projected around ourselves to express meaning (1962: 196). As part of this cultural world, identities operate in the same way—projected around the individual through a process of identity performance. These projected identities allow individuals to 'go on in each other's presence' (Bauman 1996: 19). Just as culture requires an interactive impetus or dialogue, identity is similarly shaped and driven by interaction. Social interaction, then, is central to identity formation, which in turn is one of the main 'projects' associated with 'growing up'. Stuart Hall (1996: 4) also points to the messiness of identity:

> [I]dentities are never unified and, in late modern times, increasingly fragmented and fractured; never singular but multiply constructed across different, often intersecting and antagonistic discourses, practices and positions. They are subject to a radical historicization, and are constantly in the process of change and transformation.

In his later work, Hall goes on to discuss a 'crisis of identity [...] which is dislocating the central structures and processes of modern societies and undermining the frameworks which gave individuals stable anchorage in the social world' (2004: 114). This discourse of crisis is not only a powerful commentary on late modern or postmodern forms of identity but it can also be applied as a criticism of digital expressions of identity. The fragmentation and fracturing referred to by Hall can be magnified as people move rapidly across different networks and communities and cultures. At another level, the fragmentation described by Hall also occurs in the very transmission of data, where in a digital system information is literally broken down into bits and bytes, ones and zeros, for transmission and reconstitution in meaningful ways by the receiver. An image of a friend drinking a beer in Thailand that is accessible through Facebook has made a long and complex journey to arrive on a screen elsewhere in the world; a journey of information packets that are necessarily fractured and fragmented, but eventually reorganised and rendered meaningful. We would offer this as an alternative metaphor that embraces the fragmented conceptualisation of late—or postmodern forms of identity, framing fragmentation not as a crisis but as a necessary process in coherence: assembled and impressed upon different audiences in interchangable ways.

Bennett explains that 'a central feature of postmodernity is its empowering of the individual subject [...] allowing them to construct identities which are freed from the confines and restraints of class and tradition [... providing individuals with] the freedom to choose one's identity' (Bennett 2005: 40). This mobility and expectation for individuals to embrace agency has become a comfortable reality for postmodern societies. However, in the age of the internet, Hall's 'crisis of identity' and other criticisms of postmodern identity are gaining new currency in debates around issues such as identity theft, addiction to online gaming, and the shift to social network sites and other forms of digital communication as being 'prioritised' over traditional offline forms of communication. As Frabetti (2011: 2) asks, in relation to the internet, '[i]s not access to every text always already mediated by technology (such as, e.g., by writing)?' We could extend this question to all forms of social interaction. Are our interactions not always-already mediated by bodies, by languages, by gender and other social structures, by institutions? Certainly, the internet does offer new and even unique configurations of these forms of mediation in some instances, and thus new literacies for 'being on the internet' are sometimes required. However, the familiar 'offline' rules of mediation, into which members of societies are socialised, can be (and have been, and are being) translated to the social spaces of the internet, usually with young people who have grown up with the internet, in the 'vanguard' (Livingstone 2008) of translating those rules.

In the next section, rather than considering the new and unique forms of sociality emerging 'on the internet', we are instead concerned with examining the ways in which existing social processes, such as identity and belonging, crucial to 'growing up', translate to and are reconfigured for digital social spaces.

Revisiting Goffman and the Dramaturgical Framework

The sociological perspective of symbolic interactionism offers an understanding of how identity is formed and maintained (or abandoned or imagined) that can act as a model for how identity as an ongoing process plays out on social media, despite the differences in mediation that occur across digital and physical spaces. As Blumer (1969) explains, the tradition of symbolic interactionism is underpinned by three premises: first, individuals act towards things (objects, other people, groups of people, institutions, and ideals) based on the meanings that those things have for them; second, those meanings are derived from social interactions; and third, the use of those meanings in action involve an 'interpretive process' (Blumer 1969: 5). This third premise, the interpretive process, is described by Blumer as a kind of internal reconciling whereby the 'actor is interacting with himself [sic]... the actor selects, checks, suspends, regroups, and transforms the meanings in the light of the situation in which he is placed' (1969: 5). In other words, meaning emerges (is constructed) through social interactions with others, but is then deployed to make sense in specific contexts.

One of our aims in this book, and the project that sits behind it, has been to understand how these sets of processes operate on Facebook. Conventions around 'being' in digital spaces emerge from shared social interactions grounded in physical spaces. For example, determining who has access to profiles and what constitutes a Facebook Friend, deciding what to share, what or who to delete, how to describe an event or communicate an idea, and indeed how all these things change over time. How those shared conventions (or violations of those conventions) are then applied, however, relates to the 'interpretive process' that Blumer describes as so essential to a symbolic interactionist approach.

One of the key figures in symbolic interactionism is Erving Goffman. Goffman's (1959, 1979) dramaturgical framework has become central, and even somewhat of a bingo-card cliché for understanding the presentation of self in digital spaces. Many internet researchers have used his dramaturgical framework to theorise the selection of profile pictures (Mendelson & Papacharissi 2011), the writing of 'authentic' profiles (Uski & Lampinen 2014), the management of privacy (Pearson 2009), and to understand why and how people decide who to friend and who to block (Robards 2010, and on unfriending see John & Dvir-Gvirsman 2015). Goffman likens the presentation of self in everyday life to a stage performance in which actors use props and cues from their audience to sculpt their self-presentations. He argues that when individuals interact, they are compelled to draw on available resources to know the person with whom they are interacting:

> When an individual enters the presence of others, they commonly seek to acquire information about him [sic] or to bring into play information about him already possessed ... Information about the individual helps to define the situation, enabling others to know in advance what he will expect of them and what they may expect of him. (Goffman 1959: 1)

Identity performance is a crucial component of social interaction—without this 'presentation of self' or without the ability to 'read' the identity performances of an individual, social interaction could not occur. Drawing on past experiences and available signifiers, individuals construct a narrative around the person with whom they are interacting. This narrative draws accessible markers of identity together into a cohesive story, informing appropriate forms of interaction and behaviour, providing parameters for the interaction, or points of resistance. This is the process that sits behind all manner of social interactions, from sexual attraction to racism to respect. Goffman provides the example of the 'sympathetic patients in mental wards [that] will sometimes feign bizarre symptoms so that student nurses will not be subjected to a disappointingly sane performance' (1959: 16). In other words, it is clear that identity performance is also subject to a sense of expectation; anticipation based on those narrative parameters, informed by previous experiences and assumptions.

Regions and Standards

Goffman's example of the 'mental ward' implies that the socialised individual always has some understanding of what constitutes an appropriate performance of identity in certain social situations. There are rules—often unwritten, although in some cases institutionalised—for different spaces and situations: restaurants have dress codes, laws govern responsible driving behaviours and swimwear is usually only acceptable at the beach or pool. Individuals, the actors in Goffman's dramaturgical framework, move between performances often without consciously noting it, drawing on certain markers of identity more heavily in different situations. Goffman describes different social contexts as 'regions', in which the performance of individuals is governed by two broad sets of 'standards': first, the way in which the performer engages with the audience, verbally and non-verbally; and second, 'the way in which the performer comports himself while in visual or aural range of the audience but not necessarily engaged in talk with them' (1959: 110). Thus, Goffman argues that an appropriate self-policed performance of identity—determined by the standards of the region, or the space in which the performance takes place—must be maintained, whether in direct or indirect contact with a perceived audience. These rules and codes of interaction are generally well established in face-to-face situations, as we learn them through the process of socialisation throughout our lives.

Translating norms into digital forms of sociality can be problematic as the cues transmitted in physical spaces that signal what presentation of self is appropriate are reconfigured in digital social spaces. For instance, the broad adoption of social media has created some anxiety around how people should 'act' on these platforms, an anxiety that is most intensely projected on young people. See, for instance, the section in the previous chapter on context collapse. Rather than inventing entirely new ways of being in digital spaces, social media users adapt existing norms and practices (how to deal with strangers, what constitutes a friend, how to conduct oneself in public) to work in digital social spaces. Elsewhere, we have written about the teenage bedroom as a metaphor in understanding how young people manage space, both in practical and physical terms, pointing out the limitations of such a metaphor (Lincoln & Robards 2014).

The Idealised Self and Socialisation

Central to the discussions around 'authenticity' and 'integrity' in the presentation of self in digital spaces are questions around the 'idealised' self (Uski & Lampinen 2014). Goffman approaches the 'presentation of idealized performances' (1959: 44) through a literature on social mobility, arguing that these idealised presentations are aspirational, that individuals will instinctively perform the best version of themselves, which he terms the idealised self. This isn't a fake performance or a deception, but simply a presentation of what the individual regards to be the best qualities and appearances, contingent upon the standards of the region. Goffman is not very specific on the process of socialisation, or how the individual comes to learn the standards of performance. He does offer the observation that the individual must 'learn enough pieces of expression to be able to "fill in" and manage, more or less, any part that he [sic] is likely to be given' (1959: 79). Goffman does not offer a clear argument about how and where this learning occurs—whether through parents, schools, mass media, and so on—although one can safely assume it would be a complex set of experiences and role models working in concert that lead to a sufficient number of 'pieces of expression' being mastered for the performance.

Goffman argues that when actors enact the idealised performance, they become the idealised self; constantly (or not, depending on the level of attentiveness required by the performance) fixing their hair or makeup in reflective surfaces, adjusting the hem line on a pair of shorts or tucking in errant shirts. The extent of these 'revisions' to maintain that idealised presentation varies from person to person, as does the extent to which an idealised performance is enacted on social media. The question here is the extent to which social media users have control over the presentation of self in a space where others are also able to effect and modify that presentation—not just friends tagging each other in unflattering photos or posting inflammatory memes, but also Facebook itself reconfiguring the ordering of disclosures through opaque algorithmic decision-making. We revisit this question throughout the book.

Mendelson and Papacharissi, in their study of college students' Facebook photo galleries, note that in personal photography 'the positive is always recorded over the negative, with moments of celebration emphasized' (2011: 254). This appears to map neatly on to the notion of the idealised self. However, participants in their study also found themselves being tagged in photographs that did not align with their idealised self: 'To another embarrassing photo, the subject commented: "Bad hair!!!! DESTROY! DESTROY!"' (Participant in Mendelson & Papacharissi 2011: 262). While being embarrassed by a failure to present an idealised front is certainly not unique to identity performance in digital spaces, the crucial difference is in the persistent nature of the 'bad' photograph or the incriminating status update or the geo-location check-in at a music festival when you are meant to be on a sick day away from work. While a user might 'untag' themselves in a photo, that image may persist even when it isn't linked to a user, until the person who uploaded the photo deletes it or it is flagged for deletion by Facebook. Even after an image is deleted, it is unclear as to how long the image is stored on Facebook's servers or in server backups, potentially remaining, if not readily accessible, for years after deletion (Cheng 2012). Images erased from Facebook may of course have also been screenshotted by anyone who had access to it, stored locally and potentially shared in other contexts.

Thus, in revisiting this notion of the idealised self in Goffman's dramaturgical framework and seeking to extend it to presentations of self on social media, it is important to consider not only questions of authenticity and integrity (is it possible to present a 'fake' version of self?), but also to attend to the implication that others (trusted friends or otherwise) can also play a part in this process, through tagging persistent images of the individual or making comments on the individual's wall, status updates, and so on, that do not align with that individual's own concept of the idealised self. We will return to these co-produced presentations of self throughout the book.

Sign-Equipment

For Goffman, props—'sign-equipment' (1959: 45)—are a central part of performing the idealised self. This symbolic equipment which individuals recruit to their performances includes an array of material goods. What constitutes the 'ideal', for Goffman, 'will tend to incorporate and exemplify the officially accredited values of the society' (1959: 45). In other words, the context of the presentation is again central to the performance itself. A new suit or high heels may not be appropriate for a bush rave, just as wearing flip-flops and shorts to a corporate job interview would represent a misunderstanding (or resistance to) the standards of the 'region'. In some situations, recruiting the wrong sign-equipment (wearing the wrong costume) can result in exclusion from a venue or even an arrest if the performative transgression is indecent enough. Discussing clothes, Goffman proposed that men wore three different types of costumes:

> Men are displayed in formal, business, and informal gear, and although it seems understood that the same individual will at different times appear in all these guises, each guise seems to afford him something he is totally serious about, and deeply identified with, as though wearing a skin, not a costume.
>
> (Goffman 1979: 51)

The link between clothes and identity is strongly foregrounded here by Goffman, and we dwell on this point at some length given how directly the idea of sign-equipment can be transposed to digitally mediated spaces. Women are also addressed by Goffman, although very differently, betraying the prejudices of the day. He says that women are less attached to strict performances—almost flippant in their fashion choices, 'as though life were a series of costume balls,' where one is free to 'mock one's own appearance' (Goffman 1979: 51). Goffman proposes that because women adhere less strictly to costume categories, they identify less with their clothes. There are clear problems with these assertions, especially given the shifts in attitudes towards fashion by men since Goffman's work was published. Men are increasingly likely to transgress these costume categories and blur any divisions, just as some women would probably fit the stifling typology for men's clothes that Goffman advances above. The visibility and fashion of trans and non-binary people also wonderfully complicate these rigidities.

Billington and Vasconcelos (2013) take up some of these themes in their article that explores the applicability of Goffman to notions of performance and identity in the 'online virtual world' Second Life. Their study is particularly interesting because it engages with the idea that Second Life participants 'edit facets' of their physical selves in Second Life. One of the attractions of such virtual worlds is its 'enhanced potential to edit the self', enabling users to embellish or conceal the parts of their physical selves they feel less confident about, perhaps concealing narrative aspects upon which they have been judged previously. This is manifested in avatars through the enhancement of particular features that can allude to the ideal self. Billington and Vasconcelos also consider the use of "alts" that, accordingly to their findings, rarely supplant or are totally removed from the participant's physical life: for most, there is a connection in some way to it. These findings enhance the usefulness of Goffman's work on the presentation of self, while also enhancing his work in that their study considers the complexities of 'self' as it play out in digital contexts. In their conclusions they suggest that in the case of Second Life participants, there is a range of 'different gradations in editing the self' (Billington & Vasconcelos 2013: 110) but with the digital Second Life avatar being 'anchored' to the physical body. Their findings reveal that in-between these gradations of identity there are 'grey areas', areas of ambiguity, areas of enhancement and also areas of exclusion to provide participants with a 'level play field' (2013: 107) that they might not experience otherwise. Billington and Vasconcelos contend that alongside understanding identities as they are performed in Second Life by their participants, Goffman's framework also enables us to consider more closely the boundaries and areas in-between those 'editing facets'.

Despite the flaws and limitations of Goffman's dramaturgical framework, viewed through our lens in 2019, Goffman's observations are not without their merit, especially the role sign-equipment (clothes in this instance) play in identity performance. This argument could be extended to a variety of identity devices: cars, books chosen for display in an office, ornaments that decorate coffee tables and, central to this project, the array of devices that can be used in the presentation of self on social media. While Goffman deals with fashion as a physical and embodied example of how identity is performed, it is the symbolic and cultural importance of clothes that makes his analysis pertinent and particularly resonant for our purposes. Despite the broad application of Goffman's dramaturgical framework to performances of self mediated by the internet (boyd 2006, 2007, 2014; Hewitt & Forte 2006; Menchik & Tian 2008; Robinson 2008; Tufekci 2008; Mendelson & Papacharissi 2011), there have also been various criticisms of the way in which Goffman's theories have been applied to online social spaces. In the sections that follow, we will track the application of Goffman's dramaturgical framework from the 1990s, to the 2000s, to the 2010s.

The Limitations of the Dramaturgical Framework

According to Barnes, one of the central arguments in symbolic interactionism is that 'physical bodily interaction with objects and people is necessary to develop a sense of self' (2000: 170), and thus the performance of self in a space where physical bodies are not present inhibits the development of a sense of self. Consider, for example, Miller's (1995) early attempt to apply Goffman's dramaturgical framework to digital social interactions two and a half decades ago. Miller argues that digital interactions increasingly mirror physical interactions: 'Electronic communication will become more and more human communication to the extent that there is more to it than just efficiently passing information to each other' (1995: 2). He concludes, however, that at the time of his research, the internet lacked the depth needed for 'electronic selves' to truly emerge. Miller argues that while online interaction is undeniably social, important performative cues transmitted in physical interaction (facial expressions, clothes, intonation, body language, etc.) that Goffman saw as so important were notably absent. Thus, Miller (and others, including more recently Owen 2011) bring in to question the 'legitimacy' and 'value' of digital performances of self, rendering this form of mediation as subordinate to physical interaction and thus somehow disingenuous.

Nearly 15 years after Miller, Pearson (2009) moves beyond questions of legitimacy and applies the dramaturgical framework directly to social network sites and the private/public divide, through Goffman's frontstage/backstage paradigm and the "glass bedroom metaphor". In the years since Miller conducted his update of Goffman's theory, the richness and depth of social interaction online has developed far beyond the personal homepages and text-only interactions of the 1990s found in email exchanges and discussion forums with which Miller was dealing (along with the likes of Rheingold 1994; Turkle 1995; McRae 1997; Dibbell 1998). In the 2000s, early social media platforms added a new dimension to the performance of self in digital spaces, incorporating dynamic content updated not only by the profile author but by friends and contacts. Social network sites became complicated and nuanced stages of identity performance. As Pearson argues, 'the audience and the performer are disembodied and electronically re-embodied through signs they choose to represent themselves' (2009). Pearson concludes that social network sites blur the boundaries between private and public, backstage and frontstage. Her assertion is that the nature of the internet (and thus social network sites) is inherently susceptible to third-party lurking—by individuals outside the 'glass bedroom'—that observe interactions without participating.

Also seeking to advance this understanding of frontstage and backstage, Pinch (2010) invokes Goffman's 'sociology of doors' (that we also refer to in the previous chapter), arguing that the rise of new technologies (such as social network sites) often obscures the importance of 'old technologies' and their role in everyday life. The door in a hotel restaurant, for example, functions as a technology for separating the frontstage and backstage performances of waiters and cooks, but is rendered invisible because of its mundane nature. Pinch also recalls the important role of the horse in World War 2, overshadowed by new technologies such as the microwave radar and the atomic bomb (2010: 409). Moving on to the rise of the internet, and providing a potential answer to critics of the application of the dramaturgical framework to online interactions, Pinch offers an alternate interpretation of Goffman's (1963) notion of co-presence:

> [Goffman] mainly restricted this notion [of co-presence] to full bodily presence, by which he meant something like a physical area where interactants find themselves in visual and aural range of one another. If co-presence is interpreted as only bodily co-presence, then the idea will have limited applicability to online worlds. But if co-presence is conceived of as a means whereby interactants are available and accountable to each other for their mediated interactions, it has a wider application.
>
> (Pinch 2010: 420)

While flagging this second, wider interpretation of co-presence in applications of Goffman's dramaturgical framework is not common in the literature, it does provide a viable route by which Goffman's important observations and theories on the presentation of self can be made applicable to online forms of sociality. Pinch goes on to advance this second interpretation by providing another example of an old technology that can help us think about the implications of new ones:

> The clue to thinking about co-presence and its application to an online world is again to think about mediated interactions which do not involve computers. A useful example here is letter writing. This is a mediated form of communication with its own special norms and obligations. Writing and receiving letters are accountable social

actions. The importance of the mediation and how it affects the accountability of actions can be seen when for some reason a person who writes a letter is present when the recipient reads it. The ensuing mild embarrassment is telling and derives precisely from the changed form of mediation and co-presence.

(Pinch 2010: 420–421)

Studying how people manage impressions on social media, and how people present themselves in digital spaces—as this book seeks to do—is about documenting strategies that, in Bauman's words, allow individuals to 'go on in each others' presence' (1996: 19). In digital social spaces, however, that presence (or co-presence) operates somewhat differently than physical spaces. As Pinch explains here, forms of co-presence that are mediated online are much less foreign than one might expect. A similar kind of mild embarrassment can be seen when people discuss, during physical in-person conversations, what 'goes on' on Facebook. Consider, for instance, the awkwardness involved in catching up with someone you haven't seen in-person for a while, but who you have followed closely on social media: Facebook posts about a new job and relationship, daily Instagram stories documenting weekends at music festivals and brunch, and tweets about politics and reality TV. What is left to 'catch up' on?

The cautionary criticisms of applications of Goffman's dramaturgical framework, then, are useful insofar as they invite scholars to properly reflect upon the theories they are deploying. While the dramaturgical framework is not without its limitations, if a wider interpretation of co-presence can be sustained (whereby individuals are available and accountable to each other despite physical distance) then Goffman's insights can continue to provide a rich and valuable framework from which interactions mediated by the internet can be better understood.

Performances Versus Exhibitions, as Artefacts of Self

Developing this application of Goffman's work to the internet further, especially in relation to the notion of co-presence contested in Pinch's (2010) work, Hogan (2010) offers a more nuanced understanding of the dramaturgical framework. He makes a distinction between 'performances', where 'actors behave with each other', and 'exhibitions', where individuals 'submit artifacts to show to each other' (Hogan 2010: 377). Hogan clarifies that exhibitions can also be performances of self (consider the display of photographs in a home), but that these exhibitions do not require co-presence:

> Clarifying this distinction creates an expanded theoretical repertoire for scholars, thereby enabling them to disentangle processes occurring when actors are copresent

> (in time, if not in the same geographic place) and processes that occur when actors are not necessarily present at the same time but still react to each other's data ... One of the key distinctions between exhibitions and performances is that performances are subject to continual observation and self-monitoring as the means for impression management, whereas exhibitions are subject to selective contributions.
>
> (Hogan 2010: 377, 384)

Hogan acknowledges that there are limitations to this typology, such as what he refers to as the 'hybrid spaces' of MMOs (Massively Multiplayer Online Role Playing Games) that 'share aspects of both off-line situations and online exhibitions' (2010: 382). Can all content not be considered a performance, though? In answering this question, Hogan argues that performance must be understood as either ephemeral or recorded, where the latter transforms the performance and renders it subject to a different kind of 'aura' (by way of Benjamin 1967). However, we would argue that there are examples of interactions (framed as exhibitions in Hogan's typology) on social network sites that are also quite ephemeral. Consider 'Mikalah', a teenaged participant in one of boyd's (2010) studies, who deactivates her Facebook account (rendering her profile invisible/non-existent to her network) each time she isn't directly engaged with the site, or 'Shamika', another of boyd's participants, who deletes each wall post, status update, and 'Like', shortly after it is posted. Both of these practices constitute a form of participation, but also render the recorded performances as ephemeral in different ways, troubling the seemingly neat typology Hogan is seeking to advance.

In the years since this work, there has also been a turn towards more ephemeral forms of the digital trace, with Snapchat being the clearest example. Snapchat was the first mainstream platform to allow users to send text, picture, and video messages that would last only for a few seconds (or a 24 hour period in a 'story'), ostensibly vanishing after. Handyside and Ringrose (2017) studied the role of Snapchat in mediating memory and intimacy among 18-year-olds, and found that it offered a 'temporal fastness and ephemerality' to their exchanges. At the same time however, they also found examples of 'fixity through the screenshotting of "disappearing" snaps' (Handyside & Ringrose 2017: 347), as users are able to bypass the intended temporary nature of a 'snap' and record whatever is on their screen with their phone's screenshot function. This turn to the ephemeral was adopted later by Instagram and Facebook, where users were able to create daily 'stories' that tend to chronicle more mundane everyday experiences in a 24-hour time period.

In their work on how the 'clean eating' movement (avoiding processed foods and refined sugars) plays out on Instagram, Baker and Walsh (2018) also draw upon and develop Goffman's dramaturgical framework. They explore the 'architecture of online spaces' (Baker & Walsh 2018: 4554)—namely hashtags on Instagram—raise important questions about the ways in which gendered identities are formed and performed on Instagram. They suggest Instagram is an increasingly important site for users to visually display the self, engaging with social constructs in ephemeral contexts. Critiquing studies that primarily examine the ways in which 'reflexive individuals strategically present their selves online' Baker and Walsh build on Goffman's notion of the presentation of self to consider how 'interactions are implicated in social structures and social order' (2018: 4555), primarily focussing on gender display in imagery on Instagram that uses the hashtag #cleaneating and #eatclean to 'reveal how the body is idealised online' (p. 4554). Their analysis considers narratives of gender in 'before' and 'after' shots on #cleaneating and #eatclean as they pictorially document their journey and 'transition in a physical form' emphasising progress, dedication and success towards the ideal self (Baker & Walsh 2018: 4561). Engaging with Goffman's contention that societies 'must mobilize their members as self-regulating participants in social encounters' through ritual (Goffman 1967 in Baker and Walsh 2018: 4567) the authors conclude that while we can appreciate that social media opens up a range of possibilities for individuals to explore aspects of their identity such as their gender, its uses also conform to and perpetuate existing hegemonic structures. For example, they explain how achieving top posts using #cleaneating #eatclean went beyond the online performance seeping into 'the values and practices of the clean eating community' (p. 4567). In this respect, their work revises significantly Goffman's work going beyond social media as a site of creative expression to how these 'displays of health operate as a form of collective identity' (p. 4568), thus pushing impression management beyond the individual.

Despite the various limitations discussed in this section—from any application of Goffman's dramaturgical framework to the internet at all, through to the limitations of much more nuanced interpretations and typologies advanced by Pinch (2010) and Hogan (2010) and how Baker and Walsh (2018) push the framework beyond the individual—it is clear that this framework remains useful. It is productive for understanding the ways individuals present themselves, even when the technologies of mediation are 'new' and present new challenges, beyond Goffman's imaginings in the 1950s. For this reason, we have recruited Goffman's dramaturgical framework to this project, and use it as a key underpinning in the chapters that follow, informed and revised by a growing area of scholarship discussed here. In addition, we look to the work of Anthony Giddens to provide a useful understanding of identity as reflexively constructed and in-progress, especially for the young people at the core of this project.

The Reflexive Project of Self

Giddens argues that identity formation, a crucial part of growing up, is a reflexive process. Individuals frequently undergo what he describes as a 'psychic reorganisation' (1991: 304) of their identity, negotiating the influence of large impersonal organisations that characterise late modernity. Giddens defines the 'stable individual' as someone with a 'feeling of biographical continuity which she is able to grasp reflexively and, to a greater or lesser degree, communicate to others' (1991: 54). As with the theories from scholars in the tradition of symbolic interactionism, the social aspect of identity—the act of communicating a reflexive story about self, or performing a region specific, standard-adhering sense of self—is central to stability, and what Giddens describes here as the notion of continuity. Giddens argues against assumptions that we reinvent ourselves only at crisis moments in our lives, instead contending that individuals are actively and endlessly negotiating and constructing self-identity, even amidst the mundane experiences of the everyday. This argument is consistent with Gergen's (1991) claim that the identity projects of individuals are in a constant state of construction and reconstruction, at once 'shaped by social structures' (Woodward 2000: 1) such as class and gender, while also being the product of some agency or 'choice' (Beck 1992).

Giddens describes this approach as the reflexive project of self, 'the process whereby self identity is constituted by the reflexive ordering of self narratives' (1991: 244). As Thomson explains, 'storytelling (to ourselves and others) is central to the construction of a reflexive project of self. As we rework existing narratives and forge new ones, we invent and reinvent who it is possible to be' (2007: 80). In further contextualising Giddens' reflexive project of self, Thomson makes the claim that contemporary (late modern) society demands a much more active engagement in this reflexive storytelling labour. She provides the example of a flexible and uncertain employment market, where a version of self is constantly written and rewritten through the curriculum vitae and participation in public institutions such as continuing higher education and welfare. Thomson also points towards an intensification of the 'work on self identity in private: in conversations with our parents, partners and friends, through reading self-help literature, magazines and horoscopes' (2007: 81). We will return to this focus on work and employment in Chapter Five.

One point that Thomson touches on very briefly is the added option to develop a 'personal website', which, for Thomson, would also figure in to the reflexive project of self, requiring yet another ordering of narratives. In the years since Thomson was re-reading Giddens' reflexive project of self in relation to young people's transition narratives, the 'personal website' may continue to operate as a useful professional tool, but has been dwarfed by participation in social network sites. Rather than engagement here being a 'choice', maintaining a social media presence has become mandatory for many, especially for young people, where not participating can mean being left off invitation lists for parties, not seeing photos of newborn babies or weddings, and appearing 'unavailable' to friends, along with other forms of exclusion. Digital expression of the reflexive project of self has become an important part of late modern life, not in addition to things like employment, a personal life, and a sense of community, but as a medium through which these forms of participation in the social world are mediated. For example, Miller's (2011) *Tales from Facebook* dips into the lives of people from Trinidad for whom Facebook serves an important social utility. For Miller's participants, Facebook was used to seek employment, to conduct informal study groups, and also played a role in the formation (and decline) of relationships. For these individuals, maintaining a presence on Facebook was crucial for maintaining participation in various aspects of their lives. In this way, simply being present on Facebook inscribes a digital trace of growing up over time.

The profiles that constitute social network sites can, in relation to Giddens' reflexive project of self, be understood through two different and yet related frames: first, as a tool that can be used in the process of reflexive self-making; and second, as an object (or a product) of that project. Through the first frame, the initial construction of a profile and the subsequent social interactions mediated on the site can be understood as labour involved in the ordering of self-narratives. For instance, the individual is prompted (but isn't required) to enter employment and education details, to list favourite books, films, music and television shows, to identify favourite quotes, religious and political views, and state their gender and a subsequent 'interested in' field, signalling sexuality. Thus, filling out the initial profile is akin to the ordering of self-narratives required in the writing of a curriculum vitae for Thomson (2007), but across a broader range of fields of life. While this is an important step, this initial biographical 'about me' side of the profile, at least on Facebook, is not at the core of the site's functionality. Instead, it is the social exchanges—commenting on and posting pictures, status updates, wall posts, and events; hanging out in closed groups and participating in IM (Instant Messenger) conversations; and the subsequent 'curation' (Hogan 2010) of this content (untagging, deleting, editing)—that constitute the everyday engagement with the site.

The second frame, then, is the product of this labour, of these interactions, that the individual can reflect upon. In this sense, the profile (which is not contained, but through the architecture of hypertext serves as one point of reference to other pages and profiles) operates as an archive of the reflexive project of self. The 'producers' (Bruns 2008) of social network sites can look back on their lives in a convenient format: past relationships, distant parties, previous employment, past education, even current news items posted to a network, memorialising a tragedy like the 2010 Queensland floods in Australia or celebrating a political achievement like the passing of marriage equality legislation. Through this frame, the variously public and personal conversations of self with others (and self with self) discussed by Thomson (2007) can be articulated and archived in a single place. In Kim's words, social network sites 'are both the object and process of self-formation' (2010: 109).

Some years ago now, in 2004, Cheung specifically investigated the personal homepage as a medium of identity-play, a 'form of media which facilitates the reflexive project of the self' (2004: 60). While Cheung deals with the overt performance of self that occurs on many homepages, as touched upon in the previous section of this chapter, he also discusses the generative dimensions of this process. That is, when the performance of identity functions also as a process for configuring (or figuring out) a project of self. Cheung notices that the act of performing a self can also be a negotiation of multiplicity, an attempt to localise or unify identity. The postmodern self, he observes, is often far from unified:

> [Consider] the Chinese-American lecturing in the USA, who feels passionate about gay fiction but also about heterosexual pornographic movies, who loves both academic books and PlayStation games, and who actually supports feminism yet likes Sylvester Stallone's movies a lot.
>
> (Cheung 2004: 59)

Cheung argues that writing this self into being online can be a trying experience. Indeed, it requires multiple performances in the same space, a problem that all users of social media must negotiate. As participation in digital spaces moved away from personal homepages and more towards the social media of Facebook, Instagram, and Snapchat, the nature of reflexive identity-work persists, but the ways in which this process plays out in a networked and inherently more social environment requires a much more nuanced set of approaches. Instead of the largely static form of the homepage, maintaining an 'authentic' or conventional profile on a social network site requires regularly updating and 'curating' (Hogan 2010) dynamic content. In addition to initial 'constructions of self', it is the interaction and ongoing performance of self that bestows legitimacy and 'authenticity' on social media.

Conclusion

In this chapter we have provided a set of theoretical frameworks concerning identity and mediation that this book seeks to build on. We have suggested that existing theories of identity can be applied to the identity-work undertaken in digital spaces—in 'growing up on Facebook', for instance—leading to our use of Goffman's dramaturgical framework and Giddens' reflexive project of self. In the next chapter, we move on to our own empirical project—the Facebook Timelines Project—and set out our approach that forms the basis of the subsequent substantive chapters.

References

Abidin, C., & Brown, M. L. (2018) *Microcelebrity around the globe: Approaches to cultures of internet fame*. London: Emerald.

Baker, S. A., & Walsh, M. J. (2018). 'Good Morning Fitfam': Top posts, hashtags and gender display on Instagram. *New Media & Society*, 20(12), 4553–4570.

Barnes, S. (2000). *Developing a Concept of Self in Cyberspace Communities*. New Jersey: Hampton Press.

Bauman, Z. (1996). From pilgrim to tourist—or a short history of identity. In S. Hall & P. du Gay (Eds.), *Questions of cultural identity* (pp. 18–36). London: Sage.

Beck, U. (1992). *Risk society: Towards a new modernity*. London: Sage.

Benjamin, W. (1967). The work of art in the age of mechanical reproduction. In W. Benjamin (Ed.), *Illuminations* (pp. 217–251). New York: Schocken Books.

Bennett, A. (2005). *Culture and everyday life*. London: Sage.

Blumer, H. (1969). *Symbolic Interactionism*. Berkeley: University of California Press.

boyd, d. (2006). Friends, Friendsters, and MySpace Top 8: Writing community into being on social network sites. *First Monday*, *11*(12), 1–19.

boyd, d. (2007). Why youth (heart) social network sites: The role of networked publics in teenage social life. In *Youth, identity, and digital media* (MacArthur foundation series on digital learning, Vol. 119, p. 142).

boyd, d. (2010). Social network sites as networked publics: Affordances, dynamics and implications. In Z. Papacharissi (Ed.), *A networked self: Identity, community, and cultures on social network sites*. London: Routledge.

boyd, d. (2014). *It's complicated: The social lives of networked teens*. New Haven: Yale University Press.

Bruns, A. (2008). *Blogs, Wikipedia, second life, and beyond: From production to produsage*. New York: Peter Lang.

Buckingham, D. (2008). *Youth, identity & digital media*. Massachusetts: MIT Press.

Bullingham L., & Vasconcelos, A. (2013). The presentation of self in the online world: Goffman and the study of online identities. *Journal of Information Sciences*, *39*(1), 101–112.

Cheng, J. (2012). 'Over 3 years later, "deleted" Facebook photos are still online', Arts Technica, http://arstechnica.com/business/2012/02/nearly-3-years-later-deleted-facebook-photos-are-still-online/. Accessed May 24.

Cheung, C. (2004). Identity construction and self-presentation on personal homepages: Emancipatory potentials and reality constraints. In D. Gauntlett & R. Horsley (Eds.), *Web.Studies: Rewriting media studies for the digital age* (2nd ed., pp. 53–68). New York: Edward Arnold.

Dibbell, J. (1998). *My Tiny Life: Crime and passion in a virtual world.* New York: Henry Holt.

Dobson, A. S., & Ringrose, J. (2015). Sext education: Pedagogies of sex, gender and shame in the schoolyards of tagged and exposed. *Sex Education, 16*(1), 8–21. http://doi.org/10.1080/14681811.2015.1050486.

Duguay, S. (2014). "He has a way gayer Facebook than I do": Investigating sexual identity disclosure and context collapse on a social networking site. *New Media & Society, 18*(6), 891–907. http://doi.org/10.1177/1461444814549930.

Frabetti, F. (2011). Rethinking the digital humanities in the context of originary technicity. *Culture Machine, 12,* 1–22.

Gergen, K. (1991). *The saturated self: Dilemmas of identity in contemporary life.* New York: Basic Books.

Giddens, A. (1991). *Modernity and self identity.* Cambridge: Polity Press.

Goffman, E. (1959). *The presentation of self in everyday life.* London: Penguin.

Goffman, E. (1963). *Behavior in public places: Notes on the social organization of gatherings.* New York: The Free Press.

Goffman, E. (1979). *Gender advertisements.* London: Macmillan.

Hall, S. (2004). *The future of identity, identity and belonging: Rethinking race and ethnicity in Canadian society* (pp. 249–267). Toronto: Canadian Scholars' Press.

Hall, S. (1996). Introduction: Who needs "Identity"?. In S. Hall & P. du Gay (Eds.), *Questions of cultural identity* (pp. 1–17). London: SAGE.

Handyside, S., & Ringrose, J. (2017). Snapchat memory and youth digital sexual cultures: Mediated temporality, duration and affect. *Journal of Gender Studies, 26*(3), 347–360.

Hasinoff, A. A. (2015). *Sexting panic: Rethinking criminalization, privacy, and consent.* Champaign: University of Illinois Press.

Hewitt, A., & Forte, A. (2006). Crossing boundaries: Identity management and student/faculty relationships on the Facebook. In *Computer Supported Cooperative Work Conference*, Banff, AB, November 4–8: http://citeseerx.ist.psu.edu/viewdoc/download?doi=10.1.1.94.8152&rep=rep1&type=pdf.

Hogan, B. (2010). The presentation of self in the age of social media: Distinguishing performances and exhibitions online. *Bulletin of Science, Technology & Society, 30*(6), 377–386.

John, N. A., & Dvir-Gvirsman, S. (2015). "I Don't Like You Any More": Facebook unfriending by Israelis during the Israel-Gaza conflict of 2014. *Journal of Communication, 65*(6), 953–974. http://doi.org/10.1111/jcom.12188.

Jurgensen, N. (2011). Digital dualism and the fallacy of web objectivity. *The Society Pages*, September 13: https://thesocietypages.org/cyborgology/2011/09/13/digital-dualism-and-the-fallacy-of-web-objectivity/. Accessed September 2, 2019.

Kim, Y. (2010). Service or control? A critical thought of the 'Social' in social network services. *Communications & Convergence Review, 2*, 104–112.

Lincoln, S., & Robards, B. (2014). Being strategic and taking control: Bedrooms, social network sites and the narratives of growing up. *New Media & Society, 18*(6), 927–943. http://doi.org/10.1177/1461444814554065.

Livingstone, S. (2008). Taking risky opportunities in youthful content creation: Teenagers' use of social networking sites for intimacy, privacy and self-expression. *New Media & Society, 10*(3), 393–411.

Madianou, M., & Miller, D. (2012). Polymedia: Towards a new theory of digital media in interpersonal communication. *International Journal of Cultural Studies, 16*(2), 169–187.

Marwick, A., & boyd, d. (2011). I tweet honestly, I tweet passionately: Twitter users, context collapse, and the imagined audience. *New Media & Society, 13*(1), 114–133. http://doi.org/10.1177/1461444810365313.

McRae, S. (1997). Flesh made word: Sex, text and the virtual body. In D. Porter (Ed.), *Internet culture*. New York: Routledge.

Mendelson, A. L., & Papacharissi, Z. (2011). Look at us: Collective narcissism in college students Facebook photo galleries. In Z. Papacharissi (Ed.), A networked self: Identity, community, and culture on social network sites (pp. 251–273). New York: Routledge.

Menchik, D. l. A., & Tian, X. (2008). Putting social context into text: The semiotics of E-mail interaction. *American Journal of Sociology, 114*(2), 332–370.

Merleau-Ponty, M. (1962). *Phenomenology of perception*. London: Routledge.

Miller, D. (Ed.). (1995). *Acknowledging consumption*. London: Routledge.

Miller, D. (2011). *Tales from Facebook*. Cambridge: Polity Press.

Morozov, E. (2011). *The net delusion: How not to liberate the world*. New York: Penguin Books.

Owen, S. (2011). Social network sites, surveillance, subjectification: Researching power in Facebook. *Unpublished conference presentation at The Australian Sociological Association 2011*, Newcastle, November 29.

Pearson, E. (2009). All the World Wide Web's a stage: The performance of identity in online social networks. First Monday. https://firstmonday.org/article/view/2162/2127.

Pinch, T. (2010). The invisible technologies of Goffman's sociology from the merry-go-round to the Internet. *Technology and Culture, 51*(2), 409–424.

Rheingold, H. (1994). *The virtual community: Homesteading on the electronic frontier*. Cambridge: MIT Press.

Robards, B. (2010). Randoms in my bedroom: Negotiating privacy and unsolicited contact on social network sites. *PRism, 7*(3), 1–12.

Robinson, L. (2008). The cyberself: The self-ing project goes online, symbolic interaction in the digital age. *New Media & Society, 9*(1), 93–110.

Thomson, R. (2007). A biographical perspective. In M. J. Kehily (Ed.), *Understanding youth: Perspectives, identities and practices*. London: Sage.

Tufekci, Z. (2008). Can you see me now? Audience and disclosure regulation in online social network sites. *Bulletin of Science, Technology & Society, 28*(1), 20–36.

Turkle, S. (1995) *Life on the screen: Identity in the age of the internet*, New York: Touchstone.

Turkle, S. (2011). *Alone together*. New York: Basic Books.

Uski, S., & Lampinen, A. (2014). Social norms and self-presentation on social network sites: Profile work in action. *New Media & Society, 18*(3), 447–464. http://doi.org/10.1177/1461444814543164.

van Dijck, J. (2013). "You have one identity": Performing the self on Facebook and LinkedIn. *Media, Culture & Society, 35*(2), 199–215. http://doi.org/10.1177/0163443712468605.

Vitak, J. (2012). The impact of context collapse and privacy on social network site disclosures. *Journal of Broadcasting & Electronic Media, 56*(4), 451–470.

White, R., & Wyn, J. (2007). *Youth and society: Exploring the social dynamics of youth experience* (2nd ed.). Oxford: Oxford University Press.

Woodward, K. (2000). *Questioning identity: Gender, class, nation*. London: Routledge.

Wyn, J., & White, R. (1997) *Rethinking youth*. London: Sage.

CHAPTER FOUR

Scrolling Back through Facebook Timelines: Making Sense of Digital Traces

> I think I'm a scroller. In the morning when I wake up I automatically, even without thinking, I click on my social media and I just scroll through
>
> Karen (25)

Scrolling on social media has become the dominant mode of experiencing both current and continuous 'feeds' of algorithmically sorted information. It is also how we navigate personal histories and digital traces of lives. As the quote from one of our research participants, Karen (25) above indicates, scrolling has also become a daily ritual and a routine part of everyday life.

Before we turn to our more substantive findings in Chapters Five through Nine, in this chapter we introduce our study with a particular focus on methodology and the development of what we call the 'scroll back method', a method that reflects the way that young people engage with social media in their daily lives. This method allowed us to explore the sustained (five or more years) use of Facebook among 41 young people in their twenties. As we will explain, by focusing on this group, we sought to uncover how growing up stories have been told and archived online, and how disclosure practices (what people say and share on social media) change over time. We question how we can understand the digital trace inscribed through the Facebook Timeline as a longitudinal narrative text. We introduce the notion of scrolling back through Facebook with our participants as co-analysts of their own digital traces as a productive way for better understanding how young people's lives are increasingly mediated and recorded in digital social spaces.

Qualitative Approaches to Studying Young People's Uses of Social Media

As we have noted in the introduction to this book, the *Facebook Timelines* project came about at what we believe to be a unique time in the emerging history of social media. As Facebook—the longest standing social network site—reached its tenth birthday in 2014 it became clear that there was now a population of 'established' Facebook users who had been using the site over an extended period of time. This longevity is unparalleled by earlier platforms such as MySpace, Friendster and Bebo that were the introduction to social media for many young people (see boyd 2006, for instance, on MySpace and Friendster). Many of the users of these earlier platforms went on to 'graduate' to Facebook and other now dominant forms of social media, but some of the conventions and practices that were forged on these pre-Facebook platforms persist (Robards 2012).

Fuchs (2017) describes social media as 'a complex term with multi-layered meaning'. Facebook, he says, 'contains a lot of content (information) and is a tool for communication and for the maintenance creation of communities. It is only to a minor degree a tool for collaborative work, but involves at least three types of sociality: cognition, communication and community' (7). Given the capacities of Facebook as outlined by Fuchs, it is clear to see why such a site should appeal to young people. Further, it is free[1] to join and provides young people with a 'space' within which they can share aspects of their lives, can find out about others, can communicate with people outside the realms of school or work, and can find like-minded people who have similar interests and hobbies (see Chapter Seven). Of course, the experiences of using social network sites like Facebook are not always positive as Nilan et al. (2015), Marwick and boyd (2014) and others argue, and as we discuss throughout this book, being on the site can bring unwanted trouble, drama, distress and upset—some of which is part of growing up more generally.

As much of the classic literature on youth cultures suggests, 'growing up', especially around the teenage years is one of the most turbulent periods in life (Erikson 1968; Hall and Jefferson 1975; Frith 1984; Willis 1990; Griffin 1993; Furlong & Cartmel 2007; White & Wyn 2007; Roberts 2009). During these

---

1. Over time, of course, it has become apparent that there are 'costs' to being on Facebook, including the ways in which the platform monetises content produced by users, targets advertising, and even sells access to private data (Dance, LaForgia & Confessore 2018)

years, so much change is taking place, from physical, emotional or psychological changes, or change related to personal circumstances (moving out of home, getting a new or first job) and achievements tied to socially and culturally sanctioned rites of passage (passing examinations, going to university, graduating, and so on). Within the space of around five years, in their late-teens and early-twenties, a young person makes multiple decisions about their futures while trying to make sense of their emerging adult selves and others around them, working out who their friends are, who to make alliances with, who to avoid, and so on (Henderson et al. 2007). As we have argued in the introduction, we made a conscious choice to work with young people who had recently moved out of their teenage years into their twenties, to reflect upon what those teenage experiences of 'growing up' had been like, and how those experiences had been mediated through a social network site over a sustained—and quite critical—period of their life. As we also argue above, our research makes an important intervention into the fields of Sociology more broadly but specifically in youth and internet studies because it captures those experiences as they have occurred *for the very first time*. This is the first generation that are able to say—as well as evidence—that they have grown up using one specific social network site and, importantly, have documented those experiences on it in unprecedented ways, even if social media use now appears banal and everyday.

We were also aware that young people's experiences of growing up were now documented across a range of different social media platforms as sites such as Instagram, Snapchat, and Tumblr, that have also become very popular over the life span of Facebook. This means that for many of our participants their teenage years had been documented in great detail across several social media platforms but particularly on the longer-standing Facebook where more detailed narratives of their teenage lives had been inscribed. What was particularly interesting about this was the extent to which Facebook was operating as an 'archive of life' for many young people who, as when looking back over old photo albums or diaries, were reminded of particular events, occasions, even people that were since forgotten. Indeed as we will argue later on in this book (particularly in Chapter Eight), Facebook was doing a considerable amount of 'memory work' for them, resurfacing old posts and allowing them to reflect back on their own histories. The research process revealed the enormous amount of content held on the site, ultimately, for some, making it difficult for them to contemplate life without Facebook. Indeed, drawing attention to these longitudinal digital traces of life inscribed on Facebook appears to be one of the platform's key strategies for retaining its user-base, as we also argue in Chapter One. Leaving Facebook would mean leaving behind not just channels of communication, but also traces of personal histories and memories.

The Facebook Timelines Project

It is within this context that we designed our project and developed our methodology. As sociologists of youth, our previous work examined different 'personal' spaces within which youth cultures play out: Lincoln's previous work focuses on 'teenage bedroom culture' (2012) while Robards' work considers the significance of social network sites as identity spaces (2010, 2012). We became interested in the ways in which social network sites, specifically Facebook, had become immersed into everyday youth culture and how youth culture and everyday life was mediated through the site. It was through this lens that we approached the design of this study.

An important consideration for us in the project's development was to be able to understand the 'multi-layering' of social media that Fuchs (2017) describes while at the same time understand how young people intercept and engage in these multiple layers in the context of 'growing up'. Another key consideration was to be able to effectively document how young people's uses of social media changed over a sustained period of time (5+ years) and the factors that contribute to these changes. One of the most significant findings with regards to the users of social media who took part in our study was (perhaps unsurprisingly) the quantity, quality and topic of their disclosures. As we will describe in more detail in subsequent chapters, as our participants matured so did the content of their disclosures. Their desire to share excessive amounts of information on Facebook (frequency of status updates, for instance) waned and when reflected upon through the research process early disclosures on Timelines were often deemed embarrassing, pointless, and even tedious. It was these ruptures and discomforts that pointed towards the most significant changes in practices of the presentation of self and the ordering and re-ordering of reflexive projects of self.

An important observation by the participants on their own digital traces was that often early disclosures mimicked a style of writing that was more akin to texting or to MSN (Microsoft Network messenger—an Instant Messenger that was popular before Facebook Messenger). As is often the case when growing older, looking back over traces of one's teenage years often provokes expressions of embarrassment or shame and this was no different when looking back over Facebook Timelines. While we may look back nostalgically over old photographs, diary entries, and letters, we can also find it difficult to confront elements of our past and this is even more intense on a social media platform which is owned by an advertising corporation, shared with a networked public, and co-constructed with peers and family.

Another key consideration in the development of our methodology was to do with context. As qualitative researchers we were keen to understand the common and unique contexts of our participants' disclosures so that we could learn about the motivations for different kinds of disclosure practices, as well as how these change over time. Taking our cues from participants in an interview scenario, we were interested in understanding the range of contexts and circumstances that influenced the ways in which disclosures were made, establishing commonalities as well as drawing out unique practices. Indeed the contexts of disclosure were specific to each user, and much like their use of other 'personal' spaces, influenced how the site was used as a part of their everyday lives. Lincoln (2012, 2015) in her work on 'teenage bedroom culture', for example, highlights the significance of understanding family dynamics and domestic politics when exploring the role and significance of bedrooms in the lives of young people. Family dynamics were important in this study, often being influential from the moment of joining Facebook as a number of our participants had been introduced to the site by older siblings who had helped them to set up profiles. Others had set up them up under the supervision of parents. Our data shows that both types of initiation into the world of social media impacted on how that user then went on to use the site.

When learning about the different contexts of use from our participants we were also keen to learn more about their social media use more broadly, for example, what platforms they were currently using and on which sites their 'social media lives' began. We also asked questions about the spaces in which social media was accessed. For example, a number of participants talked about their early use of Facebook taking place in their bedrooms using a laptop, while others described limited access to social network sites through a shared home PC that was located in a shared space such as a living room or dining room. A number of participants spoke about the significance of acquiring a smartphone and how their Facebook use had developed as a consequence of being able to access the platform at any time in any location. All of these scenarios were important to understand as we sought to uncover the growing up stories of our participants as they were told and archived digitally.

Facebook Timelines Participants

Our research sample was made up of 41 participants who, for matters of convenience, were based primarily in our hometowns at the time: the North West of England in the UK (Lincoln) and Tasmania in Australia (Robards). Participants were recruited through a 'call for participants' poster campaign that primarily involved placing posters around university locations, cafes, bars, libraries and other spaces in key locations where young people in their twenties might spend their time. We also shared the advert on social media. Self-selection was important because we wanted to work with people who defined themselves as active and long term (5+ years) Facebook users and who were willing to 'let us in' to their Facebook worlds. By the end of the recruitment process our sample consisted of 23 females and 18 males (one of our male participants also identified as trans) with a range of educational qualifications from minimum levels (completion of grade 10 in Australia) through to one participant with a PhD.

Our participants worked in a range of occupations including: education, medicine, childcare, retail; hospitality, service work, social media, and DJ-ing. We also had a diverse group in terms of sexuality, with two men and one woman who identified as gay, one male who identified as bisexual, and another male participant who was undecided when it came to his sexuality. The two cities where we were based (Liverpool and Launceston) are higher education 'hubs': Liverpool has four universities in a city of approximately 500,000, while Launceston is a regional hub in Tasmania where the University of Tasmania is a significant employer and occupies a central place for the community more generally. In other words, universities are key to both of these towns. It was no surprise then that many of our participants were involved in or recently graduated from higher education (Bachelor's degrees and diplomas). However, we did endeavour to ensure some diversity around education, so 13 (about one third) of our participants were not currently enrolled in or recently graduated from university.

As we explain elsewhere (Lincoln & Robards 2016; Robards and Lincoln 2016), and as you would expect, gender, sexuality, educational backgrounds and career aspirations had significant impacts on the digital traces produced through sustained social media use, and thus the diversity of our sample in this sense is important. The research was primarily conducted with the participants in locations such as researchers' university office or a cafe. Participants were invited to bring their own devices (smart phones, laptops) through which to access Facebook, otherwise they could access their accounts via the researcher's PC or laptop. When participants accessed their accounts from our own computers, we used Google Chrome's 'Incognito' mode in order to avoid login details being stored. We also made a point of ensuring our participants were properly 'logged out' at the end of the interview, encouraging them to do this for themselves. We found all of our participants to be engaging, in-depth and thorough in their conversations with us, generously taking time to talk through and reflecting upon many different aspects of their lives.

The Stages of the Scrolling Back Method

Our research method can be broken into several steps: the first involved the pre-interview Facebook 'friending', followed by an in-depth qualitative interview.

We break the interview down further into four additional parts that we use to structure the rest of this chapter. The steps in total were: (1) pre-interview friending and participant responses to it, (2) social media patterns, (3) personal mapping, (4) the scroll back itself, and (5) looking forward to social media futures. While steps 2–5 took place within a single interview, it is useful for us to separate each stage enabling us to reflect critically on the research process, as well as providing a roadmap for other researcher using social media as a research tool.

Stage 1—Friending and Participant Responses to It

In stage one, after the participant has agreed to take part in the project, we asked them if they wanted to become Facebook friends. We considered this to be useful for a number of reasons. Firstly, mimicking the way that contemporary friendships are often formed, becoming friends on the site meant that the participants were able to connect to us and to find out more about us before meeting face-to-face. Further justification for this move was received during interviews with participants who claimed that they found it strange if they met someone new and they didn't have a Facebook profile. As Cate (20) said, 'I think that is a normal thing although people don't really admit to that but it's normal.'

Additionally it would have been at odds with the research had we not each had a profile through which we could friend our participants. Both of us were already and still are (at the time of writing) Facebook users and therefore we had profiles that the participants were able to see. We did not create research-only profiles, to 'protect' ourselves, as we wanted to be as open as we were asking our participants to be with us. The longevity of this Facebook friendship raised some interesting—and quite different—responses from our respective University Ethics Committee: Lincoln's University ethics committee was keen to see the 'friendship' terminated at the end of the study (as with Miller's 2011 study). Robards' ethics committee on the other hand were willing to accept that the 'friendship' continue on beyond the formal research, in line with feminist scholarship around 'cultivating relationships with research subjects in ways that engender a sense of interaction, participation and involvement' (Rumens 2008: 17).

After sending an email to the participant confirming the details of the research, setting out the next stages and inviting them to become Facebook friends, we found that we received friend requests very quickly. This connection gave us useful insights into the social media practices of our participants, serving as a basis for the interviews that followed. However, we acknowledge that friending our research participants does raise important ethical considerations (as discussed elsewhere by Robards 2013) particularly around intentionality (who is Facebook for?), the ongoing nature of consent, and consent in the context of shared, co-constituted digital traces. We address these considerations in the sections below.

We used the friend request process as an opening point of discussion, finding out how they felt about it. Many participants were somewhat blasé about either sending the friend request or receiving one, while others explained how they responded to it in relation to their broader privacy practices:

> Generally, actually when people send me a friend request recently I've had to think twice if I actually know them or not but because I was so excited about the research and I was excited that I could be involved I was willing to have you as a friend on Facebook ... But in terms of like my privacy, I'm more cautious about it. Like for adding people that I won't be speaking to in the future and that I haven't really spoken to in the past but that's only recently. I used to just add everyone. (Neha, 20)

Neha's discussion of receiving the researcher's friend request provokes her to outline how her friending practices have changed over time, and how as she has got older and more experienced using social media, she has become more cautious about who she becomes friends with. Feeling a sense of trust is important here, and certainly our status as University researchers contributed significantly to this. In this respect, all but three of our participants became friends with us on the site. Other examples of the responses we received included:

> **Tina (22):** I was just kind of like "Well, why not?" Because if everyone else can see it then there's no issue you seeing it.
>
> **Louis (20):** I sent the request initially. I didn't have any issue with privacy settings. I feel pretty comfortable with the stuff I post up on Facebook, obviously it is a private sort of domain which I share with people but I don't have much of an issue sharing with other people.
>
> **Cate (20):** No I didn't change anything and I just think I've got my family on Facebook and when I was younger I know I'd have been a lot more conscious of that but I think now I don't just post things. I do think about what I post generally, especially because I've got my parents. So I think because I've got them, because I've got other family members, I do kind of bear that in mind sometimes. So you know, I felt comfortable with it especially because I know it's for this. It's not just like a complete stranger that I don't know at all.

The theme of trust clearly runs through the excerpts above, while additional themes also emerged around transparency, feeling comfortable with posts shared and uses of Facebook. Tina's view is that all she shares can be seen by all her friends anyway, so she had no need to edit out specific disclosures or make areas of her profile private before inviting the researcher to become friends. Her disclosures are meant to be visible to all her friends and thus her posts are made accordingly. Louis's comments highlight his default position as being at ease with his disclosures, highlighted by the types of disclosures he made which were primarily around his hobbies of travelling and football. Cate's use of Facebook is underpinned by the fact that she has a number of family members as friends. This instigates a specific kind of posting behaviour that is more measured, guarded and family-appropriate. Interestingly, Cate uses the fact that she has family members as friends as justification for becoming friends with the researcher as part of this project; there's nothing she wouldn't want her family to see which means there's nothing she wouldn't want us to see.

With the permission of the participants, we used our access to their profiles to help us approach the interview itself. Not only did the process of becoming Facebook friends present some interesting questions for us about privacy and ethics but also in relation to how personal content and access to it is viewed by Facebook users. As a site through which multiple connections are made with other users, access to participants' profiles also mean we could view disclosures made by their Facebook friends subject to their privacy settings, where our participants were tagged in posts made by others for instance. From a research perspective, the capacity to reach more data was certainly appealing as the more data we could access the richer the understanding of our participants contexts of use would appear to be. However—and importantly—we had not received any form of consent to access these posts made by others, nor did we consider it to be ethically sound to dip into these Timelines, despite them being part of our own participants' profiles. Additionally, even though our participants did consent to us reviewing their Timelines, we only used their interview transcripts as our data source, using Facebook merely as a way to confirm or check information once the interview was completed. Hence, in this book we do not use data directly taken from Facebook Timelines themselves. The goal here was to reflect on growing up narratives as mediated on Facebook as they are understood by users. We weren't 'scraping' comments or even using screenshots from our participants' timelines, but instead using them as a prompt, a starting point, for co-analysis.

A critical aspect of the research was that the participant was present to work alongside us as a co-analyst of their own digital traces. For us, analysing posts on Facebook in the abstract could not provide us with the level of understanding needed to make sense of this data, with comments very easily being misunderstood or 'taken out of context' to use boyd's phrase (2010). By inviting our participants to act as co-analysts, we were able to 'read between the lines' with them, as they explained the meanings of cryptic posts, the back-stories behind certain images, or as they mapped out friendship circles, and provided context for jokes and absences.

While this approach revealed much, it also has its own limitations. Participants would sometimes mis-remember or forget things that scrolling back would resurface or challenge their own recollection, as we explore further below through the example of Leon (29).

Stage 2—Social Media Patterns

Stage two of the research process was the first in the more traditional qualitative approach of in-depth interviewing. The interview itself was divided into four distinct steps. First, there was a discussion on more general social media use (including the uses of different social network sites), Facebook adoption (When did you start using Facebook? Why?), time spent on Facebook, routines of access, and so on. The questions in this stage of the interview were relatively straight-forward, prompting some basic recall and storytelling, to build rapport and get participants into the mode of the interview. These questions also helped to signpost Facebook content that we could explore in more depth once we were on the site (stage 4) and enabled us to begin identifying narratives of growing up in context. This stage also helped us to 'break the ice' in the interview scenario, with easy questions that did not require too much deep reflection, helping us to build rapport.

Stage 3—Mapping

While we were of course interested in seeing what was visible on the Facebook Timelines of our participants, we were equally interested to find out what was absent. What was missing? What was hidden, or erased? What kind of things don't make it on to Facebook that might otherwise be understood as 'critical' or 'fateful' moments (Giddens 1991, Thomson et al. 2004)? The mapping exercise revealed the extent to which participants relied on Facebook to do the recalling for them: a number of participants actually found it challenging to remember the years in which critical events happened, often being surprised to see different years appearing on Facebook for these events. Was it their own memory that was faulty? Or the inscription on Facebook?

Our participants were asked to complete a handwritten timeline of what they perceived to be key transitional or critical moments in their lives so far, and since they had joined Facebook. Our intention here was to explore what our participants interpreted as key or critical moments and to discover if and in what ways these events were visible on Facebook. Participants did often struggle with this, finding it a challenge to remember specific events and dates and having to confirm them through disclosures made on Facebook, sometimes going back to adjust their handwritten timeline. In this respect then, we would argue that scroll back enables users to fill in missing memories, while the site itself works as an archive within which these memories are permanently stored (an aspect, we argue in Chapter One, that Facebook has continually worked to develop). The depth of the handwritten narratives varied as the examples below demonstrate, but we are cautious that other factors were in play here: being unsure about how much to disclose, perception of a "critical moment", the context in which the timeline was written (busy cafe), time constraints, and so on.

Stage 4—Scrolling Back

In this stage of the interview, we asked participants to log into their Facebook accounts (using their own device, or Google Chrome's 'Incognito' mode on our own laptops or PCs) and navigate to their Timelines. From here, we scrolled right back to their very first disclosure, which for users who had put their date of birth into their profile, appears as the day they were born. From here we asked the participants to 'drive', navigating in reverse chronological order through the years, including years they were not actually 'on Facebook' but years in which they had later retrospectively tagged 'life events', such as the birth of a younger sibling, a graduation, travel, and so on. In years where they were 'on Facebook', at the time of our interviews Facebook sometimes provided summaries when a year was selected: friends added, photos tagged in, even algorithmically sorting some posts. At the time of writing however, this seems to have changed, revealing how the platform itself is constantly inventing and reinventing itself.

While we generally progress and scrolled back in reverse chronological order, we also let the participants take us in different directions. Sometimes we would scroll back through albums—especially profile picture albums, which were a particularly curated selection of images that some thought had gone into, serving to represent the user on the platform. Facebook profile pictures also tended to be weighted more heavily by the algorithm that chooses what is featured in newsfeeds, so they would often attract more attention, likes, reactions, and so on. In many cases, where participants were more systematic and set out to scroll back to every single post, it quickly became clear that this would be far too time consuming, and we had to nudge them along to go to a more recent year. In these situations, they would often quickly flip through dozens of posts, and settle on one every now and then to discuss at more length, as we had requested that they narrate their Timelines as they would a photo album or a diary.

As we have described above, the presence of the participant was crucial in our research design and analysis for three key reasons: First, we were always conscious of the intentionality behind the disclosures we were interested in. Their personal histories shared on social media were not made for us as researchers; they were intimate personal records of life shared between friends. By scrolling back with participants, we were radically changing the context and temporal aspects of these disclosures. We were asking our participants to explain their teenage mindsets and life worlds, which we could not have understood without them. Second, we wanted the project to be enabling for our participants: enabling for them to make sense of their own digital traces, to critically reflect on what was visible and also what was not visible, and for them to be able to control that content. Third, we wanted to understand what went on behind the scenes and between the lines: what was the story behind that vague status update? Who were the friends in the photos? What posts prompted discomfort, embarrassment, or even panic? Why did a particular post take several drafts to get right before posting and why was this important?

An excellent example of this is taken from our interview with Leon (29). When scrolling back to some photos of a night out from a number of years back, Leon was shocked and embarrassed to see photos he had since forgotten about:

> This is photos, I presume when I ... so this is from nights out. Oh God! I hope this is not visible to everybody else! It does say it's public, not really alright with that. Can I change that? [laughs] how do I stop this? Hide from timeline, hide from timeline. Just gonna go through this—hide from timeline ... Oh my God look at that—that's embarrassing! [laughs] What's this? Weird people—why's that on there? Can I delete this? Can I delete it?
>
> (Leon, 29)

We found that the process of narrating disclosures provoked participants to ask (themselves) a lot of questions about posts. As Leon says nervously above "What's this? ... why's that on there? Can I delete this?". During the interviews, participants were re-piecing together their past and remembering things they had forgotten about. Some even used the site to check dates and events based on the information being resurfaced through the scroll back method. In the context of growing up narratives, participants were not simply scrolling through content but were scrolling back through their own lives. This provoked reflections upon how much they had matured since joining the site, as noted through observations on writing style, content, uses of grammar and punctuation, as well as observations on what mattered to their much younger self and what matters to them now. Some participants expressed anxiety about how naive they felt they had been and how vulnerable some of their posts could have made them, clearly articulating an understanding of the appropriateness of disclosures as fun, silly, help-seeking, emotional and so on. Others felt hesitant to read posts because they were worried what they might be confronted with. You can almost feel Leon's hesitation and nervousness about a set of photos that he has re-discovered through this scroll back method that he also discovers are set to 'public'. The urgency in his voice ('hide from timeline, hide from timeline') represents his panic to ensure the photos cannot be seen on his profile, and he even resorts to asking the interviewer how to set the photos to a private setting.

Privacy settings, the visibility of certain posts, and the processes around revising historical digital traces are key to experiences of 'growing up on Facebook'. We will revisit these practices and themes in subsequent chapters.

Similarly during the scroll back stage of the research, Karen (27) was confronted with posts that she felt embarrassed about and like Leon she discovered that the post was public as she was looking back over her Timeline with the researcher. As with Leon, there was a sense of panic in Karen's voice as she tried to work out how to adjust the settings and as she vocalises her concerns that the post 'better not have been seen' by her friends (despite it having been their since 2012 and seemingly not seen since then either). The scroll back method revealed material that she now considered shameful and embarrassing and the research process has presented her with an opportunity to limit who can see the post there and then. In the photo she is wearing 'skimpy shorts' for a night out, probably for an 18th birthday celebration by her recollection. Her concerns come from an imagined scenario: if someone 'accidentally comes across my Facebook, I want them to see me in a, I don't know, a professional way instead of a girl who's really drunk with like shorts riding up her areas!'. Amidst her slight panic are narratives of a transition from her teenage years to her twenties from a fun, carefree time, to becoming a professional, using past images to position her current—and future—professional self. The photograph she discovered did not immediately provoke reflections of a good night and fun times, rather anxiety about how the image serves her now. Some years later, as a PhD student who also works as a sessional lecturer, Karen considers this image to fall outside of the boundaries of her present professional image—it simply does not work as part of her present narrative of self, hence the urgency to make the image private.

As with a number of participants who were confronted with posts that they believed no longer represent them, Karen does not delete the image that caused her that initial embarrassment, rather she changed the settings to private so that only she could see it. This demonstrates that while its performative function has changed, Karen still considers it to be a part of her past, a past that she does not want to completely erase, but does not want on display either. In this respect, Facebook works as this holding space; an archive of lives curated to foreground specific life narratives, but with a substantial repository of material to dip back into.

As we have argued elsewhere (Vivienne, Robards & Lincoln 2016) this process created a sort of 'holding space' for our participants who were scrolling through vast amounts of content on a daily basis, but had spent little time scrolling through and reflecting upon their own disclosures. As a result, participants often ended the research interview by thanking us for creating the time to go through their profiles, even feeling a sense of having 'cleaned out' and 'cleansed' their profiles through merely looking at the content or identifying content to edit out. This experience draws on a teenage bedroom metaphor (Lincoln 2012; Lincoln & Robards 2014) in that such practices are akin to the ways they may clean out their bedrooms and re-discover old objects that takes them back to their younger selves, re-affirms who they are or throwing away things that no longer serve a purpose (Lincoln 2012; Woodward 2015).

Stage 5—Back to the Future

To finish the interview off, we asked our participants about how they imagined things might change around social media in the future. This allowed us to move away from the scroll back process and the Facebook Timelines themselves, to debrief, but also to think forward. Will Facebook be around in another decade? What might it look like? These kinds of speculative questions helped to uncover anxieties and ambivalence about Facebook but also social media more generally. In responding to our questions and prompts in this stage of the interview, our participants also imagined their own futures. Where would they be in ten years? How might they imagine socialising their own children into social media use, having grown up using social media themselves? While the answers to some of these questions are beyond the scope of our work in this book, we will return to these themes and questions in our final chapter.

Scrolling for You

In 2015 Facebook introduced "On This Day", a feature that the site claimed presented 'a new way to look back at things you have shared and posts you've been tagged in on Facebook' (Gheller, 2015: *newsroom.fb.com*). This development followed the success of third party applications such as TimeHop that resurfaces photos from the same day from across different social network profiles enabling users to see old posts again. Rather than relying on the user to look back over their archive, this function digs back for the user, providing nostalgic reminders of times gone by, as well as times shared on Facebook. Consequently, users are reminded of the sheer amount of content—going back years—that they have stored on the site, potentially re-aligning any consideration of deleting a profile.

When talking about the 'On this Day' function our participant Shaima (29) described it as a type of 'automated scroll back', that is that the function algorithmically pulls posts from the same day in a previous year. Recent updates by Facebook have ensured that not all posts on that day are resurfaced. For example, posts about the death of loved ones that have received high numbers of comments are not resurfaced, neither are posts from an ex-partner (see, for instance, Eric Meyer's 2014 reflections on the 'algorithmic cruelty' of Facebook resurfacing images of his deceased child). Akin to the 'scroll back' method 'On this Day' undoubtedly serves to provoke feelings of nostalgia but for our participants, it also provoked feelings associated with confronting this younger self that, as we demonstrate above with scroll back, include guilt, embarrassment, shame, panic, anxiety as well as happiness, warmth, joy, love and comfort. Much like stumbling across an old photograph in an album the 'random' appearance of an old post on the timeline can initiate a number of different responses. Unlike the scroll back method we have outlined here, 'On this Day' generally resurfaces single posts although this can be more if the Facebook user is prolific in their posts.

In addition to the memories that are recalled through the function, we also argue that 'On this Day' provides daily opportunities for users to edit their profiles. Not only does the function provide an opportunity for reflection, it is also potentially presenting an opportunity for users to delete images. However, this is complicated by the algorithmic make up of the feature because primarily it is resurfaced based on the popularity of the post as well as its happy, positive content (i.e. not a post about the death of a loved one). In this respect, it is arguably not presenting images that will potentially be deleted from a Timeline—in fact, quite the opposite—but as a form of profile maintenance and preservation. In this respect, finding and deleting content from a profile is the responsibility of the user rather than an automated Facebook function. Consequently, our research approach gives users the opportunity to do this 'clearing out' work. Maintaining the archive based on popular images and positive experiences is helped along by Facebook who want their users to remain active.

Scrolling Back as Emotional Labour

Our discussion of the scroll back method has demonstrated that going back over years worth of content is labour intensive in a number of ways. This includes the physical labour required to do the scrolling; the labouring of time as it takes sometimes hours to scroll back through so much data; and the emotional labour that comes with confronting the past when scrolling back through an old archive. Consider Shaima (29) who used the scroll back exercise to reflect back on her time when she was a 'fangirl' of a Korean pop band. Shaima's story provides a useful example of emotional labour on Facebook demonstrating how this term changes over time and how scroll back can 'take you back' to a time and a place, evoking those nostalgic feelings of fandom and adoration.

Shaima was a rather cautious Facebook user and always had been, keeping what she posted to an absolute minimum. She spoke in-depth about the extent to which she would consider the content of a post before sharing it on Facebook. This caution was practised even more now that she was in her late twenties and pursuing a professional career. Shaima was an international student from Malaysia studying for a doctoral degree in Liverpool. When reflecting upon her use in her interview and when scrolling back through her Timeline, Shaima often used the language of regret to frame her own posting practises. For example she said 'I am somehow jealous of people who don't have any restrictions on posting things on Facebook because I think they are more, is it, bold'. For Shaima, being bold on Facebook is a representation of being bold in other realms and she regrets not being able to use this platform more confidently to share her views. In this respect, her cautious use appears labour-intensive as she emotionally connects to the connotations of what she really wants to say, but then regrets the modesty of her post when she eventually shares something on the site. This 'narrative of regret' continued as Shaima reflected on her friends' use of the site and she goes on to say 'It doesn't matter even if they'll put up an album of spring, like flowers and I was like "at least you do have those kinds of memories that will appear again"'. Shaima's cautious use has, for her, become synonymous with not having an archive of memories. She looks on in envy of other friends who can post the most mundane images (springtime flowers) but these images will go on to remind the user of specific times in their lives or to remind them of the things they love and enjoy. Shaima's restraint is therefore measured against other friends more liberal posts to the point at which Shaima is inferring that if the memories are not shared on Facebook then they will become invalid, forgotten or lost. There was something deeply significant about her reflection on absent memories, and how she experienced a lack of freedom in her posting practices.

These freedoms are informed by Shaima's Islamic background having grown up in Malaysia and the different experiences of freedom she is now exposed to while studying in the UK. However, there also appeared to be a significant amount of self-restricting that resulted in cautious posting practises over the years. An exception to this was in 2010, a year that represented a period in Shaima's life when she used Facebook as a space through which her love of a Korean pop singer could play out. When scrolling back through her Timeline Shaima gets to 2010 and announces: 'so this is the first time I met the Korean guy'.

During that year, Shaima was what she described as a 'fan girl' of a Male Korean singer. She describes the year as 'the ultimate, craziness or something because this was the time when I really loved that guy'. In that year the singer was touring in Shaima's home country of Malaysia and she had been selected to go on stage, meet him, and get his autograph during that tour. Scrolling back through her Timeline enabled Shaima to revisit the joys and emotions of this time. Clearly she has posted much about her 'fangirling' and about the singer she so adored. Seeing this content again enabled her to connect viscerally to that experience. While much of her reflections about her use of Facebook are tainted by narratives of regret and the fact she wishes she did have more of 'those types of memories' (the banal, the everyday), the ones that she has recorded are described as memory 'sparks'. Shaima said, 'I think it will remind you what you are doing at the time and surprisingly when you are looking at those photos it reminds you, you really remember what happens and that moment. Although when you ask me, it doesn't have that spark to remind me'. Her 'fangirling' experiences as they have been represented on Facebook enable a form of nostalgia that is clearly more interactive and stimulating than just thinking about that time or merely looking at photos collected in an album. There are elements of Shaima's practices that are akin to looking back over an old journal or diary but the Timeline offers an account of those experiences that are not just created by the user but by other fans too, and contain a range of content from status updates, photos, videos, links and so on. Those experiences are archived 'in the moment' thus preserving an account of that time that is rich enough that one can almost relive the 'sparks' of that time.

For Shaima then, Facebook facilitates important emotionally charged memory-work. The scroll back method enabled her to revisit this time and experience again the adulation of this period, while also regretting she didn't have more moments to experience like this on the site—too few 'sparks' to relive and revisit. Her narrative of regret continued further as she reflected upon the fact that she was in her final year of studying abroad and soon she would be back in Malaysia having not posted much at all about her time in Liverpool.

Int.:	So is it something you wish you had?
Shaima:	Yes. I really wish. And even now as I'm coming towards the end of living abroad here. It is kind of different from your country so I suppose there are some things I want to post to remember, who are not here. What are you going to do because let's say you keep blogs or journaling then you can track back, but this is one of the things you can do [on Facebook] but I can't bring myself to do it.

Shaima's experiences capture some of the complexities that have been unravelled by using the scroll back method, and the extent to which the method has prompted participants to critically reflect upon and analyse their years of use. Much like the definitions of use that we briefly discuss in the final section of this chapter, labour—and particularly emotional labour—on Facebook is multi-faceted and labour is just as much associated with what is not posted as with what is. It is only through engaging our participants in discussion of their Timelines that we have been able to understand these facets and the contexts within which memory-work is done.

Scroll Back and Notions of 'active' Use

In the final section of this chapter, we briefly reflect upon notions of Facebook "use" and narratives of active participation on the site when looking back over years of disclosures.

Our participants were in their twenties, and had been using Facebook for a sustained period of time from a site they used solely to one of a number as other social network sites such as Tumblr, Twitter and Instagram gained popularity (a "poly media" approach (Madianou & Miller 2012) to engaging with social network sites). Given this, and to go back to the question "is Facebook cool?" in our previous chapter, it became evident through the research process that our participants were often keen to describe themselves as inactive users of the site. They had accounts but they 'did not use it much'. This was a curious position to claim since the participants were self-selecting and had identified as a Facebook user and the scroll back method enabled us to interrogate this notion of 'active' use further with the participants. In addition, stage 1 of our research as outlined above provided us with the opportunity to understand where Facebook was positioned in the social media landscapes of our participants as well as their 'hierarchies of cool'.

Undoubtedly, their use of Facebook had changed quite drastically over the years, and inevitably given the changes and developments that have changed within the site itself, particularly with regards to privacy. Their accounts were, however, by no means dormant as scrolling back revealed. Other scholars such as Justine Gangeaux invite participants to look back over the activity log that often reveals more extensive use that the participant had perhaps realised (Gangeaux, 2018). Indeed, this would be a productive and fascinating method to employ in future studies, and also perhaps confronting for reasons other than those documented in this chapter.

An analysis of our participants narratives around use are primarily situated within narratives of their disclosure practices. One of our core arguments in this book is that disclosure practices are aligned closely with 'growing up' and maturing on the site. In this respect, participants commonly expressed embarrassment or shame (even in a comical way) when confronted with the content, length and style of very early Facebook posts that they had never revisited. The quantity of disclosures was, in most cases, overwhelmingly more in the early Facebook years, so it is fair that participants should position their use today in this context. But beyond that, there were narratives of 'cool' placed around Facebook, with the site being positioned as the much less cool relation to platforms such as Instagram or Snapchat, with comments relating to little or practically non-use now, often made before the interview had even begun.

Livingstone (2014) closely aligns different age phases with social media use. For example she says:

> By age 14–16, the increasing complexity of their social and emotional lives, as well as their greater maturity, contributes to a re-focusing on what is valuable to them. Their changing orientation to social networking online (and offline) appears to be shaped by their changing peer and parental relations, and has implications for their perceptions of risk or harm. (1)

Livingstone identifies 'changing orientations' in social media use as young people move through their late childhood and early teens that correlate to how they relate to themselves, their friends, peers and family, and complement their changing priorities. For Livingstone this also closely aligns to what users perceive to be risky or harmful on social media. For example, Livingstone (2014) explained that 9–11 year olds are concerned with what is real or fake; 11–13 year olds with what is fun, transgressive or fake; 14–16 year olds often perceive risk in the context of complex emotional and social change.

This framework for understanding changing social media literacy undoubtedly complements our findings, but in addition what we have been able to achieve with our participants is a longitudinal approach around using social media itself to reflect back over at least two of those phases that Livingstone refers to as well as beyond the teenage years into the twenties when one's priorities arguably change again, for example in relation to careers or relationships. Our findings move discussions about social media literacy away from 'snapshots' of different phases to a long term narrative that captures the nuances of growing up over an extended period of time. Importantly, the narratives constructed around their disclosures are framed within the context of growing up as we suggest above, aligning with Livingstone's (2014) observation above about the 'changing orientations' of young people in their mid-teens.

Nena and Cate reflected back over a period of 6–7 years of Facebook use, having both joined the site in their early teens:

> I think my usage of Facebook and my maturing has coincided like it's both like kind of like worked together. So using Facebook less would be to do with me growing up and just becoming a woman. Nena (20)

> I think partly just growing up as well; knowing that you don't want to be putting everything you think on Facebook. Cate (20)

Facebook plays an integral part in Nena and Cate's growing up, their use aligning with their perceptions of maturity, even stabilising the self or 'becoming a woman' as Nena says. These quotes also demonstrate how both young women have become more experienced users and thus more aware of the risks of 'putting everything you think on Facebook', operationalising more discrete patterns of disclosure and engagement with the site. Additionally the quotes suggest that avid Facebook use was an activity more closely aligned with being a young teenager and having fun with your friends, but that the site takes on new significances as the participants get older. However, Facebook does not become redundant in such scenarios, remaining part of an ageing identity: our participants did not envisage a time when they would be without Facebook as its future uses as a contacts list, storage space, and archive of memories were clearly articulated.

Other reflections on social literacy took more extreme forms, with some participants talking about scrolling back to early posts in which they had 'disclosed everything' seemingly with a limited sense of what may or may not be appropriate while also maximising on the technological affordances offered by the site. Ali (23), for example, said 'when I first got it I put everything on it. As in I gave them every bit of information they wanted to know. I put all the pictures, videos, absolutely everything you could use Facebook for I did … I used to have my mobile number on there for public, everything used to be public. My mobile number was on there. I think I even had my address on there at some point'. The key points to note here are: (1) the amount of information shared on the site and; (2) the fact that all of that information was made public. Over time, Ali learned that a 'share everything' approach was not entirely sensible and thus disclosures of personal information were scaled back and managed more appropriately using the privacy settings. But as with Cate and Nena, Ali reflects back on his early Facebook use as a marker of his maturity both on and off the site.

Cate (20) continued to reflect on how her use has changed:

> so mainly now it's kind of sharing and posting things like that. I wouldn't just write what's on my mind. I don't do that anymore. So I think that's the major change that you can now share things and also like photos as well.

Cate, like a number of our other participants has 'scaled back' on her 'performance of the personal' on Facebook to the point at which 'less' is considerably more significant than 'more' in terms of the number of disclosures made as we'll as the type of content. Further, the sharing of too much personal information on Facebook is interpreted as risky, not only in terms of the safety implications but also with regards to identity. As noted above, a significant lessening in 'what's on my mind' type disclosures is seen as a signifier of moving towards a more mature, adult identity. As Ali (20) elaborated:

> Really now, it went from me using it for everything to now it's just sort of an essential where say I've got group work at uni, I don't know who the people I'm working with, the first thing you'll do is go on Facebook and message them. So it's like a contact system rather than a social element to it. Whereas when I first got it, it was purely social and everything you did people would be like oh it's going on Facebook or let's put it on Facebook or something like that. So it was very, very social to start with. But then as time went on there is less and less information on there about me, like personal information ... I can't remember the last time I put a status. It must have been over a year and a half, two years ago.

Aligning with Livingstone's framework on social media literacy (2014) discussed above, Ali's comments reflect his 'changing orientations' and priorities that mean he is using Facebook in quite different ways in his twenties than he did in his early teens. For him, Facebook now stands as a useful communication tool through which he can maintain semi-professional relationships with fellow University students rather than using it as a site to socialise with them, although he states 'what I upload is probably edging on not really being a Facebook user'.

Scroll Back Ethics

Using Facebook profiles as texts in research is extremely sensitive. On the one hand, as qualitative researchers we cannot help but relish the prospect of being able to work with such rich archives of data and Facebook profiles potentially offer the researcher previously unseen quantities of detailed information about individuals stored in one place, often on an everyday basis and organised chronologically. Before our very eyes we have longitudinal life narratives of young people's growing up stories—sometimes the quality of which have been the stuff of dreams for qualitative researchers engaging in longitudinal research. However, what is crucial here is that for us, these are not archives that have been kept as part of our research project. These are personal archives produced through everyday interactions, 'managed' by an individual but co-constituted by a networked public of people through tags, comments, and uploads. As we have discovered, these archives can be central to the working through, piecing together, and understanding of a young person's identity. In this respect, as we have detailed here, we were extremely sensitive in our approach and this meant thinking carefully about the ethical implications of using this type of data not meant for research, for research.

One of the obvious complications that adds to this relates to notions of public and private and where in fact Facebook exists within these binary oppositions. Scholars such as Alice Marwick and danah boyd (2011) and Jessica Vitak (2012) argue that social network sites like Facebook operate in an environment of 'context collapse' when the boundaries of public and private are collapsed down and thus young people are 'moving' around, blurring previously firm boundaries. We discuss this in more detail in Chapter Two. This issue of context collapse raises important ethical questions, flagged by Thomson et al. (2014) who ask 'what might it mean for people to engage in social science research without the promise of anonymity, and how might different aspects of confidentiality be explored in relation to "context collapse?"' (p. 13). We had to consider this question carefully in our planning while finding a balance between engaging the participants as co-analysts who were very much at the 'helm' of the scroll back process with respecting their privacy and ensuring anonymity and confidentiality. Our decision to only include extracts from the interviews themselves in our writing and presentation of the data was primarily taken to be sensitive to this issue. However, new and emerging research methodologies are necessarily challenging and rethinking these ethics boundaries further. There is more work to be done.

Conclusion

In this chapter we have critically reflected upon our methodology, paying particular attention to the development of the scroll back method. Imitating the ways in which users engage with social media in their everyday life, the scroll back method presented a familiar way for our participants to engage with their own digital traces, while providing them with an opportunity to go back over years of disclosures on Facebook. The scroll back method was situated within more traditional approaches to qualitative research, namely the in-depth interview (Denzin & Lincoln 1994) and timelining (Sheridan et al. 2011) as it was crucial for us to understand the contexts of disclosures made on the site. However, the participant's role was not only to provide crucial narrative data, but to work alongside us as co-analysts of their own digital traces. As we outline above, this was a key ethical consideration for us, as we were acutely aware that Facebook Timelines have not primarily be written for research purposes, but that they are deeply personal accounts. Our methodology enabled our participants to take control of their disclosures as they scrolled back through years of data, and enabled them to provide narratives around the disclosures they chose to tell us about.

As we argue above, the scroll back method provided us with incredibly rich insights into the lives of the first generation of young people who have lived out their teenage years on one social network site. But we also argue that there were obvious gains for our participants too, namely providing them with the space and time to go back over disclosures that they had not revisited, often since the time of posting. The method enabled participants to identify content they wanted to delete, or share again with friends, and content they had forgotten about, provoking nostalgic reflection on old memories. In this respect, the scroll back method was also described as being 'therapeutic' by a participant who found it enabled them to engage in a digital 'clear out' of their teenage past, particularly as many were contemplating a professional future.

The scroll back method has enabled us to unveil personal histories and detailed growing up stories that we will explore over the next five chapters: Chapter Five relates to the arena of professional and working life as we observe our participants moving into careers from education; Chapter Six considers love and romance exploring, the dynamics of relationships as they play out on the site; Chapter Seven explores the dynamics of family life; and Chapter Eight considers different leisure activities such as music festivals, travel, and sport. In the final chapter of this book we revisit some of the themes introduced above around uses of Facebook, with a particular focus on absences on the site, arguing that non-, ambiguous, or partial disclosures can play an equally important role in understanding young people's growing up narratives on social media.

References

boyd, d. (2006). Friends, Friendsters, and MySpace Top 8: Writing community into being on social network sites. *First Monday, 11*(12), 1–19.

boyd, d. (2010). *Taken out of context: American teen sociality in networked publics.* (PhD thesis), University of California, Berkeley, USA.

Dance, G., LaForgia, M., & Confessore, N. (2018) As Facebook raised a privacy wall, it carved an opening for tech giants. *New York Times*, https://www.nytimes.com/2018/12/18/technology/facebook-privacy.html. Accessed December 20, 2018.

Denzin, N. K., & Lincoln, Y. S. (1994). *Handbook of qualitative research.* Thousand Oaks, CA: Sage.

Erikson, E. H. (1968). *Identity: Youth and crisis.* New York: Norton.

Frith, S. (1984). *The sociology of youth.* Ormskirk: Causeway Press.

Fuchs, C. (2017). *Social media: A critical introduction* (2nd ed.). London: Sage.

Furlong, A., & Cartmel, F. (2007). *Sociology and social change*. Maidenhead: Open University Press.

Gangeaux, J. (2018). *Mediated young adulthood: Using social network sites in the digital era* (unpublished PhD thesis) University of Glasgow, Glasgow, UK.

Gheller, J. (2015). *Introducing on this day: A new way to look back at photos and memories on Facebook*, Facebook Newsroom, visited 6/9/19: https://newsroom.fb.com/news/2015/03/introducing-on-this-day-a-new-way-to-look-back-at-photos-and-memories-on-facebook/

Giddens, A. (1991). *Modernity and self identity*. Cambridge: Polity Press.

Griffin, C. (1993). *Representations of youth*. Oxford: Polity Press.

Hall, S., & Jefferson, T. (Eds.). (1975). *Resistance through rituals: Youth subcultures in post war Britain*. London: Hutchinson and Co.

Henderson, S., Holland, J., McGrellis, S., Sharpe, S., & Thomson, R. (2007). *Inventing adulthoods: A biographical approach to youth transitions*. London: Sage.

Lincoln, S. (2012). *Youth culture and private space*. Basingstoke: Palgrave Macmillan.

Lincoln, S. (2015). 'My Bedroom is Me': Young people, private space, consumption and the family home. In E. Casey & Y. Taylor (Eds.), *Intimacies, critical consumption and diverse economies*. London: Palgrave Macmillan.

Lincoln, S., & Robards, B. (2014). Being strategic and taking control: Bedrooms, social network sites and the narratives of growing up. *New Media & Society, 18*(6), 927–943.

Lincoln, S., & Robards, B. (2016). Editing the project of self: Sustained Facebook use and growing up online. *Journal of Youth Studies, 20*(4), 518–531.

Livingstone, S. (2014). Developing social media literacy: How children learn to interpret risky opportunities on social networking sites. *Communications, 39*(3), 283–303.

Madianou, M., & Miller, D. (2012). Polymedia: Towards a new theory of digital media in interpersonal communication. *International Journal of Cultural Studies, 16*(2), 169–187.

Marwick, A. E., & boyd, d. (2011). I tweet honestly, I tweet passionately: Twitter users, context collapse, and the imagined audience. *New Media & Society, 13*(1), 114–133.

Marwick, A. E., & boyd, d. (2014). "It's just drama": Teen perspectives on conflict and aggression in a networked era. *Journal of Youth Studies, 17*(9), 1187–1204.

Miller, D. (2011). *Tales from Facebook*. Cambridge: Polity.

Nilan, P., Burgess, H., Hobbs, M., Threadgold, S., & Alexander, W. (2015). Youth, social media, and cyber-bullying amongst Australian youth. *Social Media + Society, 1*(2), https://doi.org/10.1177/2056305115604848.

Robards, B. (2010). Randoms in my bedroom: Negotiating privacy and unsolicited content on social network sites. *Prism, 7*(3), 1–12.

Robards, B. (2012). Leaving MySpace, joining Facebook: "Growing up" on social network sites. *Continuum, 26*(3), 385–398. http://doi.org/10.1080/10304312.2012.665836.

Robards, B. (2013). Friending participants: Managing the researcher-participant relationship on social network sites. *YOUNG: Nordic Journal of Youth Research, 21*(3), 217–235.

Robards, B., & Lincoln, S. (2016). Making it "Facebook Official": Reflecting on romantic relationships through sustained Facebook use. *Social Media + Society, 2*(4), 1–10.

Roberts, K. (2009). *Youth in transition: Eastern Europe and the West*. Basingstoke: Palgrave Macmillan.

Rumens, N. (2008). Working at intimacy: Gay men's workplace friendships. *Gender, Work & Organization, 15*(1), 9–30.

Sheridan, J., Chamberlain, K., & DuPuis, A. (2011). Timelining: Visualising experience. *Qualitative Research, 11*(5), 552–569.

Thomson, R., Hadfield, L., Holland, J., Henwood, K., Moore, N., Stanley, L., & Taylor, R. (2014). *New frontiers in QLR: Definitions, design, display*. National Centre for Research Methods. http://eprints.ncrm.ac.uk/3297/1/new_frontiers_in_QLR.pdf. Accessed September 5, 2019.

Thomson, R., Holland, J., McGrellis, S., Bell, R., Henderson, S., & Sharpe, S. (2004). Inventing adulthoods: A biographical approach to understanding youth citizenship. *The Sociological Review, 52*(2), 218–239.

Vitak, J. (2012). The impact of context collapse and privacy on social network site disclosures. *Journal of Broadcasting & Electronic Media, 56*(4), 451–470.

Vivienne, S., Robards, B., & Lincoln, S. (2016) "Holding a Space" for gender-diverse and queer research participants. In A. McCosker, S. Vivienne, & A. Johns (Eds.), *Negotiating digital citizenship: Control, contest and culture*. Lanham: Rowman & Littlefield.

Willis, P. (1990). *Common culture: Symbolic work at play in the everyday cultures of the young*. Milton Keynes: Open University Press.

Woodward, S. (2015). The hidden lives of domestic things: Accumulations in cupboards, lofts and shelves. In E. Casey & Y. Taylor (Eds.), *Intimacies, critical consumption and diverse economies*. London: Palgrave Macmillan.

White, R., & Wyn, J. (2007). *Youth and society: Exploring the social dynamics of youth experience* (2nd ed.). Oxford: Oxford University Press.

Wyn, J., & White, R. D. (1997). *Rethinking youth*. London: Sage.

CHAPTER FIVE

Shaping and Performing Professional Identities: From Education to Employment

The movement from education to employment has not been a 'linear' transition for some time (Wyn & Woodman 2006), but it is still seen as a significant rite of passage for young people navigating towards the idea of adulthood. Getting a first job is a rite of passage that can signal new freedoms such as income and associated autonomies, but also new responsibilities like meeting the expectations of employers, paying taxes, and interacting with banks. For many young people, first jobs happens alongside education: casual and part-time jobs during high school, multiple jobs during tertiary studies, and undertaking more advanced studies (Masters, Graduate Diplomas, etc.) while working full time to improve career advancement opportunities. Despite these complexities and differences, for most young people there are two key educational milestones (experienced and/or anticipated): (a) graduation from secondary/high school; and (b) graduation from tertiary/university education. For many of our participants, it was this second common point of graduation—usually undertaken in their early twenties—that was especially critical for grappling with a 'professional identity'. Twenty-six of our 41 participants were currently studying at or had graduated from university or some form of tertiary education, and all had finished high school or an equivalent secondary qualification. For some of our participants, impending graduations and the prospect of applying for jobs prompted episodes of revisiting the ways in which they were presented on social media, as they began to imagine how potential employers in their careers of choice would search for them and interpret the digital traces of their lives. In this chapter, then, we consider how narratives of 'growing up' play out in the context of the transition from education to employment. In this transition, we explicitly see participants 'editing the project of self' (Giddens 1991), mindfully working out how to present themselves in digital spaces, while curating audiences and content in ways that are markedly different from earlier years.

Two of our participants, Andrea (22) and Dina (23) were nearing the end of medical school at the time of our interview. The training and requirements associated with becoming a medical doctor are particularly gruelling and lengthy, and thus so too are the expectations of professionalism placed on these soon-to-be doctors. Both Andrea and Dina discussed how, as part of their medical training, they had been coached in a job seeking seminar about the recruitment process involving Google and Facebook searches. Dina explained:

> People came and talked to us about how to apply for jobs. And they [said] ... we'll do a Google search on you and we'll look at the first two pages ... so I think that was an incentive for people to change their name on Facebook ... [or] 'tidy up' their profiles.

We will come back to Andrea and Dina, among other participants, later in the chapter. For now, there are two key issues to unpack here that will serve as foundational organising principles for this chapter. First, is the ways in which employers and recruiters are enrolling web and social media search in their hiring processes. This should come as no surprise of course, but it also raises concerns around privacy, how young people conceptualise their personal histories as the 'backdrop' to employment futures, and the lenses through which employers make decisions based on decontextualized digital traces. The second section of this chapter will be more participant-focussed and deal with the strategies of impression management associated with 'tidying up' one's profile. Here, we will explore the practices of our participants to navigate a perceived sense of surveillance from potential employers, from changing one's name to going back through a profile to erase and revise past disclosures. These strategies have significance beyond the employment context, in terms of personal memory, but also how we position youthful experiences in the context of 'adult' employment anxieties in competitive neo-liberal 'job markets'. In this way, we consider how our participants work to shape professional impressions on social media, how they manage boundaries in workplaces, and indeed the ways in which social media use has itself become a form of paid work.

What About the Youthful Hijinks?

In 2010, the then CEO of Google, Eric Schmidt, predicted that 'every young person one day will be entitled automatically to change his or her name on reaching adulthood in order to disown *youthful hijinks* stored on their friends' social media sites' (Jenkins 2010, emphasis added). While these are the words of the journalist interviewing Schmidt, where Jenkins has paraphrased Schmidt, there is an eerie resonance between Schmidt's prediction and the strategy Dina (23) and her peers employed some years later as they were finishing medical school: changing their names to 'disown youthful hijinks' (in Jenkins' words) attached to them on social media. At the time, Schmidt's prediction could have been dismissed as rhetoric that bought into a moral panic about young people posting everything online for all the world to see, oblivious of their privacy and ruining their futures. And yet, only a few years later, there we were with Dina having this conversation about how many of her peers had indeed changed their names on Facebook as they prepared for their careers in medicine. Not just to disown their 'youthful hijinks' though, but as a very precise tactic of impression management with a narrow and quite specific audience in mind: potential employers.

So called 'Millennials', or 'Generation Y', born between the 1980s and early 2000s, experience a range of structural conditions that are significantly different to previous generations: they combine non-standard precarious work patterns and study (Furlong & Cartmel 1997; Furlong 2009; MacDonald & Marsh 2005; MacDonald 2011, 2016; Woodman 2012, 2013; Woodman & Wyn 2015) at the same time as they delay transitions out of the family home (Biggart & Walther, 2012; Furlong, 2009; White & Wyn 2013) and decisions around marriage and children for longer than previous generations (White, Wyn & Robards 2017). Increased levels of participation in higher education have also led to much higher levels of credentialism and a focus on qualifications (Robinson & Lamb 2012; van Krieken et al. 2014: 154). Coupled with high levels of youth unemployment and under-employment (Denney & Churchill 2016), these structural changes make entering into a 'career pathway' a significant and challenging rite of passage. At the same time that these structural changes are taking place in young people's lives and the wider economic landscape, crafting identities in a range of digital social spaces has become central to communication (Baym 2015), civic and political participation (Harris & Roose 2014; Highfield 2017), inclusion and belonging (Robards & Bennett 2011), as we seek to explain in this book.

Before we explore in more detail the practices our participants used in managing emerging professional identities, we will first consider some of the background on how social media are being used by recruiters and employers, to both identify and recruit employees, but also to engage in surveillance of their existing staff. In doing this, we engage with the broader cultural landscape that young people are navigating that is invariably underpinned by neoliberal frameworks within which individuals are tasked with taking responsibility for their own futures.

Social Media and Professional Identity

The most common negative stories about the discrepancy between a professional identity and personal expression are those with popular name recognition: professional athletes, celebrities and politicians (Nothling 2018; Houston & Vedelago 2018). Consider the high profile case of young progressive Scottish MP Mhairi Black. Elected to the House of Commons at just 20-years-old, the youngest MP since 1667, some of Black's tweets from when she was 16-years-old were resurfaced after she took office: "Woke up beside half a can of Tennents [a Scottish lager] and a full pizza and more money than I came out with. I call that a success!", "maths is shite", and "OASIS LIVE!!!!!!!!!!!!!! FUCKIN' YASSSSS MAN" (McKernan 2015). In Australia, conservative MP George Christensen had a Facebook post he made reported to the police. Days after a mass school shooting in the US, Christensen uploaded a photo of himself aiming a handgun with the caption: "You gotta ask yourself, do you feel lucky, greeny punks?" (Nothling 2018). The 'greeny' target in Christensen's post refers to Australia's environmentalist and socially progressive political party The Australian Greens. For both Black and Christensen, what might be seen by some as social media faux pas (or tone deaf and distasteful in Christensen's case) might also be interpreted as appealing to a voter base for others. Black's tweets might humanise and endear her, connecting her to her youth and bypassing the formality and distance politicians are often required to maintain, while Christensen's post (made while he held office) signals an irreverence that might appeal to some while others (precisely the people he seeks to alienate in order to appeal to his base) would interpret it as inciting violence.

While politicians walk a fine line between professional identities and appealing to particular groups of people to secure votes, people in other careers and lines of work might not enjoy so much flexibility in how they manage their impressions. Professional athletes in particular appear to attract a high level of scrutiny. Consider Australian Rugby player Paul Gallen who was fined $50,000 for a late night tweet containing an obscenity, while another, Josh Dugan, had a contract with the Brisbane Broncos (rugby team) terminated following an Instagram post where he told someone to "end yourself" (Carayannis 2016). Cheerleader Caitlin Davies's career was ruined after a photo of her drawing offensive graffiti on an unconscious man was shared on Facebook. UK Footballer Joey Barton and UK gymnast Louis Smith repeatedly found themselves in trouble after constantly using derogatory, often sexist language in their social media posts (Ingle 2016). In each case, utterances and phrases that might go unchallenged in some contexts can be career-ending in the traceable and persistent contexts of social media, especially on platforms athletes leverage to obtain the status of a public figure to attract lucrative sponsorship deals and attention.

While public figures face intense scrutiny, everyday people are now also scrutinised based on their social media disclosures. In 2015, a Sydney hotel supervisor lost his job after making a sexist and offensive comment on the Facebook page of a journalist (Levy 2015) and in 2010 a Coles supermarket employee was fired for comments about her co-worker on Facebook (McWhirter & Cabrera 2010). In 2015, Rachel Burns, a care assistant in a UK residential care home lost her job after posting a video and photo of a singalong at work. According to the company's head office, Burns had breached Surrey County Council policy on four counts: she had posted the image on Facebook, it identified a resident, she posted a video, and she was friends with one of the residents' family members (McDermott 2017).

While extreme enough to make it into the news, these examples serve as a reminder that both past and current disclosures on social media can be damaging in a professional context. What is less newsworthy are the many decisions made by managers and recruiters on a daily basis, informed by searches on social media.

Recruitment managers are now turning to social media to scout for talent, target potential recruits (Carrillat et al. 2014), and to vet applicants (Nikolaou 2014). Industry surveys of hiring staff indicate that as many as 90% use social media to screen potential employees (Bennett 2011). This creates both challenges and opportunities for job-seekers and recruiters alike. From a recruitment perspective, as both Nikolaou (2014: 181–182) and Jeske and Shultz (2016: 540) explain, using social media to screen potential recruits is a cost-effective way to gain useful information, but can also raise concerns around privacy and discrimination.

In their study of 448 undergraduates in the US, Drouin, O'Connor, Schmidt and Miller (2015) found that 42% did not think a person's social media should be used to make hiring or firing decisions. Another 28% were neutral on this question, and only 30% thought social media should be taken into consideration around hiring and firing. Drouin et al. also asked whether or not it was 'acceptable' for a teacher to post 'a picture on her Facebook site of her holding a beer during a vacation to Ireland' (2015: 125)—a very specific scenario that gets at a range of assumptions around impression management, employment, and context. 52% of their respondents said it was acceptable, 24% were neutral, and 24% said it was not acceptable. When it came to whether or not that same teacher should be at risk of losing their job for posting photos depicting lewd behaviour, however, 44% said there should be some repercussions there (27% neutral, 29% thought there should be no threat to losing one's job). This paints a complex picture of how the young people in this study conceptualised what was appropriate or not in terms of how employers might use social media to make hiring and firing decisions: okay in some situations, but not in others. Drouin et al. conclude that 'this generation of upcoming workers must be informed that regardless of their opinions of the fairness of these policies, as it currently stands, their short-term social media use could have a long-term effect on their future careers' (2015: 128). This kind of responsibilising discourse firmly places young people as the bearers of their own success and failure when it comes to impression management. This ignores the responsibilities of and standards we should demand of employers or platforms when it comes to privacy, respecting boundaries around work, and allowing young people to have space where every action and utterance is not weighed against entire future careers.

Comparing Facebook and the less widely used but professionally-focussed LinkedIn, José van Dijck (2013) argues that these platforms afford opportunities for self-expression, self-communication, and self-promotion. She suggests that maintaining 'multiple personas across platforms' can potentially be a powerful strategy for managing identities, with certain audiences in mind for each. Indeed, research has demonstrated the strategic and nuanced ways in which some young people exercise control over their use of different social media, across different contexts, especially as that control relates to 'social privacy' (Raynes-Goldie 2010). In contrast to Drouin et al. (2015), this approach emphasises a much more nuanced and 'empowering' approach to thinking about impression management strategies across social media profiles where the 'threat' of 'implications' for future careers do not have to loom heavy over everything young people do or do not do on social media.

The Reflexive Project of the Self for Hire

As we explored in Chapter Three, Anthony Giddens (1991), in his theory of the reflexive project of the self, explains that selves are made, not inherited, or static. People are expected to continuously work on, reflect on, and revise their self-projects as they build careers, progress through education, negotiate loss and failure, and deal with trauma. Expressions like 'I'm taking some time to work on myself' or 'pick yourself up and get back on the horse' after a disruption to the self-project are examples of how this self-work is individualised. Giddens describes the 'stable individual' as someone with 'a feeling of biographical continuity which he or she is able to grasp reflexively and, to a greater or lesser degree, communicate to others' (1991: 54). While Giddens has been criticised for placing too much emphasis on agency at the cost of carefully considering cultural and structural forces that also shape reflexive projects of the self (Adams 2003), the concept nonetheless still carries much theoretical weight in discourses of identity and is operationalised in various contexts.

Rachel Thomson (2007), for example, considers the curriculum vitae (CV) to be a modern, employment-focussed manifestation of the reflexive project of the self. As she argues, the CV, or resumé, requires a very specific ordering of self-narratives for a particular outcome: finding a job. CVs document and craft stories around educational background, past employment, future trajectories and goals, experience related to the particular job one is applying for, and even hobbies or personal interests for young people applying for entry-level jobs. The CV requires a particular kind of storytelling, embellishing some truths and leaving out others. Different careers require very different kinds of CVs: To include a photo or not? What kind of referees are best, and how many should be provided? Should the CV be emailed, attached to a form, or delivered in-person? The reflexive project of the self is not just about communicating one's self to others (although this is an important part of Giddens' (1991) formulation), but also about organising stories about ourselves *for* ourselves. As Thomson (2007: 80) explains, 'story-telling (to ourselves and others) is central to ... the reflexive project of the self. As we rework existing narratives and forge new ones, we invent and reinvent who it is possible to be'.

The very idea of the CV, resumé, or portfolio as a material object is perhaps passé in some industries. At least in the creative industries, an Instagram profile has become a portfolio of work that serves a similar function. Florists, tattoo artists, hairdressers, and fashion designers can all leverage the visual focus of a platform like Instagram to attract potential clients or buyers, and find work. Walzer and Sanjurjo (2016) in their study of tattoo artists, found that being present on social media was essential for these artists to find work, but also exposed them to risks. One of their participants explained 'today, if you don't put something that's yours on the Internet, you don't exist, but if you do, you get it stolen in the same minute' (Participant in Walzer & Sanjurjo 2016: 74). Being able to refer potential clients to an Instagram profile or draw in new clients through social media has become crucial to the point that not having a presence in these spaces can mean you don't exist for some audiences.

There are of course entire social media platforms dedicated to helping users find work, with LinkedIn being the most well-known. Established in 2003, LinkedIn's vision is to 'create economic opportunity for every member of the global workforce' (about.linkedin.com, 2018). Users can create professional profiles that document their employment history, identify 'career interests' for recruiters, and even compare salaries. Despite their vision of creating opportunity for everyone, according to van Dijck (2013: 207), LinkedIn's user base is 'mostly male ... middle-aged (corporate) professionals', looking for or already in high-income jobs in large firms. Van Dijck argues that LinkedIn is more than just a CV however, and instead LinkedIn profiles actually serve as 'inscriptions of *normative* professional behavior: each profile shapes an idealized portrait of one's professional identity by showing off skills to peers and anonymous evaluators' (2013: 208, emphasis original). In Goffman's (1959) terms, LinkedIn is very much an example of a digitally mediated presentation of a professional self—the kind of self we might also present in a job interview or at a conference. As we will demonstrate through the accounts in this chapter, Facebook complicates these neat comparisons because of the way it collapses various social contexts, as discussed in Chapter Two.

When it comes to employment, we can also read social media through the lens of social capital. As the saying goes, sometimes it's not what you know, but who you know. According to Haythornthwaite (2002: 389) computer-mediated communication (CMC)—with social media being a contemporary extension of the chatrooms and email they were interested in—can help to maintain and strengthen various social ties, and 'activate' latent ties. We employ a range of social ties in our daily lives, from the strong ties we share with close family and friends, built on intimacy and familiarity, through to weak ties we share with less familiar acquaintances and colleagues. According to Haythornthwaite, these ties can be assessed by factors such as 'frequency of contact, duration of the association, intimacy of the tie, provision of reciprocal services, and kinship' (2002: 386). While strong ties are crucial for social support, weak ties are also critical for accessing resources and information, allowing us to expand our social networks outside of our immediate close friends and family. Latent ties are those connections we might share with others that have not yet been 'activated'. For instance, working in a large organisation, or being part of a supporter base for a football team, or being a fan of a book series, places us in a constellation of other employees, supporters, and fans. When we meet someone and acknowledge that connection, the latent tie is activated and becomes a weak tie.

In the years since Haythornthwaite wrote about CMC having an impact on how these ties are maintained and strengthened, social media has of course become a key channel through which people are doing the work of maintaining and building social ties. In an employment context, Facebook has even developed an organisational arm called Workplace which is essentially Facebook for work. While none of our own participants talked about using Workplace, it is an interesting example of Facebook's expansion. It looks very similar, operates on a profile/timeline and newsfeed interface, you can join groups within your organisation, create events, and so on. Workplace builds on Facebook's existing philosophy of 'communicate, collaborate and connect' (Facebook.com), transcending desks, connecting desktops and mobile technology, claiming to enable employees to work together more effectively via a social network site already familiar to them. This undoubtedly means that staff need no or little training to use it because they already have personal experience of using its interface through their own Facebook use. Facebook's Workplace further embeds the logics of social media—sharing and connecting, but also surveillance and hyper-visibility—into an institutional employment environment. This might be an astute business move for Facebook, but raises new questions about how companies and Facebook itself make use of the data produced through Facebook Workplace, and how this has an impact on employees themselves.

The profiles and timelines that constitute social network sites can also be read as 'transition texts', as modern manifestations and archives of Giddens' (1991) 'reflexive project of the self'. On the Facebook Timeline, for instance, formal educational and professional transitions are marked out through explicit posts and changes to biographical 'about me' information ('Sarah started working at …'). At the same time, this particular manifestation of Giddens' reflexive project are also co-constructed by Facebook friends such as being tagged in a graduation selfie, a parent posting about the milestones of a child, the naming and visibilising of new friendships with new work colleagues, and so on. Like the professional CV, social media profiles are limited and shaped by social conventions, intended audiences, and technical affordances. They are also subject to revision and change over time.

Conceptualising the Facebook Timeline as a manifestation and archive of Giddens' reflexive project of self has allowed us to interrogate the narratives crafted through social media (by ourselves, by others, and by the affordances of the platform itself) in these terms: as reflexively ordered (sometimes more intentionally than others), ongoing and subject to constant change, and for the purposes of communication (with self and with others). Crucially, recruiting our participants as co-analysts of their own digital traces, we were able to engage in discussions with them about how they made sense of their digital traces, of what was visible, of what was missing, and learn about their motivations for certain kinds of disclosures. For a number of our participants, the Facebook Timeline is the ultimate visual manifestation of the reflexive project where their lives and the lives of their friends are constantly being revised, updated, and reworked. Even as our participants reduced their Facebook use in terms of how frequently they were posting, many still acknowledged that Facebook continued to be a platform for sharing important and significant things, like graduation, the birth of a child, a marriage proposal, a first home, and so on.

We also acknowledge that there are technological and commercial shaping effects at play in interpreting a social media profile or timeline as a manifestation of a reflexive project of self. As Bucher (2012, 1168) explains, '[a]kin to the algorithmic logic of search engines, Facebook deploys an automated and predetermined selection mechanism to establish relevancy ... ultimately demarcating the field of visibility for that media space'. Thus, the ordering of narratives in the News Feed is not entirely within the control of users themselves, at least in terms of Bucher's 'fields of visibility'. Sometimes-opaque algorithms summarise disclosures for 'years in review', and present users back to themselves and their friends. In our own project, when we scrolled back through years of Facebook use with our participants, they were seeing amalgamations of their own posts, posts made by their friends, all organised in particular ways by Facebook itself. Why did Facebook choose those six friends to highlight as new friends for 2014, for instance? Why are some posts highlighted while others must be uncovered through more rigorous searching?

For our participants who had future employment in mind when scrolling back through their own profiles, many were imminently concerned with reading these digital traces through the eyes of potential employers. What kind of assumptions would a hiring manager at a hospital make about me based on this photo of me, visibly drunk, tagged at 2AM at a nightclub on a Sunday morning? How might an editor of a newspaper I want to work at think about me if they saw that post I made about kicking out the government with a few choice expletives? Can the manager of the bar I just applied to work at see that I never go out and that I'm pretty antisocial? Why would they hire me? What kind of person are they looking for? How do I look on Facebook?

Learning to Shape Professional Impressions

Some of our participants discussed 'cleaning up' and 'making presentable' their profiles to a new audience of potential employers as they got closer to graduation from university. As already flagged in the excerpt from Dina (23) at the beginning of this chapter, two of our participants were even coached at university on how to prepare their social media presences for scrutiny by potential employers. Dina and Andrea (22) were the most explicit about this, although others (as discussed below) hinted at the role of social media in managing boundaries around professional identity. Andrea explains the feeling associated with being on the precipice of starting her career in medicine that she has been in training for at university for some years:

> I suppose, it's a big deal, starting my career, not just as a part time job but this is the rest of my working life. So it's a pretty big deal and I guess in relation to Facebook everyone, you know it is suggested we make it private and to be honest there wasn't a lot on mine that I was worried about. A lot of people changed their names. I didn't change mine, I didn't think there was anything that would make me look bad to an employer.

The pressure Andrea and Dina were under to think of themselves in professional, 'respectable' terms, was clear. As Andrea said multiple times, 'it's a big deal'. Whether this pressure was self-imposed, from their peers, families, educational institutions, or likely some broader social amalgamation of influences, was less clear. Of course in a linear neoliberal narrative of 'productive citizenship', for a young person in their early twenties who has spent 17 or more years in formal education (from primary school to postgraduate qualifying internships) successful entry into a professional career is a 'make it or break it' moment. So much hinges on that transition from education to employment. For our purposes, however, the way this pressure manifests around the scrutiny of digital traces on social media is particularly revealing. It reveals a 'futuritive' imperative where young people's lives are framed as the backdrop to productive professional careers, only useful as the training grounds for adulthood rather than as generative in and of themselves. Under this imperative, youth (including mistakes, over-indulgence, boundary-work, failure, and trouble) must be cleansed, and even erased, to contextualise a period of life to serve the next chapter. To explain this, Andrea repeated her friend Dina's observation from the beginning of the chapter about the Google search:

> They say, "just to let you know we will do a Google search of you and we will get everything on the first two pages". I think that was an incentive for a lot of people to change their names on Facebook and they are actually developing a social media kind of—something to do with social media committee, in medicine because it's been a problem, people just say whatever they want to and then get in a lot of trouble from the uni and beyond.

Dina (23), was able to provide a more extended example of the kind of trouble her peers got into on social media:

> I think we'd been aware for a while that transitioning from student to someone who's employed [and] working, particularly in the medical field, we're responsible for other people, there was a certain accepted kind of way that you're meant to conduct yourself on social media. Particularly for photos but also what you post and talk about. As students we got a scare quite early on where one boy—I think we were in the first year—wrote a comment about a question on an exam paper which was unexpected, the question. He essentially said, F-U and then put the lecturer's name and then didn't

put any context or anything like that. This was minutes after we came out of the exam. Probably over 15 people in my year liked it. Some people commented just not thinking going, "yeah that was really tough, where did that come from?" The university found out. They all were given warnings. He had to write an apology and I think all of the students who liked it were meant to write an apology and it went on their professional academic transcripts … I didn't like it, I was lucky.

This story illustrates several key points: First, Facebook was a space for a student to collectively express dismay over an exam and connect with peers who felt the same way. Second, there was institutional surveillance of this particular disclosure, but it was unclear if this was direct or indirect. After further discussion with Dina of privacy settings and norms and conventions of the day (this event took place some years before our interview), it was still unclear whether or not the student in Dina's story had posted this to a public profile or it was a private, 'friends only' post that had been captured and reported to the university—perhaps the lecturer, perhaps a disciplinary body with the university—for them to become aware of it. Third, and perhaps most crucially, the university took responsibility for managing the conduct of students on social media (and there are of course now many more examples of this elsewhere). This is important though, because it points to the ways in which 'professional identities' are being shaped and enforced even from the very beginning of university studies.

On the one hand, universities have a responsibility here to prepare their future graduates for successful employment, and so instructing them on (and perhaps enforcing their) professional identities practices is important. On the other hand, what of private or even shared spaces for young people to connect and—yes—complain? About teachers, parents, about the pressures of youth in a neoliberal order where further education is more and more compulsory at the same time as employment prospects and future stability is more and more precarious? The 'F-U' from Dina's classmate was not meant to be directed at or even read by the lecturer in question, it was meant for his friends. The problem was of course that the post was recontextualised either by being discovered by the lecturer or university, or because it was captured and sent to one of the former by someone with access to the disclosure (a friend). That this led to disciplinary action reads as a rupture of convention: it was not appropriate. In a more recent social media landscape, where Facebook has become one of many concurrently used social media platforms, there would be other channels for this kind of manner of 'letting off steam', among which Facebook might be read as the most 'public'. For example, a more ephemeral Snapchat message sent to a dozen or so close friends that would be erased after 10 seconds and where the sender would also be alerted if anyone took a screenshot. As young people have grown up with social media, so too have social media platforms evolved and incorporated more nuance around privacy and impression management, as we discuss further in Chapter Two.

Later in our discussion, we asked Dina to reflect on the disciplinary action taken by the university in relation to the 'F-U' post:

Int.: So do you think that the university was right in making that decision?

Dina: In a way it's bullying. It's saying something in a very public way about someone and naming them, not just first name but last name as well. You couldn't do that to their face without them being able to defend it. This was their way of defending it I guess.

Int.: Do you think that because you are med students there's a—you mentioned before that because of the profession that you're going into and you're responsible for people and there's a duty of care—do you think that has an impact on the conduct that's acceptable?

Dina: It probably shouldn't. People are going into professions all over the place and there shouldn't really be a double standard but I think in some ways there is. That's just because you are put in this very trusted place in society and so you do have a bit of that to maintain.

There are a few things to discuss here. First, Dina's likening of the 'F-U' post to a form of bullying, and the university's disciplinary action as a response to defend against that. It's also worth noting the way in which Dina reaches for examples from the more familiar physical space—'you couldn't do that to their faces without them being able to defend it'—in order to make sense of the conventions and practices that shape sociality in digital spaces. Of course this is how we have developed conventions for being in digital spaces, as we have written in more detail elsewhere (Lincoln & Robards 2016). By transposing metaphors of bedrooms and public agora and schoolyards on to digital spaces, we apply existing conventions for what is appropriate and was is inappropriate (Fernback 1999; Hodkinson & Lincoln 2008). Of course, these transpositions are almost always inherently flawed because of the obvious differences in spatiality, the way we think about audience and presence, and the ways in which physical and digital spaces are technically coded differently, variously with implications for control, revision, persistence, and ephemerality.

The second point to return to from Dina's reflection on the disciplinary action resulting from the 'F-U case' is the pressure both Dina and Andrea described to act a certain way because of their career paths in medicine. This is at the very core of how the university they were studying at worked to shape how professional identities should be conducted on social media. Of course it isn't just medical students who are held to such high standards. This also came up in our interview with Erin (21) when she explained how a friend who was a music teacher maintained a professional identity on Facebook by having two separate accounts:

Erin: So I mean, even if you wanted to not have [Facebook] on a personal level, instead of disconnecting from it completely maybe just have an account that you use for business purposes as well, for promotional stuff.

Int.: Do you know many people that have two [profiles/accounts]?

Erin: Yep. My friend Rebecca is a music teacher, and she has two, but she also makes sure that if she has students ... she also has students, because she teaches. She's only young herself, she's got students like me [age 21], I actually attend one of her vocal workshops once a week, and she also makes sure she is careful with the content she puts on her own account as well, because she does link them both together. Even though they are separate they're not completely separate at the same time.

Erin's description of how her friend Rebecca keeps her personal and professional lives separate on Facebook (although with some intermingling) by way of two separate accounts, is a good example of what Goffman (1959) described as 'audience segregation' (see Chapter Three). Facebook hasn't always had the option to have separate accounts, where users can switch between public-facing 'page' and their personal profiles. In 2009 in an interview with Kirkpatrick (2011), the CEO and founder of Facebook, Mark Zuckerberg, was explicit about identity being singular and that having multiple identities amounted to a 'lack of integrity':

> "You have one identity," [Zuckerberg] says emphatically three times in a single minute during a 2009 interview [...] "The days of you having a different image for your work friends or co-workers and for the other people you know are probably coming to an end pretty quickly," he says [...] "Having two identities for yourself is an example of a lack of integrity," [...] "the level of transparency the world has now won't support having two identities for a person" (Kirkpatrick 2011, p.198).

There are multiple kinds of privilege going on in this kind of 'philosophy' on identity, when we think about why someone might want to keep their professional lives separate from the rest of their lives. Consider lesbian, gay, bisexual, and trans employees who live in places where there is no discrimination legislation to protect them from dismissal due to prejudice from their employers. Or where a person from one religious background works with people from a different one, and fears exclusion or marginalisation at work. Even a person who needs to project confidence and authority at work—as a manager or a negotiator—might need to use their personal Facebook profile to seek help, ask for support, and be vulnerable.

For Shaima (29), who grew up in Malaysia, Facebook had become a site of personal tension as she lived and studied for a doctorate in the UK. For her, managing a professional identity was not primarily for potential employers but a performance for her family in Malaysia. Her 'growing up narratives' are often ones of regret at the restrictions she feels stop her posting honestly about her experiences of being abroad, and posting about the things she does outside of her study time. In this respect, not posting helps her to maintain her profile in ways that avoid questions, ambiguities or confrontations. As we will explore further in later chapters, impression management is crucial not just in terms of managing boundaries with potential employers, but also with families and friends.

That Zuckerberg sees himself as part of, or perhaps even a leader of a movement that is fundamentally changing the way we relate and interact to others and manage our own identities is particularly concerning. Given the directions Facebook has gone in over the last decade, perhaps Zuckerberg's philosophy on identity has evolved. For example, allowing musicians and artists and public figures for example to set up public pages, but also creating the aforementioned 'Workplace by Facebook', perhaps indicates a shift in thinking here. If Zuckerberg is so committed to the idea of a single identity, why allow celebrities to have multiple profiles? And why allow Facebook Workplace to set up a distinction between 'work Facebook' and 'main Facebook'?

After Erin told us about how her friend who was a music teacher managed friendships with students on Facebook, we asked her about her own career ambitions and whether or not she would consider multiple profiles:

Int.: Do you think that people who are going in to a professional life, and you've been talking about going into journalism, is that something that you think about doing as well? Having a separate professional profile?

Erin: Not yet. I feel like, I don't know, that's not going to … I did apply for the police force earlier on as well. I didn't get in, but it was just something that it was an option I thought I'd give it a go. I didn't mind if I didn't get in because I was still halfway through uni or what not. But they're going to find out stuff about your personal [life], through your personal Facebook anyway. If they want to know something they'll find out about it, so I don't think having a different account could stop that necessarily as well. And if there's stuff that you didn't want people to find out about it, it's up to you, for your own disclosure. Or it's your own fault for doing what you've done I suppose in a way too.

There is something quite resigned about how Erin describes privacy here, at multiple levels. First, 'they' (The police? Or all potential employers?) will find out about your personal life regardless of the privacy strategies you employ on Facebook. Second, she is rehearsing the same kind of discourse we saw with Dina and Andrea, where individuals must take responsibility for their own disclosures on Facebook, where what goes on Facebook should be considered public automatically. And third, if there is an unflattering or problematic disclosure on Facebook, it reflects some 'reality' that is also your own responsibility, like getting drunk or high, saying something racist or homophobic, or having a particular worldview.

At all three levels of what Erin is saying here, the clear burden is on the individual to take responsibility for their own disclosures and actions. There is no responsibility assigned to employers as they surveil potential employees, nor does Facebook itself seem to have any responsibility in mediating the privacy of its users.

In discussing her process around 'tidying up' her profile as we scrolled back through her Facebook history, Dina complicated this individualised responsibility to appear a certain way on Facebook by also being conscious of not going *too far*, to avoid coming across as a 'prude':

> When I was doing [job] applications I did go back and do the function where you check what people who aren't friends with you can see. That was in the end how—it was the make or break what went and what didn't even get through ... this kind of stuff [looking at a photo where Dina is pictured with other people, some of whom are smoking], I don't know that it should be on there but I suppose *I'm* not smoking—in terms of profession but I think you've got to just remember not to be a prude with some of these things.

There are clearly gendered dimensions to these narratives, and parallels with the ways in which especially young women are expected to walk a razor thin line between appearing to be a 'prude' as Dina puts it, but also being professional and 'respectable' (Rose at al. 2012; Lyons et al. 2016; Carah & Dobson 2016). This kind of uneven gendered labour in self-representation is important to note here. While many of our male participants also discussed their own practices of impression management, related to employment or otherwise (as we discuss below), our female participants were able to be more explicit with examples. This reveals the added pressures women face in navigating these processes of impression management especially in the context of employment futures.

Dina also took on the perspective of how patients might perceive her, when she was making decisions about which photos to delete on Facebook around the time she was applying for jobs:

> I didn't delete all of them but I deleted the ones where you look messy. Either you're sweaty from all your dancing, you're very drunk or people are doing silly things in the background because you do think what would a patient think of that? They'd want to know you were having fun so dressing up or having a couple of drinks, that's fine but when you maybe start to make bad decisions and look like you're making bad decisions, that's probably where you have to draw the line.

As with Erin, Dina is explaining here a complex process of identity-work and impression management, occupying multiple audience perspectives on her own profile, to imagine how these different people might perceive or read her: potential employers, patients, friends and family. There is a great deal of identity-work that goes into this process, consciously sifting through years of images and disclosures, and recontextualising their interpretation for employment and a professional career trajectory. The work involved in managing these presentations of self on Facebook does not simply vanish when the transition into employment is made, either, but instead is re-modulated.

Managing Boundaries at Work

After navigating the transition into work, managing impressions and boundaries on social media *at* work is a whole new story. This account from Robert, a 25-year-old man who worked in a hospital, illustrates some of the tensions involved here:

> Robert: I don't really have a professional identity. The most is what I do, like it says what I do and where [on Facebook] but, other than that ... it's personal.
> Int.: How then do you negotiate when people in your work life request be a friend on Facebook?
> Robert: There are some of my work friends there. It depends on how I've related to them during my time at work ... If I feel they're cool people ... Either sometimes they send requests to me or I send requests ... Then if I've moved on to another rotation I don't see them as much at work ...
> Int.: They're mostly peers? Or is it senior people, junior people?
> Robert: Mostly peers. I have peers that I consider are senior definitely that at work, if things are serious at work, they are the boss, they tell me what to do. But when it's just at work and things are not too intense or whatnot we'd just be chatting away.

Robert's account about professional identity, friendships, and seniority at work points to the ways in which Facebook is a site of social collisions. At the outset here, Robert insists he does not have a professional identity on Facebook, and that Facebook was personal for him. However, during the interview as we scrolled through his timeline, much of the content Robert would post and read on his newsfeed was work related: medical articles, stories about emergency room resources, and in his own words 'work related things like how to improve myself at work, so clinical stuff'. In this sense, Robert saw a disconnect between work-related content on Facebook, and his presentation of a 'professional identity' there, which is perhaps a more serious and formalised set of ideas about how to act and behave.

Robert's explanation of friending practices also reveals multiple hierarchies, in terms of who gets added as a friend, but also who is in charge 'if things are serious' at work. It makes sense that the decision-making that goes into who to add or accept as a friend on Facebook is determined by how he got along with them, how he 'related to them', if they were 'cool' or not. This also raises a potential issue though around who *doesn't* get accepted or added, and how this might visibilise social networks in workplaces by the naming of the ties. Within the hospital workplace, that turns on rostered shifts and movements between hospitals, Robert also comments on the temporal flow of people who might be 'moved on to another rotation'. When this happens for him, Facebook continues to provide a connective link to colleagues and workmates who he otherwise may see only infrequently or never again.

Despite saying at the outset 'I don't really have a professional identity', Robert has also given some thought to how he presents himself on Facebook, and how his common name also affords him some protection from search. This account aligns with the examples from Andrea (22) and Dina (23) covered earlier in the chapter, where they too were encouraged to change their names on Facebook to make them harder to find:

> **Robert:** I don't have photos of myself [on Facebook] dead drunk or anything like that … I know in my class when people would get internships a lot of people did change their name, abbreviate them or whatever so other people can't find them on Facebook. But for me my name is very common so if someone tried to Google me it would take a while. Even if they do find me I'm fairly restricted. Even if they somehow could see all my stuff there's nothing I'm worried about.
> **Int.:** You maintain a relatively tight sense of control over what's on your profile?
> **Robert:** Yeah.
> **Int.:** When people tag you in stuff?
> **Robert:** Yeah, nothing comes up on my feed or whatnot unless I approve the tag.

Searchability—the extent to which one could easily be 'found' on Facebook—was an important theme that came up multiple times in our interviews in relation to professional boundaries and impression management. University lecturer Sam (27) took a rather more pragmatic approach to managing her professional self on Facebook, instigated by five years' work on summer camps for young people. Given the popularity of the site during those five years, Sam explained how, in addition to upping her privacy settings, she had taken the decision to tell the young people she was caring for during the camps, that she was not on Facebook. In addition, in order to ensure she did not receive any 'friend' requests that could potentially present awkward face-to-face interactions in which she would have to explain why she couldn't accept them, Sam changed the name on her profile to her first name, which was quite common, and abbreviating her surname. Using her common first name and obscuring of her surname made her more or less unsearchable on the site and thus if asked, she could easily claim not to have a profile:

> **Sam:** So I think the increase in my privacy settings started due to professional reasons, and I was working in … I worked in summer camps for five years, later on at uni, and then while I was doing my Masters as well I think, maybe before my PhD as well, so it's fairly … up until a few years ago. And I found that it was easier to say to young people that I wasn't on Facebook rather than having to explain why I couldn't be friends with them because it was part of our child protection training in work that were weren't allowed to be friends with them. And I was often working with vulnerable young people as well so that was … it was professional reasons. I just thought if I just hide on Facebook then they can't search me so I can just lie and say, you know, I'm not on there and I don't have to explain why I can't be their friend.

This example demonstrates the fragile boundaries between professional and personal life and the fragility of those boundaries should they be crossed on a social network site like Facebook. For Sam, being on Facebook presented an area of potential antagonism between staff and children, who on the one hand want to develop strong ties and bonds with those in their care while at the same time maintaining professional boundaries and adhering to child protection policies. Facebook just further complicates those professional and personal boundaries and thus Sam made the conscious decision to 'hide on Facebook', using her anonymity to make explicit the boundaries between personal and professional life.

Social Media as Work

Beyond using social media to find work (or modifying the digital traces on social media to avoid impinging on the quest to find work) and using social media to manage relationships within workplaces, social media is now also increasingly becoming a serious form of work in itself. Abidin (2015: 1) has studied social media influencers in Singapore, Australia, and Scandinavia. She defines influencers as:

> everyday, ordinary Internet users who accumulate a relatively large following on blogs and social media through the textual and visual narration of their personal lives and lifestyles, engage with their following in digital and physical spaces, and monetise their following by integrating "advertorials" into their blog or social media posts.

Abidin argues that the everyday lives of these influencers, as told through social media but also supplemented by face-to-face meet-ups, is their primary 'output'.

By inviting followers into these everyday lives, intimate bonds can be formed where followers feel connected to these microcelebrity influencers through a range of processes of reciprocation. For example, Abidin's influencer participants describe how they may retweet tweets from followers, thank followers who have written personal emails to them in blog posts, or agree to take selfies with followers when they see each other in physical publics (Abidin 2015: 12). Abidin's work has also revealed the depths of labour involved in work as a social media influencer, from 'calibrated amateurism' to negotiating family boundaries around the inclusion of children in influencer labour (Abidin 2017: 11).

Although none of our participants described themselves as social media influencers, several discussed how they leveraged social media in work-adjacent ways. Erin (21), for instance, talked about how she sometimes helped friends out in promoting their bands on Facebook. It was not a full-time job, but a supplement to her income, and also afforded her access to local live music and helped her friends. While he didn't describe himself as an influencer, Nathan (28) did describe himself as a 'social media manager'. He managed the Facebook accounts of several professional sports people in the UK, and was charged with 'curating' very particularly identities as well as promoting them. While not an influencer according to Abidin's definition, his backstage role in managing profiles has the purpose of building up the number of followers and managing reputation in ways that may supposedly attract lucrative sponsorship deals, although Nathan did not talk about the role in these terms. While the examples in our own data of social media *as* work are sparse, this area of employment and making a living is only expanding.

Conclusion: The Problem with Futurity

In this chapter we have set out some of the ways in which social media figure into the transition from education into employment careers for many young people, from shaping a professional identity on social media to managing boundaries at work. A critical concern here is the way in which young people's lives—as mediated on Facebook—are seen as the backdrop to productive, work-focussed futures. This lens of futurity, where young people are only valuable because of what they might contribute and do in the future, is limited and potentially destructive. There is a duality here. On the one hand, we might celebrate young people being proactive and aware of how they present themselves on social media, conscientiously untagging themselves from questionable images or not posting things that 'might come back to haunt them' or that 'might make their grandmother cringe'. On the other hand, there is an intense pressure in this expectation, and an implicit call to erase and sterilise formative youthful experiences of experimentation, celebration, rebellion, and figuring out their own boundaries. The ways in which many young people now occupy multiple social media platforms—from Facebook to Instagram to Snapchat to Tinder, and managing different audiences through these platforms—is an individualised solution. Here, individual young people take personal responsibility for their impression management across profiles and media channels. The broader issue of the neoliberal lens of futurity—young people as future workers—is left unchallenged, and indeed even internalised, as the accounts of especially Dina, Andrea, and Erin in this chapter illustrate.

In the next chapter, we move on to the next area of life: love and relationships. In this chapter, drawing on our research data we continue to explore the significance of articulating (or not) a romantic relationship on Facebook, particularly taking into account the decisions users make about sharing particular aspects of their relationships and how they use the site to manage them, validate them, and end them.

References

Abidin, C. (2015). Communicative intimacies: Influencers and perceived interconnectedness. *Ada New Media*, *11*(8). http://doi.org/10.7264/N3MW2FFG.

Abidin, C. (2017). #familygoals: Family influencers, calibrated amateurism, and justifying young digital labor. *Social Media + Society*, *3*(2), http://doi.org/10.1177/2056305117707191.

Adams, M. (2003). The reflexive self and culture: A critique. *The British Journal of Sociology*, *54*(2), 221–238.

Baym, N. K. (2015). *Personal connections in the digital age*. John Wiley & Sons.

Bennett, S. (2011). 91% of employers use Twitter, Facebook and LinkedIn to screen job applicants. *AdWeek*, http://www.adweek.com/digital/social-media-job-screening/. Accessed September 6, 2019.

Biggart, A., & Walther, A. (2012). Coping with yo-yo transitions. Young adults' struggle for support, between family and state in comparative perspective. In C. Leccardi & E. Ruspini (Eds.), *A new youth?: Young people, generations and family life*. Farnham: Ashgate.

Bucher, T. (2012). Want to be on the top? Algorithmic power and the threat of invisibility on Facebook. *New Media & Society*, *14*(7), 1164–1180.

Carah, N., & Dobson, A. (2016). Algorithmic hotness: Young women's "Promotion" and "Reconnaissance" work via social media body images. *Social Media + Society*, *2*(4). https://doi.org/10.1177/2056305116672885.

Carayannis, M. (2016). Sports stars squander money by not using social media to its full potential. *The Daily Telegraph*, https://www.dailytelegraph.com.au/sport/more-sports/sports-stars-squander-money-by-not-using-social-media-to-its-full-potential/news-story/fab8640d9617d86cd41b773b1df6ca66. Accessed March 15, 2017.

Carrillat, A. F., d'Astous, A., & Morissette Grégoire, E. (2014). Leveraging social media to enhance recruitment effectiveness: A Facebook experiment. *Internet Research*, *24*(4), 474–495.

Denny, L., & Churchill, B. (2016). Youth employment in Australia: A comparative analysis of labour force participation by age group. *Journal of Applied Youth Studies*, *1*(2), 5.

Drouin, M., O'Connor, K. W., Schmidt, G. B., & Miller, D. A. (2015). Facebook fired: Legal perspectives and young adults' opinions on the use of social media in hiring and firing decisions. *Computers in Human Behavior*, *46*, 123–128.

Fernback, J. (1999). There is a there there: Notes towards a definition of cybercommunity. In S. Jones (Ed.), *Doing Internet research: Critical issues and methods for examining the net* (pp. 203–21). London: Sage.

Furlong, A. (2009). *Handbook of youth and young adulthood: New perspectives and agendas*. London: Routledge.

Furlong, A., & Cartmel, F. (1997). Risk and uncertainty in youth transition. *YOUNG: The Nordic Journal of Youth Research*, *5*(1), 3–20.

Giddens, A. (1991). *Modernity and self identity*. Cambridge: Polity Press.

Goffman, E. (1959). *The presentation of self in everyday life*. London: Penguin.

Harris, A., & Roose, J. (2014). DIY citizenship amongst young Muslims: Experiences of the 'ordinary'. *Journal of Youth Studies*, *17*(6), 794–813.

Haythornthwaite, C. (2002). Strong, weak, and latent ties and the impact of new media. *The Information Society*, *18*(5), 385–401.

Highfield, T. (2017). *Social media and everyday politics*. Cambridge: Polity.

Hodkinson, P., & Lincoln, S. (2008). Online journals as virtual bedrooms?: Young people, identity and personal space. *YOUNG: Nordic Journal of Youth Research*, *16*(1), 27–46. http://doi.org/10.1177/110330880701600103.

Houston, C., & Vedelago, C. (2018) Top cop resigns in disgrace over link to racist and obscene posts. *The Age*, https://www.theage.com.au/national/victoria/top-cop-resigns-in-disgrace-over-link-to-racist-and-obscene-posts-20180226-p4z1u5.html. Accessed August 5, 2018.

Ingle, S. (2016). Louis Smith lands British Gymnastics ban after video appearing to mock Islam. *The Guardian*, https://www.theguardian.com/sport/2016/nov/01/louis-smith-banned-british-gymnastics-video-mocking-islam. Accessed September 6, 2019.

Jenkins, H. (2010, August 14). Google and the search for the future. *Wall Street Journal*, 1–3. Retrieved from https://www.wsj.com/articles/SB10001424052748704901104575423294099527212

Jeske, D., & Shultz, K. S. (2016). Using social media content for screening in recruitment and selection: Pros and cons. *Work, Employment and Society*, *30*(3), 535–546.

Kirkpatrick, D. (2011). *The Facebook effect: The inside story of the company that is connecting the world*. New York: Simon and Schuster.

Levy, M. (2015). Hotel worker Michael Nolan sacked over Facebook post to Clementine Ford. *The Sydney Morning Herald*, https://www.smh.com.au/national/hotel-worker-michael-nolan-sacked-over-facebook-post-to-clementine-ford-20151201-glc1y4.html. Accessed September 6, 2019.

Lincoln, S., & Robards, B. (2016). Being strategic and taking control: Bedrooms, social network sites and the narratives of growing up. *New Media & Society, 18*(6), 927–943. http://doi.org/10.1177/1461444814554065.

LinkedIn. (2018). 'About LinkedIn', https://about.linkedin.com/. Accessed October 22, 2018.

Lyons, A. C., Goodwin, I., & Griffin, C. (2016). Facebook and the fun of drinking photos: Reproducing gender regimes of power. *Social Media + Society, 2*(2) http://doi.org/10.117/2056305116672888.

MacDonald, R. (2011). Youth transitions, unemployment and underemployment: Plus ca change, plus c'est meme chose? *Journal of Sociology, 47*(4), 427–444.

MacDonald, R. (2016). Precarious work: The growing precarite of youth. In A. Furlong (Ed.), *Routledge handbook of youth and young adulthood*. London: Routledge.

MacDonald, R., & Marsh, J. (2005). *Disconnected youth? Growing up in Britain's poor neighbourhoods*. Basingstoke: Palgrave Macmillan.

McDermott, S. (2017). I lost my job over a Facebook post—was that fair?. *BBC News*, https://www.bbc.com/news/stories-41851771. Accessed December 4, 2018.

McKernan, B. (2015). We enjoyed reading Mhairi Black's NSFW tweets as a teenager. *Indy100 from The Independent*, https://www.indy100.com/article/we-enjoyed-reading-mhairi-blacks-nsfw-tweets-as-a-teenager--xyvV8th3lb. Accessed September 6, 2019.

McWhirter, F. & Cabrera, M. (2010) Woman fired for Facebook threat. *The Advertiser*, https://www.adelaidenow.com.au/news/south-australia/woman-fired-for-facebook-threat/news-story/55a085c70e83cad0d4695187e2af1b88. Accessed March 15, 2017.

Nikolaou, I. (2014). Social networking web sites in job search and employee recruitment. *International Journal of Selection and Assessment, 22*(2), 179–189.

Nothling, L. (2018), George Christensen under fire over 'greenie punks' Facebook post. *ABC News*, https://www.abc.net.au/news/2018-02-18/facebook-post-mp-george-christensen-feel-lucky-greenie-punks/9459476. Accessed March 2, 2018.

Raynes-Goldie, K. (2010). Aliases, creeping and wall cleaning: Understanding privacy in the age of Facebook. *First Monday, 15*(1) http://firstmonday.org/htbin/cgiwrap/bin/ojs/index.php/fm/article/view/2775/2432.

Robards, B., & Bennett, A. (2011). MyTribe: Post-subcultural manifestations of belonging on social network sites. *Sociology, 45*(2), 303–317.

Robinson, L., & Lamb, S. (2012) 'How Young People are Faring 2012', report by the Foundation for Young Australians, https://www.fya.org.au/report/how-are-young-people-faring-report-card-2015/. Accessed September 6, 2019.

Rose, J., Mackey-Kallis, S., Shyles, B., Biagini, D., Hart, C., & Jack, L. (2012). Face it: The impact of gender on social media images. *Communication Quarterly, 60*(5), 588–607.

Thomson, R. (2007). A biographical perspective. In M. J. Kehily (Ed.), *Understanding youth: Perspectives, identities and practices*. London: Sage.

van Dijck, J. (2013). "You have one identity": Performing the self on Facebook and LinkedIn. *Media, Culture & Society, 35*(2), 199–215. http://doi.org/10.1177/0163443712468605.

van Krieken, R., Habibis, D., Smith, P., Hutchins, B., Haralambos, M., & Holden, R. (2014). *Sociology: Themes and perspectives* (4th ed.). Melbourne: Pearson Education.

Walzer, A., & Sanjurjo, P. (2016). Media and contemporary tattoo. *Communication & Society, 29*(1), 69–81. http://doi.org/10.15581/003.29.1.69-81.

White, R., & Wyn, J. (2013). *Youth and society* (3rd ed.). Melbourne: Oxford University Press.

White, R., Wyn, J., & Robards, B. (2017). *Youth and society* (4th ed.). Melbourne: Oxford University Press.

Woodman, D. (2012). Life out of synch: How new patterns of further education and the rise of precarious employment are reshaping young people's relationships. *Sociology, 46*(6), 1074–1090.

Woodman, D. (2013). Young people's friendships in the context of non-standard work patterns. *The Economic and Labour Relations Review, 24*(3), 416–432.

Woodman, D., & Wyn, J. (2015). Class, gender and generation matter: Using the concept of social generation to study inequality and social change. *Journal of Youth Studies, 18*(10), 1402–1410.

Wyn, J., & Woodman, D. (2006). Generation, youth and social change in Australia. Journal of youth studies, 9(5), 495–514.

CHAPTER SIX

Love, and Making It 'Facebook Official'

In the previous chapter we considered the multiple ways in which our participants managed 'the self' on Facebook within the context of employment, professional identity, and professional life. We explored the extent to which the 'project of self', to use Giddens' (1991) term, was curated and edited by our participants within these narratives, and how moving from the teenage years towards the twenties bought new ways of using Facebook (and other social media) that participants described as more mature, thoughtful and responsible. In addition, our participants envisioned new audiences, often undergoing a 'Facebook cull' as they streamlined their friends list to fit their evolving professional identity. In this chapter we continue to explore Facebook as a platform for the curation of self, turning now to our second 'arena' of life: love and romantic relationships.

Going 'Facebook Official'—naming a relationship, and being listed as 'in a relationship' with someone else on Facebook—has become a socially and culturally significant marker of romantic progression, making romantic relationships visible and formalised on the site. However, going 'Facebook Official' can also be a contested process, fraught with drama and repercussions associated with naming relationships in semi-public spaces. In this chapter we ask: What is the significance of articulating a romantic relationship on Facebook? Why do some choose to make socially and culturally critical moments like the beginning and ends of relationships visible on Facebook, whereas others (perhaps within the same relationship) do not?

How do these practices change over time? When is it appropriate to go 'Facebook Official'? In this chapter, expanding our previous work (Robards & Lincoln 2016), we discuss four kinds of non-exclusive 'relationship-trace' practices: (1) overt relationship status disclosures, mediated through the 'relationship status' affordance of the site; (2) implied relationship disclosures, mediated through an increase in images and tags featuring romantic partners; (3) the intended absence of relationship visibility; and (4) later-erased or revised relationship disclosures. We finish with a critique of the ways in which Facebook might work to produce normative 'relationship traces', privileging neat linearity, monogamy, and obfuscating (perhaps usefully, perhaps not) the messy complexity of romantic relationships.

Romance and Love in the Context of 'growing up'

Romantic relationships occupy a particularly central place in individual life narratives, alongside employment, education, and family (Thomson et al. 2002). According to Viejo, Ortega-Ruiz and Sánchez (2015), love is an important source of well-being and happiness. Love, of various kinds (between friends, towards dependents, and passionate love including sexual intimacy and physical closeness) makes people happy. Happiness, in turn, makes people more sociable, and leads to stronger intimate relationships (Diener & Seligman 2002; Peterson & Seligman 2004). The psychological literature also points to the ways in which dating relationships during adolescence are important sources of emotions, with associated positive and negative implications for self-esteem (Dion & Dion 2006), health, psychological adjustment and general well-being (Bouchey & Furman 2003; Grover & Nangle 2007). In their own work, studying young people's experiences of romantic relationships in Spain (n = 3258), Viejo et al. (2015: 1231) found that 'low-quality' relationships contributed to 'lower levels of psychological adjustment' (including verbal aggressiveness, 'delinquency', and sexism).

For many young people, entering into early romantic relationships and falling in love is a crucial rite of passage. In their writing on love, Jackson (1993) argued that while love might be understood as a private phenomenon, it is in fact 'very much a part of our public culture'. Jackson explains that 'we are surrounded by representations of love in what is deemed "great" art and literature as well as in soap opera, popular music and fiction and advertising' (1993: 202). 'Young love' is a pervasive genre of storytelling in itself. From Shakespeare's 'Romeo and Juliet' to Ariana Grande's 'thank u next', stories of youthful love found and lost are omnipresent. These texts that both celebrate and lament love, also figure into how young people conceptualise and place themselves within understandings of romance.

Of course, in the decades since Jackson was writing, social media are now also central to the circulation of representations of love and romance. Song lyrics, short sequences from film and television, and celebrities on red carpets are transmuted into memes and reaction GIFs that are circulated across social media platforms and in private message threads. Images and reaction GIFs that capture a moment of elation in love or the utter despair of a breakup, grabbed from a larger recognisable text (from *The Little Mermaid* to *Mean Girls*), can come to stand-in for an individual's experience or emotional response. In her work on Tumblr, Kanai (2017: 6) explains how social media attention economies rely on 'imagined commonalities' and the 'relatable value' of content. Commonality itself, Kanai suggests is 'not necessarily enough to catalyse the re-circulation of posts'. Instead, she contends that posts have to 'reflect the thoughts or experiences of others in a *pleasing*, or at least, non-compromising way' (Kanai 2017: 6).

Beyond popular culture, and the transmutation and re-combination/re-circulation of popular cultural narratives on love, individual and everyday stories of love are now also easily circulated through social media. In Jackson's (1993) terms, the actors in widely circulated representations of love are no longer just celebrities or distant historical figures, but are also our friends and family—perhaps even our own ex-partners. In the remainder of this chapter we consider the ways in which romantic relationships are made visible (or not) on social media, especially through the lens of Facebook.

Romantic Relationships on Facebook

Facebook invites users to display their 'relationship status' on the site, and even link their profiles to their partner's profile, reflecting a social order that privileges monogamous, long term couplings. In the 'about' section of the user's profile (in the early-2019 iteration), the order of biographical information is as follows: current employment, education, current town/city of residence, contact and basic information (e.g. gender), birthday, relationship status and link to partner's profile if provided. Relationship statuses that can be listed on Facebook include: single, in a relationship, engaged, married, in a civil partnership, in a domestic partnership, in an open relationship, it's complicated, separated, divorced, and widowed. This information is optional. Thus, the relationship status is folded into the performance of what Giddens (1991) described as the reflexive project of self, as it manifests through the Facebook profile (Robards 2014).

Because of the quasi-public but controlled nature of Facebook (Livingstone 2008; Marwick & boyd 2014b; boyd 2014), deciding when to go 'Facebook Official' with a partner can be a hotly contested issue. For some it might happen early on in the dating ritual, whereas others may never explicitly disclose their relationship status. Others still may 'shadow' a relationship, indicating its existence through image and location tags, or posting images and links to their partner's (or anticipated partner's) wall. When relationships end, disclosures on Facebook related to relationships dissolution can of course also be highly contentious. As we will explain, given the relative longevity of the site, practices around going 'Facebook Official' or not have changed over time, which is made clear when users reflect on their Facebook Timelines over years of use as they do in our study. It is our argument that Facebook can act as an archive of at least a partial relationship narrative, subject to revision and later erasure.

In this chapter, we reflect upon how romantic relationships are mediated through Facebook and the various ways in which these relationships are played out on the site over a sustained period of time. Scrolling back through profiles with our participants revealed often quite complex relationship narratives written over a period of time. It also revealed how the nature of these disclosures changed over that time, reflecting participants' maturing social media literacy, and how the documenting of relationships on the site represented a broader context of 'growing up'.

Social network sites play a key role in understanding contemporary relationships. Sites such as Facebook have become key portals through which users communicate with their friends, maintain or intensify existing relationships or begin new ones. Ellison, Steinfield and Lampe (2007: 1144) argue that the affordances of Facebook 'constitute a rich site for researchers because of its capacity to 'bridge on and offline connections'. Facebook is a platform through which social bonds can be made in an instant and its 'logic of sharing' (Kennedy 2015) encourages forming and maintaining connections with friends, family and acquaintances. In the context of romantic relationships, Facebook is a site through which we learn the relationship status of our 'friends' (Ellison, Steinfield & Lampe 2007) as the site has 'centralised' much of the romantic information we learn about people captured through changing status updates, posting images of a couple together and so on (Utz & Beukeboom 2011; Ito et al. 2010). Baym (2010) argues that users' disclosures of this type of information is crucial for 'maintain[ing] ongoing relationships and turning strangers into relational partners because it is a necessary part of getting to know each other and building trust' (Baym 2010). Our data aligns with Baym's view, as we demonstrated in Chapter Two through the examples of participants such as Neha, Louis, and Cate, whose views affirm the use of Facebook to build relationships. In the context of dating, not having a profile can even be disconcerting, as it's a mean by which people learn more about a romantic interest. Consequently, the site becomes central to relationship 'impression management' as the connections between users are displayed and reflected upon (Utz & Beukeboom 2011: 512).

Papacharissi and Gibson suggest 'SNSs cultivate practices that prompt users to be more public with their information by default. While it is possible for users to edit these settings, the code that belies the structure of the network makes it easier to share than to hide information' (2011: 77). In this respect, Facebook has been written about as a site of 'intimacy' (Livingstone 2008; boyd & Ellison 2008; Lambert 2015). Hinton and Hjorth (2013) contend that 'intimacy is a crucial concept for understanding social and mobile media, which make various intimate relationships "available" in new ways through different technological forms' (in Lambert 2015:2). They argue for what they describe as the 'intimacy turn' in people's use of social media more broadly and how intimacy on sites like Facebook 'can be used to understand some of the erosions between public and private spaces'; (Hinton and Hjorth 2013: 3) or as others have described it, how intimacy plays out in the context of 'networked publics' (boyd 2007, 2014) and 'context collapse' (Vitak 2012).

Yang, Brown and Braun (2014), who studied college students use of different technologies to conduct relationships, argue that an intimacy 'hierarchy' existed for their participants whereby different platforms for communicating with a romantic partner were used at different stages from 'initiation to intimacy' (18). For them, Facebook very much featured in the early part of a relationship, at the initiation and 'getting to know each other' stage. This resonates with Livingstone's earlier work in which she suggests 'teenagers must and do disclose personal information in order to sustain intimacy, but they wish to be in control of how they manage this disclosure' (2008: 405). Livingstone draws on the work of Giddens (1991: 94) who argues that 'intimacy is the other face of privacy'. Both Yang et al. (2014) and Livingstone (2008) demonstrate young people's strategies for engaging in different types of intimacy and to recognise when interactions need to be pulled from different 'networked publics' (boyd 2014) like Facebook into more private, potentially more ephemeral spaces.

Focusing on sustained narratives of romantic relationships on the site reveals the 'working out' young people do before posting about a crucial moment in their relationship history. Our data demonstrates how our participants often spoke of developing, in their own words, more 'mature' approaches to their disclosures on Facebook as they used the site for longer periods of time and as they themselves got older. As we have demonstrated in earlier chapters, while scrolling back, participants often identified language, emoticons and images that they felt represented their younger, 'less mature' selves and what they deemed as sometimes embarrassing representations of an earlier relationship. Often participants referred to the temporal aspects of their disclosures, viewing earlier posts made in their teenage years as hasty, and lacking thought, versus a more measured, considered approach before a disclosure about a romantic relationship is made. 'Intimacy' becomes more significant in the context of growing up too as participants talked about the appropriateness of Facebook for certain types of communication, with close friends and partners, for example. Yang et al. (2014: 5) refer to this as 'layers of electronic intimacy' whereby as a relationship becomes more intimate, the platform for intimate exchanges shifts from quasi-public disclosures to Facebook messenger, and eventually moving off the site to texting, speaking on the phone and in person. For our participants, these 'layers of electronic intimacy' occur across of a wider polymedia landscape (e.g. Instagram, Snapchat, Twitter, and dating apps like Grindr and Tinder). While our discussion here focuses on Facebook, their use is underscored by their movement between different social media platforms.

A factor that can be important when moving across these different 'layers of digital intimacy' is that of drama and what sort of drama might be created by the action about to be performed. We borrow here from Marwick and boyd's (2014a: 1187) use of 'drama' as an 'emergent concept describing performative, interpersonal conflict that takes place in front of an active, engaged audience, often on social media'. For Marwick and boyd's participants, Facebook was a key space through which drama was compounded and mobilised with drama regularly moving in and out of Facebook between other domains (for example, school) (1188). Their participants spoke of Facebook as making events more dramatic if they are shared on the site as those dramatic events are 'deliberately written into being' (1195). For them, the concept varies in gravity with drama being played out on the site for fun when bored and when acting up to peers through to more serious examples of conflict and aggression. Often the boundaries between 'conflict, jokes, hurt and entertainment' can be blurred (11). While Marwick and boyd were focussed on drama between teens in the US, we believe this concept has wider purchase and resonates with the experiences our own participants described when discussing the role of Facebook in mediating their romantic relationships. As we draw out below, the drama that can unfold from a post on Facebook is mediated in various ways on the site. For a number of our participants, whether a disclosure may or may not create or avert drama provides a judgment on whether something should or shouldn't be posted. References to 'drama' or 'being dramatic' as voiced in interviews were also used as a way of emphasising 'growing up' or maturing on the site.

Giddens (1991) has argued that one of the core characteristics of the 'ideal-typical' form of the 'pure relationship' in late modernity is the declining significance of external validation. He claims that institutions like marriage are no longer 'anchored in external conditions of social or economic life', but have instead become centred on the 'emotional satisfaction … derived from close contact with another' (Giddens 1991: 89). While the division of labour and economic necessity may not be as central to late modern relationships (although, Giddens himself acknowledges this is not true for all socioeconomic groups), it is still clear that the performance of romantic relationships continues to be significant. Continuing debates about marriage equality (especially in Australia most recently) point to the enduring significance of making relationships visible and celebrating them with friends and family. While we are not suggesting that going 'Facebook Official' might be in the same realm of socio-cultural significance as a wedding, there are interesting parallels in terms of the performativity of the act and the ways in which naming and announcing a tie might work to cement it.

Going 'Facebook Official' (or not) might seem pithy and banal for some. And yet, for anyone who has ever 'gone Facebook Official' with a partner, there is an undeniable sense of significance to it. As our participants explain, this sense of significance may be accompanied by drama, anxiety, elation, dread, or any number of other complicating emotions, but the recurrent theme appears to be around significance. As our discussion below demonstrates, Facebook has become a key platform through which relationships are played out, and made visible.

Disclosing, Shadowing, Hiding, and Revising Relationships on Facebook

The 'relationship status' on Facebook is a point of messiness and complication for many of our participants, yet their engagement, disengagement, and revisions of this status play a crucial role in their growing up narratives, both explicitly on the site and in the spoken narratives elicited in interview scenarios that run alongside the digitally mediated narratives. Like the formalisation of friendship experienced when users decide whether or not to send or accept a friend request on the site (Robards 2010), the act of naming a tie on Facebook can bring that relationship into stark and sometimes awkward focus.

In the following sections we demonstrate how our participants communicate their romantic relationships on the site. We draw out various 'performances of connection' (Lambert 2015), that we describe here through four types of relationship disclosures (and non-disclosures), ranging from the explicit, to the implied or 'shadowed' relationships, through to the more actively hidden and later-erased. We use the term 'shadowed' or 'shadowing' here to describe practices that hint at or refer to something in an implied rather than an explicit way, as we will explain further below.

What these four non-exclusive, overlapping and temporally situated types of relationship disclosures highlight is the extent to which Facebook serves as a key site through which relationships are mediated and how public declarations on the site can impact on relationships in other realms. As forming romantic relationships is understood to be an important part of normative understandings of 'growing up', these relationship-trace practices on Facebook further constitute the wider narrative around growing up that we are centrally concerned with in this book.

Type 1—Overt Relationship Disclosure Practices: It's 'Facebook Official'

For Mitch, a 20-year-old Australian, studying full-time and working in his family business, his relationship with his girlfriend of four years was an important part of his identity, and his Facebook profile reflected that. He and his girlfriend went 'Facebook Official' early on in their relationship, embodying a linear, heterosexual, monogamous, 'high school sweetheart' coupling. When we were scrolling through his profile, Mitch's girlfriend was prominent, and almost all of his profile pictures over the past four years included her:

> So that's my girlfriend there ... we were friends ... it was a week after that picture was taken we started going out ... Yeah, so this would have been just after we started going out in early 2012. And she tends to feature in my pictures from now on.

Mitch and his girlfriend also had matching profile pictures, taken at the same events or on the same day. While we were looking through his profile pictures, Mitch explained that he had gone back to delete some old profile pictures from before he met his girlfriend. These pictures no longer 'reflect[ed]' who he had become. He explained that the ones he had deleted were edited with effects, filters, and other photoshop manipulations, and represented (for him) a more childish past. He now saw himself differently, and his girlfriend, as featured in the majority of his more recent profile pictures, was central to that.

Louis, aged 20, was a full time student in his second year of study. He started to use Facebook in 2008 and his profile had, until recently been primarily centred around his interests in music from posting videos of new bands he had discovered to using his profile as a 'commercial space' to promote his own bands. It had a 'professional' feel to it and as Louis said 'I want the page to look good, I want it to represent how seriously I want to take music as a profession'. In March 2015, Louis met Emma. While up until this point Louis' profile had been dominated by music-related content, in April 2015, he and Emma made the decision to make their relationship 'Facebook Official', at which point they both disclosed that they were 'in a relationship' with each other on the site. Louis received 75 'likes' and 57 comments for this post, the most he had received for anything he had posted on Facebook at the time. Louis explained that this was because for him, it was a critical moment in his life as it was the first time he had updated his profile to 'in a relationship' and he hoped that all the 'likes' and comments were indications of his friends' happiness for him in his new relationship.

This kind of public disclosure, and the validation that comes from being acknowledged by friends and family, is not unique of course to going Facebook Official. Long-standing cultural practices like taking a partner home to meet one's parents, introducing a partner to a friendship group, even marriage itself, are all different permutations of this performative act. The act formalises a relationship, rendering it more serious and even stable.

When talking with Louis about why he and Emma had decided to make their relationship official on the site, it became clear that Facebook played an important 'behind the scenes' role in their relationship, using 'Facebook Official' as a marker of how serious they were about each other. Louis explained: '[we] were in a relationship a month before we updated our Facebook profiles. I think the reason we took this long to do this was, partially, to test how serious our relationship was going to be—we didn't feel like seeing how we would work as a couple and then possibly having a falling out, changing the information on Facebook twice in a short space of time'.

Going Facebook Official too early in a relationship brought with it the risk of unnecessary drama and pressure for the new couple. Once they had made the decision to go Facebook Official, their relationship was fore fronted on Louis' profile that began to feature photographs of them together, at their University prom and so on. Louis also changed his cover photo to an image of him and Emma. Like Mitch (20), being in a relationship was an important part of Louis' identity that he wanted represented on the site as a sign of 'progress in my life' and while his profile had not become dominated by images of him with his girlfriend, they certainly played a key role in it with new images regularly being added either by Louis or Emma in amongst a continuing flow of music-related posts.

Type 2—Implied and 'shadowed' Relationship Disclosures

Tina was 22. Her relationship with her girlfriend, Bec, as represented on Facebook, was complicated. Tina had broken up with Bec around 6 months before she was interviewed, however, they were still 'friends' on the site despite having no other contact (via phone, text or in-person). According to Tina, de-friending her ex-girlfriend was not really an option: 'all hell would break loose ... she likes drama and it would end up being an argument'. Tina's relationship with Bec as it was mediated through Facebook had always been complicated because they each projected their relationship with each other in quite different ways. Tina would tag Bec in photographs posted on her profile so they would appear on Bec's profile. Bec, on the other hand, did not. Tina had updated her status to 'in a relationship' and had named Bec. Again, Bec had done neither.

Tina and Bec were living out their relationship in two different 'modes' of exposure and disclosure on Facebook. For Tina, their relationship was performed in explicit terms. For her girlfriend, posts only hinted at or 'shadowed' their relationship. We use the term 'shadow' here to describe a form of disclosure that is implied or indirect. For example, like 'sub-tweeting' or 'vague-booking', a post can suggest or hint at a meaning that can be deciphered by some but not by others, or perhaps is written for one person in particular. boyd and Marwick have described this as a kind of 'social steganography' (2011) where social media users hide certain disclosures in plain sight, with only friends in the know being able to decode and understand the intended message. Oolo and Siibak (2013) suggest that this kind of social steganography is part of a wider assemblage of privacy strategies, including strategic information sharing and self-censorship, that young people employ on social media.

To return to the 'implied' or 'shadowed' types of relationships disclosure practices, unlike 'vague-booking', the objective is sometimes not necessarily to seek attention, but rather to avoid being explicitly and overtly performative. The subtlety of a 'shadow post' seemed much more appealing for our participants. The post needs no obvious definable features such as a person's name, but leaves enough of a reference for it to be understood by its intended audience. As we see in the example of Tina below, shadowing is also a form of protection. As her relationship ends she is able to 'take shelter' on Facebook using the site to reflect an image of the relationship as still alive until she feels ready to deal with the reality of no longer being with her partner.

In discussing how the end of romantic relationships play out on Facebook, Tina articulated how, in her own words, a series of 'fading out' stages were performed on the site. In the first stage, the relationship status is hidden so that nobody can see it. Hiding the status represents a sort of suspension of the relationship, leaving time for personal reflection on the end of the relationship before going 'Facebook Official' with the breakup. Next, and while the status is hidden, Tina described how she removed Bec's name from the 'in a relationship' status, breaking the tie between accounts. Once this was done, Tina made visible 'in a relationship' (without Bec's name) once again. This meant that Tina was not obviously stating their breakup on Facebook; rather her profile was edited subtly, over a period of time so that eventually the status could be removed altogether without attention being drawn to it. Meanwhile, outside of Facebook the relationship had already ended with close friends aware of the 'real' relationship status.

What we see here is how a relationship status is managed in quite complex ways that do not always marry up to what is happening in the relationship outside of the site. Being able to perform 'in a relationship' on Facebook even though she was no longer in one, helped Tina to come to terms with the break up, with the eventual removal of the 'in a relationship' status signifying a point at which she felt reconciled with her single self. The Facebook status temporally served as a bridge through which her relationship status could remain connected to her ex-girlfriend, when actually the relationship had come to an end. Facebook was used to mediate the relationship in a way that was useful to Tina, serving as a therapeutic tool to help her to come to terms with the split.

Mark was a 22-year-old Australian DJ, student, and LGBTIQ activist. Mark was a trans man in a long term relationship with his girlfriend, and was largely open about his relationship on Facebook. His girlfriend, however, had a relatively conservative family who did not approve of her relationship with Mark. Thus, like Tina (22), Mark had to negotiate a sometimes uncomfortable duality with the way he disclosed his relationship with his girlfriend, and also how those disclosures were rendered visible (or not) on his girlfriend's own profile. For example, Mark would post images of romantic dinners, with descriptions like 'date night with my girl', and hashtags like #girlfriend, #love, and #mygirl. His girlfriend, however, would rarely be visible in these images, and never tagged. These posts 'shadowed' their relationship, making it visible but not explicit.

Mark himself managed his visibility on social media in contrasting ways. On YouTube, Mark shared his experience as a trans man honestly and openly, and he saw this as part of his activism to help other young trans people to find their place in the world and to feel like they were not alone. In this capacity, Mark felt connected to a global brotherhood of other trans men, and this could be understood in very public terms. On the other hand, Mark was very strategic in who he would friend on Facebook, especially with new peers he had met through university or while travelling. We quote Mark at some length here to provide depth to his friending process, and the sometimes awkward dance he would do around not friending people in order to maintain boundaries in his life:

> I'm very selective of who I add on Facebook. I'm private. You can't find me. I can only find you. You can't add me even if you do find me. Like I just don't have that add button because I don't want people who just meet me to be able to just add me on Facebook because obviously I don't meet someone and go, hey I'm friends, this is my life kind of thing …

It's a security thing. You don't want to be able to—you don't know how everyone is going to take it [being trans] so if I have to be guarded in that I can't just add whoever on Facebook because they're going to see whatever. But I've figured out that I just put it off as long as I possibly can. I get to know somebody and then if I feel like I like this person, I want to let them in a little bit more in my life I will add them on Facebook. Then I think essentially maybe if they do Facebook stalk me they probably would figure it out, maybe they wouldn't …

Normally what happens is it's quite easy because you'll meet somebody. It's normally like you meet somebody out or I went to Thailand, you meet somebody in Thailand. They're like, "oh my god, add me on Facebook". You're like, "yeah sure, put your number into my phone, put your name in my phone, I'll find you tomorrow". You just don't and then there's no loss because they don't know your name and it's fine.

But I think that it becomes more and more awkward when you go to uni with people and you're seeing them every day. You're becoming quite close to them and they're kind of going, "why don't you add me on Facebook?" It gets to the point where it's kind of like, we're friends. We're not just uni buddies, we're friends. We've hung out, we've gone out partying together. Why aren't you adding me on Facebook?

Relationship-trace practices are part of this wider constellation of boundary management strategies that Mark is describing here, which elsewhere are also described in relation to privacy, impression management, and audience segregation. To return to Mark's relationship-trace practices with his girlfriend, in the images where Mark's girlfriend was pictured—a selfie of the pair kissing, for instance—those images were not linked to his girlfriend's profile. Thus, like Tina and her girlfriend, while Mark's relationship was front-and-centre on his own profile, it was mostly hidden for his girlfriend, producing two very different relationship performances. While this kind of practice does not guarantee Mark's girlfriend would never be identified—screenshots could be taken, mutual friends could potentially see the two sides of the disclosure practices being employed—this approach seemed to work for the couple, managing the delicate boundaries many queer relationships operate on.

Type 3—The Intended Absence of Relationship Traces

As we have explained, there is a certain significance and resonance to the declaration of a relationships on Facebook for many. However, changing a status from 'single' to 'in a relationship' and then, often, back again is not straight-forward. To reiterate one of Facebook's original status suggestions, 'it's complicated', and there are varying degrees of complication as we have started to unpack above. This complexity and the associated drama intensifies as we consider our final two types of relationship disclosures/non-disclosures: the intended absence of relationship traces, and the termination or erasure of those traces.

Nathan (27), a social media manager and sports fan, primarily used Facebook to document his frequent trips to sporting events, mostly football all over the world. Nathan used Facebook as a sort of 'travel log', although one driven by images rather than text. As a social media manager, his use of Facebook was particularly interesting because he was managing multiple profiles in his professional life as we discuss in the previous chapter, including the profiles of upcoming sports people as well as his own. In this respect, he would often find himself working each day with multiple profiles open; updating and switching between them constantly.

Since joining Facebook in 2006, when he first started university, Nathan had never really made personal or self-reflexive comments on his profile page. He rarely posted a status update or photos in which he featured. The few photos that did exist that he could be seen in were mostly posted by other people who had tagged him in them, again reiterating the significance of others in co-performing identity through the affordance of the tag. Nathan recalled one occasion when tagging had created some tension between him and his then girlfriend with whom he was having a long distance relationship.

As a very private person, Nathan had chosen not to display a relationship status on his profile when he was with his girlfriend. She, on the other hand did. Like our examples with Mark and Tina above, where relationship disclosures often only played out through 'shadow posts', in this scenario Nathan's girlfriend was the one seeking to name up and make their relationship explicit, not Nathan. Despite several trips and experiences together, Nathan chose not post any photographs of them together, continuing his relative anonymity on the site. Here, Nathan was not even 'shadowing' their relationship, preferring instead to keep it intentionally invisible. Nathan explained that this was because the 'self' he presented on the site was as that of a sports fan maintaining a fairly professional, anonymised profile. However, these efforts to present a very particular self on the site became compromised when his then girlfriend tagged him in small number of photographs of them together.

In one instance, Nathan recalled being tagged in a photograph, which he subsequently un-tagged. His girlfriend then 're-tagged' the photo, only for Nathan to un-tag it again. The repeated un-tagging by Nathan was not well received by his girlfriend: 'she shouted at me, yeah, I do remember her shouting at me'. Nathan explained that for his girlfriend, this was a signifier of how he felt about their relationship (embarrassed, secretive and so on) while she wanted to share their relationship openly. Nathan's decision to leave the image tagged eventually was simply to 'stop an argument', despite his persistence in creating a 'depersonalised' profile. This example also represents the mediating role that Facebook can play in relationships, to the point at which the relationship itself can seemingly be made meaningful or meaningless by what is disclosed (or not) on the site.

Robert was a 25-year-old medical doctor in Australia. Robert identified as gay, and explained this was difficult for him as he had conservative parents from Hong Kong. Robert was out to his parents as bisexual, which for him was intended as an intermediary step that he did not progress from after he met disapproval from his parents. When scrolling back through his Timeline, Robert was able to pinpoint when he had come out to his parents (as bisexual only at the time) and how this corresponded with a difficult time in his life, directly after the end of his first relationship with a man. The breakup and then coming out to his parents was difficult for Robert, but after working through this period it also marked the beginning of a new 'chapter' in his life where he became less of a 'hermit': 'For the next two-ish years … I was in the party scene'. This led to Robert entering into other relationships. While Robert was 'out' on Facebook (interested in: men), and at the time of our interview had been in a serious relationship for the previous year, this relationship was not visible on Facebook, either explicitly or implicitly. He was very conscious of not articulating or even hinting at or 'shadowing' his relationship with his partner, out of concern for how his conservative family might view this. In the previous chapter, Robert was also very conscious about how he managed his professional boundaries on Facebook as a medical practitioner who worked in a hospital. Clearly, this kind of boundary-work took place across multiple different arenas of life for Robert.

Whereas for Nathan and his girlfriend, the intended absence of a relationship trace on Facebook was a point of tension and drama, for Robert and his boyfriend, the intended absence of a relationship trace was part of an accepted survival strategy. Like Mark and the tactics of visibility he employed with his girlfriend in the previous section illustrate, LGBTIQ+ people must often walk a particularly challenging line when it comes to visibilising (or not) relationships on social media (see also Duguay 2016a, 2016b).

Type 4—When It's No Longer Facebook Official: Erasure and Revision

Ending a relationship that has been articulated and recorded on Facebook can be a significant undertaking. As Light and Cassidy (2014) explain, disconnecting *with* Facebook is an important part of how the site operates, and how users manage their presence through the site: blocking, de-friending, unfollowing, hiding. Despite a focus in the literature on how Facebook works to connect users, disconnection (especially when it comes to the separation of romantic partners) must also figure into our understandings of the site, as Light and Cassidy (2014) argue. In terms of relationships, whereas Tina (22) did not de-friend her girlfriend on Facebook after they broke up, other participants saw de-friending as an important and sometimes even necessary act after the end of a relationship. Mary, a 27-year-old Australian finance worker, was one of them. Scrolling back through Mary's Facebook Timeline, a comment from an ex-boyfriend caught her attention:

Mary: That's my ex-boyfriend ... wishing us a Merry Christmas. That's funny to see.
Int.: How so? Is that weird?
Mary: Yeah, it's kind of weird because I guess I don't really remember those days very much anymore. A lot of it's blocked out ... Most of the photos have been deleted.
Int.: You did that?
Mary: Yeah, [current boyfriend] wasn't happy with seeing those kind of things ... I did get caught out the other day. He found a picture of us on there so that was awkward.
Int.: You deleted a lot of that stuff after you started seeing [current boyfriend]?
Mary: Yeah.

Mary went on to explain that her relationship with her ex-boyfriend of four years had ended poorly. Scrolling through posts from during this time, she recalled sleeping on her father's couch, and generally going through a difficult time. Because so much of their relationship had been mediated on Facebook, Mary considered deleting her account and starting over in order to get away from those memories ('It was a four year relationship so pretty much everything on there was based on that part of my life'), but did not want to erase the rest of her life as mediated on the site in the process. She also recalled being 'sick of people' and wanting to be 'left alone' during the breakup, and habitually accessing Facebook only exacerbated that, so she deactivated her account for several weeks. This aligns with Tina's (22) experience of her breakup with her girlfriend, where she gradually 'faded out' the relationship tie over a month, in order to avoid unsolicited sympathetic contact from friends.

After Mary started seeing her current boyfriend, and it became clear that he was uncomfortable with the images of her and her ex together on her Timeline, she scrolled back to erase these images, removing these traces of her previous relationship. Even at the time of our interview, several years into her relationship with her current boyfriend, she remarked that she had been 'caught out' recently, with her current boyfriend finding a picture of Mary with her ex still on Facebook in an old album. That Mary's current boyfriend was scrolling back through old photos of her reveals something about how users of the site interact with and return to the digital traces of the people in their lives. In this way, for Mary's boyfriend,

Facebook wasn't just a way to 'get to know her' at the beginning of her relationship, as we described earlier. Rather, there is some kind of interplay here with an archived version of Mary. To enrol Hogan's (2010) metaphor of the identity 'exhibition' (over the more widely used 'performance', in line with Goffman's (1959) dramaturgical framework), Mary's boyfriend is returning to previous elements of her digital trace to wander this enduring exhibition. It's unclear if Mary's boyfriend was 'checking up on her' or reminiscing or simply scrolling idly through his partner's profile, but that he resurfaced this image with Mary, and that she deleted it, points to the ongoing significance of Facebook in mediating relationships even long after they have ended.

Ali (23) a student, was adamant that he would avoid going 'Facebook Official' in the future after a rather turbulent five year relationship with an ex-girlfriend in which 'every problem we had you could source back to [Facebook].' He explained: 'it was small things to big things, so I was really good friends with a girl at school, really close but it was completely platonic, but if she would even like a status of mine I'd get it in the neck for a week from my girlfriend'. There were a number of instances where Ali's girlfriend appeared to be very jealous and would use Facebook to 'check who I was talking to, what I was doing, where I was, all these things.' These problems persisted even when his girlfriend moved overseas. When they got back together for a final time, they took the decision *not* to be friends on the site acknowledging that Facebook had been so damaging to their relationship up to this point. Thus, they attempted a 'Facebook Free' relationship, which meant they had no access to each other's profiles. However, the relationship ended, and even though they were not friends on the site, Ali's ex-girlfriend circumnavigated this by using her mother's profile (who Ali was friends with) to find out if he was with another girl and what he had been up to. In this respect, even though they were no longer 'Facebook Official', in a relationship or friends on the site, his girlfriend found 'a way in' to continue monitoring his life. To return to Light and Cassidy's (2014) enrolment of 'disconnection' as a necessary component of social life as applied to Facebook, in Ali's case disconnection here (from his ex-girlfriend) was subverted. His attempts to inscribe some boundaries around this relationship—even after it ended—seem to have failed, given the relative invisibility that Facebook's design can afford to audiences.

As our discussions have demonstrated, Facebook is a central point for our participants through which relationships are played out. For many, the site has come to play a crucial role in mediating the many stages of a relationship from beginning to end, and even beyond as people reflect on past relationships and are prompted to delete pictures of exes by new partners. Going 'Facebook Official' might offer a sense of legitimacy to a relationship for some, but getting to this point is often fraught with complexities and influenced by the ways the relationship is lived out both on and outside of the site.

For the young queer people in our study, seen through the examples of Tina (22), Mark (22) and Robert (25), the ways in which relationships are performed, made visible, and named on Facebook can be even more contentious, especially for those with conservative family members. In other instances, for example with Tina (22) and Nathan (27), variances in how relationships are disclosed on Facebook within couples can hint at what Goffman (1959) might describe as 'backstage' juggling acts, complicated by drama, miscommunications, and power imbalances that have always caused tension in romantic and couplings. Growing up on Facebook, however, can surface these complexities and backstage negotiations in challenging ways.

Tracing Relationships in Digital Spaces: Identity, Wellbeing, Secrets and Ruptures

Our use of four types of relationship disclosures go some way to unraveling these complexities and to understand the role Facebook plays in contemporary relationships as well as in everyday life more broadly. Take our first type of relationship that considers overt relationship disclosures. Our examples draw on two participants who were openly sharing the fact that they were now in a romantic relationship, declarations of which were unequivocally made on the site. For both this marked a confidence in this relationship. However, the combination of the scroll back method and in-depth qualitative interview meant that we were able to draw out the nuances of each of their experiences and motivations enabling us to further understand the contexts and processes of decision-making between a couple. For Mitch (20), sharing his relationship represented an important stage of maturity that sparked him to delete images of his single days that were replaced by photos of him and his girlfriends: his 'new' life supplants his old. For Louis, his relationship became embedded into a profile that already had a dual purpose to connect with friends and to promote music. In this respect, his relationship was integrated into Louis's Facebook Timeline adding to his life narratives rather than supplanting them.

In our second type of relationship trace in which partnerships are in some way shadowed or implicitly hinted at, we can find narratives that allude to wellbeing. Tina for example, uses the site to 'fade out' her relationship while she still tries to come to terms with it ending. Implying some element of continued connection to her ex-girlfriend provided her with an invisible tie to her, despite the fact that the relationship had broken down. Mark similarly has to negotiate a duality since he is not able to overtly link his comments and photos to his girlfriend. For Mark, Facebook provides an opportunity for him to share the joy of his relationship but with using cautious posting practices, a duality that is, at times, frustrating and challenging.

The third relationship trace type refers to those relationships that are intentionally kept off the site, drawing out some of the explicit and clear cut stances that participants take regarding privacy and protecting identity in digital spaces. For Nathan and Robert, this involved keeping content that they perceived to be highly personal and private off the site. Nathan for example was upfront in his views that a social network site was not the place to live out relationships; these play out strictly in face-to-face situations. His hard line was met with conflict when he did become involved in a relationship that resulted in his clearly defined borders around Facebook use becoming infiltrated with a romantic narrative for a short time. For Robert, as we explain, there are serious issues around the acceptance of his relationship by his family as he is a gay man who has not be able to fully come out. For him, a complete absence of any aspect of his relationship is a crucial survival strategy. Robert's situation also connects to those narratives of wellbeing and the role that Facebook plays in this. He has found a way to be in the relationship he wants to be in, but clearly his decision *not* to share any aspect of it in this space was a critical part of this relationship working.

Finally, disclosures can be erased and revised, particularly at the end of the relationship. Tina's experiences provide an excellent example of how she used Facebook as a way to 'phase' out her relationship with Bec, reflecting the emotional ties she still had to the relationship despite it ending. Other participants, however, opted for more direct, purposeful erasure, often with future relationships in mind, or as a result of a new relationship beginning. Posts about previous relationships retain some significance, but inevitably this significance changes over time and in different circumstances. Mary, for example, erased posts when her new boyfriend called her out on still having them in her Timeline. This sparked a look back over her disclosures, resurfacing memories of a challenging and difficult time. The fact that Mary was seemingly encouraged to delete content from her past by her current boyfriend reveals some problematic power dynamics embedded into such practices over personal and private content. At the same time, this example also points to the ways in which the profiles of partners become interrelated in a hyperlinked Facebook assemblage. Mary's current boyfriend perhaps understood Mary's profile as an extension of his own, and thus the presence of Mary's ex-boyfriend on her own Timeline may have confronted him. Those challenging gender dynamics are also found in Ali's experiences when his attempts to cut all Facebook ties with his ex-girlfriend were thwarted as she used her mother's account to access his profile. Both examples raise important questions about gendered ownership, responsibility, and conduct on social network sites while reinforcing the extent to which such platforms are patently part and parcel of contemporary romantic relationships. Both examples also emphasise the challenges in trying to attain complete erasure of past relationships.

The boundaries of Facebook as a site of *disconnection* are porous, often unclear and not neatly definable highlighting the ways in which Facebook privileges connection, neat linearity and monogamy in relationships. Our research demonstrates how disclosures of intimacies to networked publics are navigated by users as part of everyday life. We have made use of Marwick and boyd's (2014) concept of 'drama', a term that emerged from many of the discussions we had with our participants about disclosing their relationships on Facebook. Facebook is a site on which drama is constantly mobilised and thus our participants talked about the various ways in which drama was avoided, averted, created, embraced and manipulated on the site. We have also utilised Light and Cassidy's (2014) application of 'disconnection' as 'social lubricant' on Facebook to illustrate how disconnecting from Facebook features in the 'fading out' or ending of a relationship, or erasing a past relationship when a new one begins. Use of this term has also enabled us to illustrate how 'disconnecting' from Facebook can be subverted by users finding (relatively easy) alternative ways to access a profile even if 'de-friending' has 'officially' taken place. Beyond the context of love and romantic relationships, we will return to an analysis of processes of disconnecting through Facebook later in the book (Chapter Nine).

It is also clear that in many ways, Facebook troubles the complexity and messiness of these relationships simply by asking for them to be named, making them visible in different ways, and by privileging specific kinds of normative relationships. Consider Mary's (22) experience of going 'Facebook Official':

Int.: Do you remember whether you and [current boyfriend] were Facebook Official in that there was a relationship status update?
Mary: Not for ages.
Int.: Not for ages?
Mary: Like seven or eight months. We were seeing each other but just, I don't know. There were a lot of ups and downs.

The 'ups and downs' that Mary is referring to here are difficult to articulate on Facebook. The performative dimension of going 'Facebook Official' is anchored to a linear and uncomplicated narrative about romantic relationships with a heteronormative progression from dating to engagement to marriage to having children at its core. While Facebook provides opportunities for separation and ending relationships, drawing attention to these ruptures appears at odds with the overall 'positive' forms of disclosure that Facebook appears to foster, at least for our participants. Further, during the early stages of a relationship, as Mary (27) explained above, going 'Facebook Official' can be very awkward. Perhaps someone has just come out of a relationship and doesn't want to be seen to be jumping into something new too quickly. Perhaps in the early stages of 'seeing each other', a couple might also be seeing other people and until they name their relationship and put borders around it, there is an unspoken openness. Thus, for some of our own participants, it became easier to ignore going 'Facebook Official' altogether, as they avoided it early on and then it seemed inappropriate after a year or so when the relationship had already become serious. Others like Louis (20) and his new partner Emma considered carefully when it was the right time to go 'Facebook Official'. When they did make it official, not only did this formalise their relationship and make it public to their 'friends', it also served as a (highly visible) marker of the progress Louis was making in his life: a critical moment in his growing up narrative as documented on the site.

Conclusion

What our discussions illustrate overall is that Facebook is a key platform upon which contemporary relationships are performed, mediated, and formalised. As we discussed earlier, romantic relationships can be crucial in young people's lives, with impacts (both positive and negative) on self-esteem, well-being, happiness, and psychological adjustment (Viejo et al. 2015). Even for young people who seek to avoid or are ambivalent about romantic and/or sexual attachment (see the asexual and aromantic movements, for instance), popular culture continues to be dominated by narratives that centre on love and romance (Jackson 1993). Unsurprisingly, within this context, making a relationship 'Facebook Official' is anything but straightforward: it is imbued with drama, complications, tensions and emotions. Even when relationships on Facebook are not explicitly named however, digital traces of relationships can be inscribed on the site, shadowed, implied. Even a mutual friend tagging a couple at a location check-in, or a nightclub posting a photo of a couple kissing in the background, can constitute digital inscriptions of relationships that can be read and interpreted. This relationship-trace-work is not always easily controlled. At the same time, naming and making visible relationship ties on Facebook has clearly entered into a popular, normative understanding of how romantic relationships progress and are marked out by rites of passage, especially for young users.

The long term implications and conventions around going 'Facebook Official' (or not) remain to be seen, but as we have demonstrated, attending to the increasingly longitudinal digital traces that constitute enduring digital media can reveal much about contemporary relationships and how they are remembered.

In the next chapter we move to consider other types of relationships, namely those that exist within the family. As we have hinted at in this chapter and in earlier ones, the use of Facebook by different family members influences the ways in which young people engage with the site, revealing the often sophisticated ways they manage audiences and content and how different types of identity performance translate within and outside of Facebook.

References

Baym, N. (2010). *Personal connections in the digital age*. Cambridge: Polity Press.

Bouchey, H. A., & Furman, W. (2003). Dating and romantic experiences in adolescence. In G. R. Adams & M. Berzonsky (Eds.), The Blackwell handbook of adolescence (pp 313–329). Oxford: Blackwell.

boyd, d. (2007). Why youth (heart) social network sites: The role of networked publics in teenage social life. In Buckingham, D. (Ed.) *Youth, identity, and digital media* (MacArthur foundation series on digital learning, Vol. 119, p. 142). Cambridge, MA: MIT Press.

boyd, d. (2014). *It's complicated: The social lives of networked teens*. New Haven: Yale University Press.

boyd, d., & Ellison, N. B. (2008). Social network sites: Definition, history, and scholarship. *Journal of Computer-Mediated Communication, 13*(1), 210–230.

boyd, d., & Marwick, A. (2011). Social privacy in networked publics: teens attitudes, practices, and strategies. Paper presented at the *A Decade in Internet Time: Symposium on the Dynamics of the Internet and Society*, September 2011, https://papers.ssrn.com/sol3/papers.cfm?abstract_id=1925128. Accessed August 27, 2019.

Diener, E., & Seligman, M. (2002). Very happy people. *Journal of Psychological Science, 13*(1), 81–84. http://doi.org/10.1111/1467-9280.00415.

Dion, K. K., & Dion, K. L. (2006). Self-esteem and romantic love. *Journal of Personality, 43*(1), 39–57. http://doi.org/10.1111/j.1467-6494.1975.tb00571.x.

Duguay, S. (2016a). "He has a way gayer Facebook than I do": Investigating sexual identity disclosure and context collapse on a social networking site. *New Media & Society, 18*(6), 891–907.

Duguay, S. (2016b) Lesbian, gay, bisexual, trans, and queer visibility through selfies: Comparing platform mediators across Ruby Rose's Instagram and vine presence. *Social Media + Society*, April–June: 1–12.

Ellison, N. B., Steinfield, C., & Lampe, C. (2007). The benefits of Facebook "friends:" Social capital and college students' use of online social network sites. *Journal of Computer-Mediated Communication, 12*, 1143–1168.

Giddens, A. (1991). *Modernity and self identity: Self and society in the late modern age*. London: Palgrave Macmillan.

Goffman, E. (1959). *The presentation of self in everyday life*. London: Allen Lane.

Grover, R. L., & Nangle, D. W. (2007). Introduction to the special section on adolescent romantic competence: Development and adjustment implications. *Journal of Clinical Child & Adolescent Psychology*, 36(4), 485–490. http://doi.org/10.1080/15374410701649342.

Hinton S., & Hjorth, L. (2013). *Understanding social media*. London: Sage.

Hogan, B. (2010). The presentation of self in the age of social media: Distinguishing performances and exhibitions online. *Bulletin of Science*, 30(6), 377–386.

Ito, M., et al. (2010). *Hanging out, messing around and geeking out*. Cambridge: The MIT Press.

Jackson, S. (1993). Even sociologists fall in love: An exploration in the sociology of emotions. *Sociology*, 27(2), 201–220.

Kanai, A. (2017) On not taking the self seriously: Resilience, relatability and humour in young women's Tumblr blogs. *European Journal of Cultural Studies*, 22(1), 60–77.https://doi.org/10.1177/1367549417722092.

Kennedy, J. (2015). Conceptual boundaries of sharing. *Information, Communication & Society*, 1–14. http://doi.org/10.1080/1369118X.2015.1046894.

Lambert, A. (2015). Intimacy and social capital on Facebook: Beyond the psychological perspective. *New Media and Society*. Epub ahead of print, 1 June 2015. http://doi.org/10.1177/1461444815588902.

Light, B., & Cassidy, E. (2014). Strategies for the suspension and prevention of connection: Rendering disconnection as socioeconomic lubricant with Facebook. *New Media & Society*, 16(7), 1169–1184. http://doi.org/10.1177/1461444814544002.

Lincoln, S., & Robards, B. (2014). Editorial special theme issue: 10 years of Facebook. *New Media and Society*, 16(7), 1047–1050.

Lincoln, S., & Robards, B. (2016). Being strategic and taking control: Bedrooms, social network sites and the narratives of growing up. *New Media & Society*, 18(6), 927–943. http://doi.org/10.1177/1461444814554065.

Livingstone, S. (2008). Taking risky opportunities in youthful content creation: Teenager's use of social networking sites for intimacy, privacy and self-expression. *New Media and Society*, 10(3), 393–411.

Marwick, A. E., & boyd, d. (2014a). "It's just drama": Teen perspectives on conflict and aggression in a networked era. *Journal of Youth Studies*, 17(9), 1187–1204. http://doi.org/10.1080/13676261.2014.901493.

Marwick, A. E., & boyd, d. (2014b). Networked privacy: How teenagers negotiate context in social media. *New Media and Society*, 16(7), 1051–1067.

Oolo, E., & Siibak, A. (2013). Performing for one's imagined audience: Social steganography and other privacy strategies of Estonian teens on networked publics. *Cyberpsychology: Journal of Psychosocial Research on Cyberspace*. https://dx.doi.org/10.5817/cp2013-1-7.

Papacharissi, Z., & Gibson, P. L. (2011). Fifteen minutes of privacy: Privacy, sociality, and publicity on social network sites. In S. Trepte & L. Reinecke (Eds.), *Privacy online: Theoretical approaches and research perspectives on the role of privacy in the social web* (pp. 75–89). New York: Springer.

Peterson, C., & Seligman, M. E. P. (2004). *Character strengths and virtues: A handbook and classification*. Washington, DC: American Psychological Association.

Robards, B. (2010). Randoms in my bedroom: Unsolicited contact on social network sites. *Prism*, 7(3), 1–12.

Robards, B. (2014). Mediating experiences of "growing up" on Facebook's Timeline: Privacy, ephemerality and the reflexive project of self. In A. Bennett & B. Robards (Eds.), *Mediated youth cultures: The Internet, belonging and new cultural configurations* (pp. 26–41). Basingstoke: Palgrave Macmillan.

Robards, B., & Lincoln, S. (2016). Making it "Facebook official": Reflecting on romantic relationships through sustained Facebook use. *Social Media + Society*, 2(4). https://doi.org/10.1177/2056305116672890.

Thomson, R., Bell, R., Holland, J., Henderson, S., Mcgrellis, S., & Sharpe, S. (2002). Critical moments: Choice, chance and opportunity in young people's narratives of transition. *Sociology*, 36(2), 335–354. http://doi.org/10.1177/0038038502036002006.

Utz, S., & Beukeboom, C. J. (2011). The role of social network sites in romantic relationships: Effects on jealousy and relationship happiness. *Journal of Computer-Mediated Communication*, 16(4), 511–527.

Viejo, C., Ortega-Ruiz, R., & Sánchez, V. (2015). Adolescent love and well-being: The role of dating relationships for psychological adjustment. *Journal of Youth Studies*, 18(9), 1219–1236.

Vitak, J. (2012). The impact of context collapse and privacy on social network site disclosures. *Journal of Broadcasting and Electronic Media*, 56(4), 451–470.

Yang, C., Brown, B. B., & Braun, M. T. (2014). From Facebook to cell calls: Layers of electronic intimacy in college students' interpersonal relationships. *New Media and Society*, 16(1), 5–23.

CHAPTER SEVEN

Mediating Family Life

As Facebook has been taken up by all ages, and as the site has become more embedded into everyday life, so too has it become a space for family dynamics and connectivity, but also tension and 'drama' (Marwick & boyd 2014). In this chapter, we consider the impact of wider inter-generational adoption of Facebook, which highlights mismatched conventions around disclosure practices. Our data offer insights into both positive experiences of Facebook's role in mediating family life, but also reveals tensions and trauma in familial relations both on and off the site. Here, we return to concepts established earlier in the book around context collapse and social media literacies, examining how young people are inducted into Facebook often under the guidance of parents, friends, and older siblings, and how disclosure practices are regularly moderated through the imagined audience of parents and grandparents. In scrolling back with our participants through their Facebook Timelines, complex and contested family lives were revealed, pointing not only to how families are mediated on Facebook, but also to the ways in which Facebook offers co-constructed narratives about family histories. In this sense, we close the chapter by considering what is often left unsaid on Facebook and how family dynamics inform how disclosures are made (or not). We return to this theme in Chapter Nine.

Performing Family Life on Facebook

Facebook founder Mark Zuckerberg asserts that family life is a core part of his 'bringing the world closer together' philosophy and underpins the role of Facebook as a site deeply embedded into everyday life. As of February 2019, Zuckerberg's Facebook profile highlights his marriage (to Priscilla Chan in 2012) and the birth of his two children (Max in 2015 and August in 2017) as key life events. Images of family life featuring his wife, children, and (farm) animals are frequently posted on Zuckerberg's Timeline with hundreds of thousands of 'likes', 'loves', 'laughs' and 'gasps' reactions (there are practically no 'angry' or 'sad' reacts on these posts). For Zuckerberg, Facebook is most certainly a family affair.

The history of Facebook is a well known tale, parts of which we have traced earlier in this book. The social network site was launched in February 2004, having been developed by Mark Zuckerberg and three of his Harvard classmates. The site followed from 'Facemash', also developed by Zuckerberg the year before, which was a "hot or not' on campus' site where students were rated against each other. Facebook was initially accessible only to students at Harvard, but within a month expanded to Columbia, Stanford and Yale. The growth from then on was exponential; first limited to educational institutions to the point at which it was referred to in *The Guardian* as a 'social network site with an educational focus' (Phillips 2007) but since September 2006, open to everyone over the age of 13 with a valid email address. One of the features of Facebook that makes it different to other social network sites other than its longevity, is the fact that despite its beginning within educational institutions, it has become a site for people of all ages to use. Importantly, central to Facebook was a mode of sharing and connecting that offered new ways to be a 'family' in contemporary times.

In the US, the Pew Research Center's data collected in 2019, indicate that Facebook use among 18–29 year olds and 30–49 year olds is now the same, at around 79%. 68% of 50–64 year olds are on the platform, along with 46% of those aged over 65 in the US (Perrin & Anderson 2019). In Australia, commercial market research by 'Yellow' indicates similar patterns of broad use. They found that 88% of their respondents (n = 1516) used social media, and of those social media users Facebook was clearly the most dominant across all age groups: 91% of their 18–29 year old respondents used Facebook, 89% of 30–39 year olds, 84% of 40–49 year olds, 74% of 50–64 year olds and 63% of those 65+ (Yellow 2018). These figures would seem to indicate higher levels of social media use in Australia when compared to the US, but the reliability of the commercial market-based research is unclear. The overall pattern, however, is that while younger people are still very much using Facebook (despite narratives of flight unpacked in Chapter

Two), Facebook is now dominant across all age groups and there are only small differences in use between young people and people in their 40s and 50s. While Facebook use seems to drop off for those aged 65+ (46% in the US, 63% in Australia), this is still a significant uptake.

As we will explore, the adoption of social media—and Facebook in particular—among older demographics brings both positive and negative experiences for our participants. They find themselves suspended in complex networks of family life online as well as offline: networks that both free but also restrict their abilities to be themselves. As we argue, these family networks do not exist in isolation but are inherently connected, informing how young people use and manage Facebook and their social media profiles. In this first section, we consider: what is it about Facebook that has made it so appealing intergenerationally? What is it about the site that has gradually lent itself to different family members and to ways of 'doing' family life online?

Unlike its predecessors MySpace and Bebo, that were both youth-based and youth-focused, Facebook's early marketing campaigns were not primarily aimed at young people and as we argued in Chapter Two, the site has arguably never traded on a status of being cool. Instead, Facebook was quick to pick up on the narratives of nostalgia emerging from people's longitudinal uses of the site as they spent more and more time on it, inscribing their lives as they went. The very fact that you could 'find' old friends from the past and extended family from far and wide, was predicated on social curiosity and the capacity for Facebook to act as a resurfacing tool. Subsequently, narratives of nostalgia have been capitalised upon in some of the key design developments on the site from the introduction of the Timeline in 2011 which made the storage of years' worth of disclosures much neater and easier to navigate, through to the recent 'Friendversary' whereby users can generate short videos with other users that they have been (Facebook) friends with for an extended period of time. Like the 2014 'look back' videos (see Robards 2014 for an extended analysis), the 'Friendversary' videos are algorithmically generated one-minute-long videos that set a series of images and posts that 'capture' the friendship of two users, and set it to emotive music and celebrate a connection between two people as mediated on the platform.

In 2012, and to celebrate reaching 1 billion users, Facebook launched their first video advert. Produced by the acclaimed advertising agency Weiden and Kennedy (whose clients include Nike, Coca-Cola and Samsung) the advert entitled 'chairs are like Facebook' hones in on its core philosophy of sharing and connecting with a constant flow of words such as together, people, connect, share, belong, build, remind, nation, universe. The advert begins with the following narration:

'Chairs. Chairs are made so people can sit down and take a break. Anyone can sit on a chair and if the chair's large enough they can sit down together and tell jokes and make up stories or just listen. Chairs are for people. And that is why chairs are like Facebook.'

The advert was met with mixed reviews in the media at the time. For Shamberg (2012, HuffPost) it was seen as celebrating the technology rather than its users: 'The problem is that we haven't seen a brand like Facebook before because it is literally built on emotion. Every action their users take is driven by some emotion'. While the simile of the chair does seem rather obscure or pretentious—arrogant even—reflection on the content of the advert does give us some interesting insights into why Facebook is a family affair and not just the domain of the young.

It was a shrewd choice to choose a chair as an object to be like. It captures the ubiquitous nature of Facebook; the fact that it is something used by a lot of people across the globe, in different contexts for different things. It is something that can just 'be there' (many users just leave their Facebook profiles open all the time, dipping in and out as they please), it is a 'thing' we go to when we have a break or a rest, it has become part of the fabric of everyday life, to the extent that it is a given—just like the inanimate chair. It can be moved around, used in different formations alone or with different groups of people: large or small. 'Pull up a chair' is inviting as is 'send me a friend request'. The narrator claims 'anyone can sit on a chair' which is accompanied by people of different ages sitting on chairs. It is meant to be read that Facebook is for everyone, no matter what your age; it's a space for all. It is an object we pull up when we want to bring people together or when we just want to be by ourselves. Crucially, it is an object that is found in practically all family homes. Indeed, the simile of the chair does in many respects work with the underlying philosophy of the site which is about connectedness and bringing people together. However, as Shamberg points out, the advert fails to engage with the emotional aspects of its users and rather focuses on the object/technology. The site is undoubtedly a place in which emotion and intimate exchanges play out as we have discussed in the previous chapter and will continue to explore here. However, the focus on the domestication of Facebook in this advert is important because it reinforces its place in everyday life as an extension of the domestic sphere within which family life primarily resides. It emphasises the collapsing down of domestic boundaries and refiguring what family life means—and where it is performed—in the digital age.

Family Life, Facebook and the Teenage Years

It was inevitable that Facebook should become the social network site on which family life is performed given the number of users and its longevity as a sharing platform that is now spanning generations of users. While our data revealed many positive aspects to this, living out family life on a social network site can also cause tensions and conflict, especially for our participants who had experienced their teenage years while on the site. The teenage years are often one of the most turbulent periods in the lifecourse, marked out by a series of critical transitions and rites of passage in multiple spheres such as education, employment, family and home life. In this way, Facebook can be employed by young people to 'impression manage' an identity for the benefit of family members alongside other types of identity play that aligns to other social and cultural worlds. Here we see how 'the family' is used as a prompt to filter disclosures, how activity on the site can cause tensions and drama and how having family members on Facebook has driven young people off the site, or at least modulated their use.

As part of the research process described in Chapter Four, our participants were invited to produce handwritten timelines on which they charted what they perceived to be the key events in their teenage years, experienced over the time that they had been using Facebook. In doing this we enabled our participants to identify what they deemed to be important moments in the context of their lives as well as being able to use the handwritten timelines alongside their Facebook Timelines to identify the motivations for documenting some events and not others. In the handwritten timelines, participants identified more 'formalised' transitions such as taking exams, getting their first job, going to university, dropping out of university, passing driving tests even in the case of one participant being able to go out in public without a chaperone. Other moments identified were to do with social experiences such as going to a gig or music festival, having an alcoholic drink or going to a club for the first time, travelling abroad with friends rather than family, and personal critical moments such as coming out, being in a romantic relationship, a relationship ending, a relationship beginning again, meeting current friends, illness or injury, having house parties with friends, learning to play a musical instrument, starting bands, moving house, attending a high school prom, or in the case of one of our participants a '2014: traumatic event', and another 'sneaking out to malls'.

In a number of instances critical moments were identified as those related to family life and key family events. This was particularly the case for participants who had been brought up in Islamic communities where the wedding of a family member featured significantly as a key moment or transition in the participant's life. One of our participants, Nena (20), noted down four family weddings in her handwritten timeline, clearly standing out as significant in her memory. Nena also explained that she was 'in charge' of managing the social media aspects of her family during these weddings, which included sharing wedding photos with other family members primarily using Facebook Messenger.

Other family related moments that were common in our interviews included siblings moving out of the family home, the death of a family member (particularly grandparents), family holidays, annual celebrations such as Christmas, or milestone birthdays such as an 18th or 21st were also recorded. In many cases, it was seemingly banal images or posts that prompted deeper reflections on family and the importance of familial ties. Ari (21) reflected on a photo of a family vacation when we scrolled back to it in his Facebook timeline: 'Family trip to Queensland … which is pretty significant because it's the first family trip we did'. Ari further explained, prompted by the image, that his family was 'pretty close' and they had come together at a time when he was ill before the travel photo was taken. 'I was pretty sick in 2011 … I had to take three months off school … it was glandular fever … I had to go to hospital … it was pretty shit'. There were no photos of Ari's time in hospital or explicit references to this significant time away from school, but the photo of the first family trip away resonated with him and connected in the interview to that longer narrative about the importance of family, which he further linked back to this traumatic experience.

It is evident then, that the teenage years are often highly eventful and what is deemed as an important or critical moment is often part of a very personal trajectory, where family is closely implicated. While there were many key moments in common across our sample such as taking exams, getting a job, or going to university there are also a number of interesting diversions mapped out though each participant's personal experiences and circumstances. In addition, what we have also learned from our research is the extent to which these stories and experiences are not only mediated through Facebook but also through *family life on Facebook*. As young people who find themselves on the brink of independence, often what they disclose on social media is subject to an additional filter beyond those set by the site itself, for example parents who insist they are 'friends' with their children on the site for safety and monitoring of activities as well as for genuine friendship.

Signing Up: Parents, Facebook & Online Safety

The participants who took part in the *Facebook Timelines* project were in their twenties. For many, joining Facebook had happened in their early teens—typically around 13 or 14 years old. Given their age, this often meant that their first steps into the world of social network sites was under the supervision of parents, or sometimes older siblings if not their friends. Alice (20) for example, spoke about the role of her father when initially setting up her Facebook profile, and earlier a Bebo profile:

Alice: I think for Bebo I sat down with my Dad just so he could watch to make sure the information going in wasn't like age or like home or whatever. I think he sent me a picture of myself that had like a hat over my face so that you wouldn't see my face so that I could upload that as my profile picture.
Int.: Your dad gave you that?
Alice: Yeah, my dad sent me that. So they allowed me to have it but they were like if you use a picture that …Like sees you … but for Facebook I was older so I knew what I was doing then … I think my friend might have come over to help me set that one up. Just because I wasn't really sure how it all worked and they kind of just brought up the page and told me what to do and then I filled it all in when they left.

At the start of her social media use Alice was guided by her father, who wasn't on social media himself at that point. They discussed privacy and the extent to which one should reveal details about themselves on social network sites. In effect, what Alice's father was doing was ensuring she made informed choices about the story she would tell about herself online, setting boundaries of disclosure for her as a novice user before she posted anything. The boundaries of disclosure in this scenario are set through the use of an anonymised photograph that was selected for her to use as her profile picture. Such practices then translated (at least in the first instance, while still 'new' on the site) onto Facebook. However, after several years of use and with a self-proclaimed maturity, Alice disclosed 'critical moments' on the site including images in which she is identifiable. When scrolling back with the researcher, Alice revealed a photograph of her drinking before a night out with friends at which point she announces: 'this is pre-drinks. That's my first fishbowl'—a large fish bowl shaped glass to drink from. So while her family, namely her father, was significant in socialising her into social media use, Alice's disclosure practices clearly evolved over time as she became more independent and developed her own conventions for being visible in networked publics.

Initially getting on Facebook was clearly a family affair for other participants too. Dina (23) explained, 'I think one of my cousins signed up with me, sat there and forced me to'. Sarah (28) and her high school-sweetheart-turned-husband initially had a joint couples profile before they both set up their own separate accounts: '[Husband's name] and I had a joint one and it was mostly him using it, and then I got on the bandwagon when I started adding people from high school'. For Mitch (20) it was his brother who got him into it: 'He told me how he could meet people on there and one of his friends assigned him a profile picture when he didn't really want to have it, they made a profile for him. And yeah, he said that I should add him on there so I did.'

For other participants, negotiating family through Facebook was much more fraught. Claudia (20) grew up in the foster care system, and had strict institutionally mandated boundaries around communication with her biological family:

> Claudia: I've had to do it [strict privacy settings] because I was a foster child. When I left foster care a couple of years ago, like my security was ... it's hard to explain. Like when you're in the foster care system you have like security and no-one's going to contact you from your family, like my biological family ... as soon as I turned 18 my biological family tried to contact me. I had to change my settings.
> Int.: So, that was part of, protecting yourself?
> Claudia: Yeah.

Claudia's experiences point towards the ways in which being visible and searchable on Facebook can be a real risk when family is linked to trauma and state-enforced processes of separation. Claudia went on to explain how her foster sister also played a role in her initially signing up to Facebook: 'I saw my foster sister, she had Facebook and she was talking to all these people from school, and I was like, "I want to talk to people who go to my school. I want to let everybody know what I'm doing"'.

Our participants joined Facebook when there were still many 'unknowns' about how the site would develop and what it would become. In these early days when they first joined the platform, users were unlikely to be considering long term digital traces or the notion that Facebook might come to be considered an 'archive of self' and it was likely that users considered the site as something of a fad given the back catalogue of similar social network sites at that point (Bebo, MySpace, LiveJournal, and so on). What this indicates then, is that while user guidelines set by the site itself were in place, all users joining the site were new to it and learning how to be on it as they created their profiles and growing networks of friends.

There was no precedence as we have now which makes the role of the parent an interesting one in this context, and one that has been placed under the microscope as social network sites have become embedded into many aspects of our everyday life. Alice's (20) example above reveals the potential awkwardness of a father—who did not use Facebook at the time—trying to help guide his daughter in how to 'be' in networked publics. Today, young parents themselves have grown up using social media or at least in contexts where social media use is normalised, and it remains to be seen how these differences will map onto the ways parents guide and manage their own children's social media adoption and use.

The work of Sonia Livingstone and colleagues has been pioneering in this respect, offering insights into children and young people's uses of social media, enabling us to have a better understanding of internet safety, privacy, media literacy and everyday life online as experienced, navigated and negotiated by young internet users themselves. The research projects of Livingstone and colleagues include *Global Kids Online*, *EU Kids Online*, *Parenting for a Digital Age*, *Children's Rights in the Digital Age* and *Children's Data and Privacy Online*. Their research highlights many of the ongoing challenges in the relationship between young people, their parents and other family members online. For example, a report (written by Dongmiao Zhang and Sonia Livingstone in January 2019) from their national survey of UK parents, part of the *Parenting for a Digital Future* project, highlights digital inequalities and how these are influencing 'parenting, socialisation and the family'(1). Overall, the report comments on 'possible digital inequalities between more or less societally advantaged groups focussing on gender, ethnicity, socioeconomic status (SES), parental education, family composition and special educational needs (SENS) and disabilities' (1). One of its key findings is about online risks and parental mediation and the contexts within which parents mediate and manage their children's online practices. Their findings show that parents do adopt a range of mediation practices that encourage children to use the internet in positive ways as well as being able to alert them to risks but that this mediation can have some variations. For example, more educated, higher SES parents, single parents and parents of children with SENS reported more online harms for children compared to parents from other educational backgrounds and socioeconomic groups, and thus these parents also did more parental mediation of their children's internet use.

In terms of the role of parents, the report found that mothers do a little more than fathers in terms of parental mediation but that mostly mothers and fathers are on a par when it comes to setting rules about what a child can do online, rules of use and use of parental controls. Parents from a higher education background tended to be the ones who were engaging their children in discussions about online safety and talking about their internet use. Such nuanced discussions are now possible as we now have a history of young people using the internet. While the internet had been around for some time before social network sites like Facebook became so popular, use was not comparable to how it is today, and thus for our participants being a user of a social network site did not exist within the social, cultural or economic contexts within which it operates today. However, as Facebook reaches its 16th year in existence in 2020 we know the extent to which it is now embedded into so many lives across generations.

Family as a Facebook Filter

The role of the family infiltrates many aspects of Facebook use from the initial set up to current use of the site. Family relationships on Facebook can be complex with both positive and negative experiences that are shaped by narratives of growing up and new forms of independence for young people that see them changing the way they interact on the site, as well as moving to other social media platforms. Alongside the explicit privacy settings and sharing filters available through Facebook, we argue that there is also a 'family filter' on Facebook that produces an additional level of profile management—sometimes even control—that governs how and what our participants disclose on the site.

Take Essa (20) for example, who described her use of Facebook as 'fairly basic' given that she was 'pretty reserved socially'. This basic use was informed by the 'scary stories' she would sometimes hear in films and in the media about social media being used to track down and prey upon young people. She explained that, in her own words, in her young, 'naive teenage years' she would pay attention to these stories. In addition, she said that her mother was 'very clear' about her being careful when posting anything online: talking to her about online safety and encouraging her to always post with caution:

> When I'm home they're always like 'you can't put that in a post' and pictures and everything. And I think as well they're a bit reserved. My brother posted pictures of him and his girlfriend at the time. My aunt kind of lost it ... got really mad and made him take it down. So I think especially when we were in high school they were just a bit reserved about what we posted especially ... you're not supposed to. And even though we stayed in Dubai we still had family back in India so it was more like if you have a picture with a boy it's kind of like 'who is that?' In my culture it's a bit reserved.

This kind of 'family filter' was direct and explicit, where family members governed what can and (in Essa's case) cannot be said on social media. In Chapter Nine we consider the above scenario through the lens of absenting content, as it emerges in our interview with Essa that her reserved online practices were tied up within a web of family politics and traditions that do not translate into her social life. Her leisure time is often defined by behaviour that the family would not approve of, such as missing tuitions to go to the mall with friends. Here however, we consider her situation through the lens of family as a Facebook filter that sets the parameters for her disclosure practices on the site. Clearly Essa's parents are vocal about her and her brother's online practices, using opportunities when they are at home to remind them to be careful about what they post.

The example of Essa's brother posting photos with his girlfriend highlights a key concern around religion and relationships and Essa's brother posting photos with his girlfriend can be read as an act of rebellion that he was subsequently confronted about by a family member—his aunt. Reputation is at stake here and any image that might raise questions about the status of a relationship is consistently flagged up as to be avoided. We understand from this quote that Essa has family in Dubai and in India and that family members in both countries have profiles on Facebook. This dynamic creates a complex terrain for Essa to navigate as her family spans different cultures, hence her decision to absent material from the site as we discuss later in the book as a mechanism for avoiding miscommunication or sharing of content that may be considered inappropriate depending on who is reading it.

This reserved approach to posting was not always the way Essa disclosed on the site, however. In her interview, Essa talked about the process of going back over her Timeline at various intervals and making changes to the content, especially going back over denser periods of disclosure when elements of her social life were revealed. This would include deleting or changing privacy settings, often in response to new family members joining the site. This notion of the family as an active filter through which past disclosures would be re-interpreted through the eyes of a new 'audience member' points to the complexity of impression management processes occurring here. As Essa said 'I've also adjusted some photos that aunties and uncles can't see.' This is a clear example of the 'family filter' in action, using the technical sharing and privacy affordances of Facebook informed by the social conventions that determined what was appropriate and what was not appropriate to share with family.

These kinds of strategies to negotiating family on Facebook was set amidst other considerations about Facebook content. As young people in their early twenties who have been using the site for a sustained period of time, 'doing my Facebook' is a conscious process. Much like the phrases 'doing my makeup' or 'doing my hair', 'doing my Facebook' is positioned as a critical form of maintenance that if not done regularly reflects poorly on the present self. As Essa said: 'I read it all last week and I was like oh my God I need to do my Facebook because it represents me when I was like 16'. While she may not wish to get rid of that content as 'it's nothing inappropriate or anything it's just a different time' there is a sense that there is a need for ongoing maintenance and assessment for contemporary relevance. What this example illustrates is that relevance does not stand still, and alongside the use of Facebook by different family members, with new ones still joining, makes the process of 'doing Facebook' essential—but very challenging—to the ongoing representation of the self.

Using family as a Facebook filter is found in other arenas of Facebook use also. Continuing with Vanessa and Essa's discussion, we see that different family members influence different types of Facebook use. For example, Vanessa considers the ways in which Facebook disclosures mobilise discussion between family members either with or without her being involved. With her mother, there is clearly open channels for discussion and as her next of kin, it was not unusual for her parents to ask her directly about content they were unsure of. However, Vanessa seems frustrated as the gossip or drama that may be mobilised by other members of her extended family who have read the same content.

> I'd rather have my mum and stuff on Facebook because I know if there's anything they'll come and ask me but I know if it's extended family they kind of just assume stuff and then just make their own stories up.

Essa reflects on some of the practices that her school friends used in order to keep family and friends separate, namely setting up dual accounts, one with an unsearchable name to significantly reduce the risk of parents finding the other account. So cryptic is the other account name that even friends have to be added; they cannot search for the profile. Duffy and Chan (2019) have written about similar practices Instagram, where young people will create multiple accounts including 'finstas' or 'fake Instagram profiles' where they will post more curated and semi-public images to a larger network on one, and more everyday, banal, less highly surveilled disclosures on the other. In this way, finstas operate as social spaces where young people can 'evade the concerns about surveillance and possible disciplinary outcomes' (Duffy & Chan 2019: 127) especially when it came to family and teachers.

Undoubtedly there is certain appeal in this approach for teenagers who are using social network sites as spaces of rebellion in which their 'real' teenage life plays out. On the family site, an edited and strategically managed version of the self is present, as Essa (20) explains:

> I think that my friends at school used to have two different accounts; one for family and one for school. … And you had to keep up both accounts obviously so the parents didn't know that they had this one so they'd have to write, post appropriate pictures in one and then post the rest on the other. They keep the other profile completely private so even if you type it in you can't find it. Yeah there are certain profiles which unless they add you can't add them. You can't add them unless they add you so that's what they used to do.

While we do not know the motives for Essa's friends deciding to make up new, second profiles (which technically breached Facebook policy on owning multiple accounts), this scenario highlights some interesting dynamics that pertain to the notion of the family as a Facebook filter. In this example, the family is completely filtered out of their Facebook activity because their disclosures for an audience of friends is taking place on another profile. Presumably, the profile on which family members are friends, is subject to ongoing filtering in that an edited version of that person is being shared on that site, fit for the audience. Essa's point about receiving different responses to her posts by different family members brings into focus the complications that can emerge from crossing the boundaries between family and personal life, and it is often the repercussions of a disclosure 'taken out of context' (boyd 2008) that triggers different kinds of 'drama' depending on how they 'read' particular information (Marwick & boyd 2014).

This kind of boundary-work also brings us back to our wider theoretical approach informed by Goffman's (1959) dramaturgical framework unpacked in more detail in Chapter Three. Maintaining multiple profiles on the one platform—to manage boundaries between family and friends, in Essa's case—is a specific form of impression management, which as Duffy and Chan (2019) also suggest, is linked to Goffman's conceptualisation of impressions that are 'given off' and 'given'. These tactics of boundary-work have always occurred and occur in a wide range of ways in physical spaces, but in the last few decades, as young people have been growing up in digital spaces, these conventions and practices of boundary-work have been translated and adapted.

Facebook, Family & Surveillance

Participant's discourses around their changing use of Facebook over time often connect to narratives about their family relationships, particularly with parents. Reflections on parents' use of and interaction with Facebook often emerged within our participant's narratives of maturing over time on the site and the politics of crossing boundaries between personal and family life. While a number of participants spoke of the positive relationships hey had with parents online, others spoke of this relationship sometimes being awkward and challenging, especially when the site became a surveillance tool through which parents could check out their children's activities. In turn, parental use of Facebook is often termed as 'amusing' as they comment perhaps inappropriately on their son or daughter's posts, alerting Facebook friends to the fact that someone's parents are now using the site.

Age plays an important factor in how those comments are responded to. For example as Karen (25) illustrates below, her mother 'liking' or commenting on a photo is interpreted as a form of surveillance, a reminder that she is looking in on posts. These reminders used to irk Karen as a teenager when she considered spaces like Facebook to be 'her' space, not one that should be invaded by parents but used with friends. In turn, Karen became more mindful of her posting practices (being careful not to use 'bad' language and so on) which then made her use of the site more cautious. However, now in her twenties Karen does not mind her mother's comments as she used to, instead finding them amusing. Thus her irritation towards her mother's posting has evolved to a position whereby she is observing her mother's posts and interpreting her mum's use of the site as 'quite funny'. No longer is there the stigma of having your mother comment on your posts that the teenage years brought. Additionally, Karen's more mature social media literacy enables her to use terms like 'quite funny' to enforce a naivety of use by her mother that works to separate their social media worlds.

> Int.: How do you feel about, say like your mum being on Facebook?
>
> Karen: I don't really mind. I think it's quite funny. I think maybe some people would feel differently about it but I don't mind too much. She's, she sort of just watches I think [laughs]
>
> Int.: So, are there any situations where you've got family and friends interacting on posts ...
>
> Karen: Yeah, yeah I think definitely. I think if I post like a new profile picture or something my mum will automatically comment on and my friend will like my mum's comment because they're like 'oh, you're mum's on Facebook'. Erm so that's like a kind of a situation. But I think I'm older now so I'm not so worried about my mum seeing me like write a swear word or seeing one of my friends do something like that but when I was younger I'd be really like 'don't look at my stuff' but now it's like it doesn't matter too much.
>
> Int.: So when you were younger do you think it would have horrified you a bit more?
>
> Karen: Yes. I would have been like you can't be my friend! Definitely, yeah. No, I don't think I would have accepted her to be honest.
>
> Int.: So, do you think when you were younger social media was more like your space?
>
> Karen: Yeah. I think it was much more like a social, friends type thing. I think yeah, definitely.

In this example, Karen's own relationship with her mother—and how she relates to being seen by and surveilled by her mother—has changed over time, as most parent-child relationships do. In this case though, the process of growing up on Facebook has also been modulated through that relationship.

Using advanced social media literacy and skills as a tool to manage the dynamics of family life online was a common theme that ran through the Timelines project. Participants saw themselves as being more experienced than their parents, more 'in the know' and savvy about the appropriateness of posting, commenting, and sharing information on the site. For Jess (25), looking back over her Timeline enabled her to reflect on the influence her mother had on her posting practices, even if she only had her own Facebook account for a short period of time. The complication for Jess was that when her mother was using Facebook, she also had friends who used the social network site too, and those friends would often 'report back' to her mother about things Jess had been doing in addition to her mother querying Jess's Facebook activity herself. In this respect, Facebook had become a site of multiple angles of surveillance that did impact on Jess's posting practices. Reflecting on this, Jess frames her early use of Facebook and 'all the crap [she] used to post' within discourses of naivety. She is rather disparaging of her younger self who didn't even consider that people would scroll back through masses of disclosures to find out what she had been up to.

Her mother's decision to stop using Facebook seemed a welcome one for Jess. However, her mother remains a Facebook user to some extent as she then begins to use Jess's account to 'stalk people'. For Jess, her mother using her Facebook profile is OK because it mitigates her having her own profile, which for Jess is far more problematic. As Jess proclaims 'I don't mind as long has she hasn't got Facebook!'. But this will inevitably impact on Jess's use because her profile is not a space in which she can get away from family life and be with her friends. The content is constantly open for surveillance, but Jess accepts this position and sees it as a way to maintain some control of what aspects of her Facebook life are communicated to her mother and how:

Jess: Oh ok, so around that time were people your parents age getting Facebook? I can't quite remember. I just remember being asked to add them online one day by my mum and then thinking—the worst thing isn't it?

Int.: But you said your mum still hasn't got Facebook now?

Jess: No, she just uses mine to stalk people. Which I don't mind as long as she hasn't got Facebook. If she doesn't see what I'm doing it's fine!

Int.: But did that matter more to you, so when you were younger is that something that you were more conscious of than now?

Jess: Of my mum seeing it? Yeah, yeah. Well, to be fair I wasn't really worried about my mum 'cos she's not exactly tech savvy. There was quite a few times when I had to go and turn the laptop on for her, so that wasn't really a problem. But my mum's friends are so nosey, so very nosey. So they would have told them everything.

Int.: And do you think at the time that was a conscious decision not to put that on Facebook because that is something that you wouldn't?

Jess: Yes. Mainly, you know what, it was probably mainly because I knew my mother would be looking at it or somebody might tell her about it. Thinking about it now it was absolutely ridiculous because all the crap I used to post before and why would I think somebody else wouldn't go through all that. Although I don't know perhaps friends can't see all this stuff—I should check that one day!

Using experience that surpasses those of parents to create time and space boundaries in a context when those don't exist in a traditional sense suggests that young people distance themselves from the 'embarrassing' parent comments. As the first generation who have grown up online, our participants find themselves operating within a context in which their position is somewhat superior by default: they joined the site at a young age, have the excuse of youth for their mistakes online but also have a track record of use that has matured and refined in context. However, this is not to position our participants as wholly at the forefront of social media use. Interviewing them in their twenties has captured a period in which 'looking back' over a number of years' worth of disclosures has become important. As we have discussed in Chapter Five, our participants were moving into new phases of their lives in which they were beginning to think about professional life and careers. As Jess's comments affirm above, checking back over content posted in those more carefree, teenage days becomes relevant in those new, emerging narratives of the responsible self.

Mediating Family Life on Facebook: Co-constructed Narratives, Drama & Tensions

Family life on Facebook is always 'under construction' and thus the narratives around a family are constantly evolving. As we have demonstrated so far being part of a family online can be highly contested and challenging, but it can also be fulfilling and empowering, perhaps enabling families who find it hard to come together in an offline context to find the space to live out family life in mediated context. Facebook provides a space within which family can interact without being in face-to-face situations, or creating a virtual equivalent when face-to-face contact is not possible or appropriate.

In her thesis on adoptive family experiences of technological forms for post-adoption contact Sarah Greenhow (2015) considers the role of social network sites such as Facebook for adoptive families who increasingly find themselves negotiating the digital realm as part of the adoption process. Her findings suggest that Facebook can offer considerable benefits in terms of adoptee identity and for building family relationships, but that the unmediated nature of the site also meant that it was by no means risk-averse. Much like our work on Facebook, Greenhow's research, that drew on qualitative and quantitative findings, emphasised the specificity and uniqueness of different family experiences that determine how family life in adoptive contexts can play out online. The site offers real dangers inasmuch as the boundaries between public and private are blurred, even absent and as we have demonstrated elsewhere, finding a way into a profile is not contingent on being Facebook friends. This is a real concern for adoptive families. However, sites like Facebook provide a space for virtual contact, particularly between siblings, enabling adopted children to ask questions to 'satisfy curiosity' (Greenhow 2015: 123) about their birth parents and family. This in turn enables adoptees to feel a sense of identity, knowing where they have come from. The site also provides easy and quick contact when siblings live apart and in different geographic locations. Finally, and pertinent to our research that considers the extent to which Facebook mediates everyday lives, the site can be used as a way of 'getting to know' family members before face-to-face contact (Greenhow 2015: 123).

Families are configured in different ways and, much like the context of the romantic relationship, uses of Facebook can vary between family members, sometimes causing tension and friction, or a point of negotiation and discussion. Take Phil (29) for example who had a daughter but was no longer with her mother. Phil and his ex-partner had quite radically different ways of interacting with Facebook when it came to their daughter. As the quote below demonstrates, this did not seem to create tensions in their relationship, but Phil's decision not to post is bound up in narratives of the private and his perceptions of what he deems to be of interest to his audience.

> I've got a daughter but I never really post any photos up. Her mum does, her mum posts like crazy but I don't. Just because don't really see the appeals of posting up every little detail about your daily family life like (Phil, 29)

While Phil's comment might not be typical of others in similar relationship formations, his views do emphasise the extent to which Facebook is embedded into everyday family life and relationships. Phil's comment demonstrates an acceptance of different posting practices which is potentially connected to his sustained use and years engaging with the site. It is presented as a given here that he and his ex-partner have different ways of sharing their experiences and the experiences of their daughter on the site.

This example raises some interesting questions about Facebook as an archive of family life and how those histories will be read in the future (Lincoln & Robards 2016). Which version of her life might Phil's daughter connect more to? What role will Facebook play in helping her to understand the relationship between her parents? Of course the notion of a co-constructed family history is not unique to Facebook: photographs can be curated in different ways in a photo album and the verbal narratives of their meaning will undoubtedly shift and change over time, as well as change depending on who is doing the story-telling and to whom. Similarly on Facebook, narratives of family life are curated in different ways by different family members, each telling their version of the story their own way. Inevitably, sometimes this story-telling compromises family life, especially when the parameters of what constitutes appropriate discussion are challenged.

In recent years there has been a building discussion about whether or not it is appropriate for parents—like Phil—to be posting on social media about their children at all. Should children be asked for consent to be represented in digital spaces? Do they have a right to not have photos of themselves as infants circulated online? Or on the other side, aren't children extensions of their parents, so shouldn't parents have the right to include their children in representations of their own lives? What about the case of prenatal ultrasound images shared on Instagram (see, for instance, Leaver & Highfield 2018)? Leaver has suggested that in the future, children may have different readings of these kinds of practices. On the one hand, this kind of 'intimate surveillance' could be 'an indication of their parents' affection' or on the other could be interpreted as an invasion of privacy to be resisted as they grow older and develop their own sense of agency and self awareness' (Leaver 2017: 8). In this way, perhaps Phil is ahead of his time.

Often our participants spoke of a generation gap when it came to using Facebook which on occasions lead to quite significant complications off the site. For example when a parent makes an inappropriate comment on his son or daughter's Timeline that compromises the identity of that user and thus results in a child 'de-friending' their parent which inevitably creates an awkward offline relationship, at least temporarily. An example of this comes from Mary, a 27-year-old Australian finance worker who regularly reflected on her family—especially her father—when scrolling back through her Facebook Timeline. Her parents were divorced and remarried to new partners, and Mary has both full—and step-brothers and sisters. She talked about Facebook as important in keeping in touch with this big and dispersed family, and as we scrolled back through her Timeline, it was clear that family played a significant part in her life as mediated on the site. She recounted stories of sleeping on her father's couch after a particularly bad breakup, and how certain images on her profile reminder her of that time in her life. She mentioned her father 17 times during the interview, prompted by the images and disclosures on her profile. However, her father would also tend to post 'emotional stuff' on Facebook that she felt was not appropriate and sometimes upset her. Despite describing their relationship as close, she made the decision to remove him from her 'friends list' on Facebook (de-friending or 'deleting' him):

> **Mary:** I'm not friends with him [Dad] on Facebook anymore just because he posts emotional stuff about family, friends and stuff. There's a time and place for that and Facebook shouldn't be one. So Dad and I aren't friends anymore on Facebook

Int.: How did he take that?
Mary: He was a bit offended but I don't like ... if I sit there at work and if I open Facebook and see something that pisses me off it ruins the whole day.

Despite being close to her father and talking about Facebook as a useful way of keeping in touch with family, Mary deleted her father on Facebook because she didn't want to see his 'emotional' posts. This might appear ruthless in one sense, but there's also a clear strategy of self-care here. For Mary, this was a kind of strategic form of context control as she sought not just to order and re-order the projection of herself on the site, but also how she consumed (or did not consume) the disclosures of others.

Managing Content and Constructing Different Narratives of Self

As we have established so far, having family members as friends on Facebook was common for many of our participants and the fact that this was the case impacted on the stories they could tell about their lives on the site. Decisions about what to share on Facebook were by no means 'snap' decisions—as Mary's example reveals—but often made 'behind the scenes', with consideration given to the implications of posting (for example whether the content would create 'drama' Marwick & boyd 2014). As Cate (20) says 'I do think about what I post generally, especially because I've got my parents. So I think because I've got them, because I've got other family members, I do kind of bear that in mind sometimes ...'. However, as we have argued elsewhere, the continuous flow of data within the site created algorithmically by site design, by other users or by the user themselves, can complicate this process and thus some users found themselves constantly making decisions about what to post and to whom on the site.

Nena (20), who we introduced earlier in this chapter, for instance, was an avid Facebook user and the self proclaimed 'manager' of content shared on the site with her large family. At big events such as weddings, parties or graduations, Nena was often relied upon to take then upload photos onto Facebook to share with her family and friends, a role that she was happy to take on. However, aside from the family-friendly content she would share with them, the fact that she was 'friends' on Facebook with so many family members meant that Nena had to consider carefully the information she was sharing about herself on the site, outside of family events and occasions. In this respect, she would manage her Facebook profile in such a way that certain sections would be hidden, or accessible to a particular group of friends and she would carefully manage which disclosures were seen by whom. For example, Nena, whose family were originally from Uganda—some of whom were Christian and Muslim—had to be careful about who shared posts about her boyfriend with. While she didn't feel her family would necessarily disapprove of him, she preferred not to discuss him 'publicly' on the site because she didn't want family members (for example cousins) to interfere as they inevitably would if they knew any details about the relationship. There were aspects of her life (Nena was a university student) that she wanted to keep private, and between her University friends. Nena said: 'I really wouldn't want my cousins to know like what's going on really with my current boyfriend and stuff. They don't know that I'm with him ... not that I wouldn't be allowed but just that I would rather that be completely private.' For Nena, absenting this narrative from the family 'portion' of Facebook audience was an important part of managing her identity as an independent woman at university. Absenting such narratives from the public parts of her Timeline gave her privacy; and this was a privacy that she might not be able to secure elsewhere so enabled her to engage in some aspects of her life outside of the family.

As is common—particularly in one's teenage years—family life and a strong family identity can sometimes be stifling (Lincoln 2015) and so there were certain aspects of Nena's life as she lives away from home as a university student, that she wanted to keep for herself or just between close friends. Being away from home made this easier, and more broadly becoming an adult—or as Nena says above 'becoming a woman'—signals greater independence and a break away from some aspects of the family. However, while this distancing may occur in other arenas of life offline, managing this position within the family on Facebook can present challenges and absenting certain disclosures on the site is a way in which our participants deal with this. For Nena, the absence or presence of particular disclosures enables her to manage multiple narratives about her life on the site: a family narrative, a university narrative, a romantic narrative, a social life narrative, moving to a professional narrative in the future. The management of her Facebook content in carefully curated ways enables these narratives to play out to particular audiences on the site. There is no doubt that this is labour intensive—as well as emotionally intensive—an aspect of Facebook life that we discuss in previous chapters. Importantly, this level of management of boundaries and privacy settings and social worlds is key for Nena if she is to have any kind of private life and enables her to have some distance from her family. It also means that she maintains a strong connection with her family through specific connection and disconnection practices on the site (Light & Cassidy 2014), thus her role managing photos of family occasions enables her to maintain those strong ties in clear, deliberate ways.

Conclusion

Given the rapid uptake and its enduring existence of 15 years (in 2019—the time of writing), it comes as no surprise that Facebook has been taken up by different family members, across generations. Our research demonstrates that having family members on Facebook and living out family life through the site can be positive and fulfilling, but it can also be stressful and compromising. Often it is not consistently a positive experience with moments of drama and tension arising at times. In this respect, understanding how family life is mediated on Facebook is not straightforward, but is as unique as the families themselves using the site. Sometimes there is clear evidence that Facebook is a space of family support, but at other times inappropriate comments and posts compromise family life. We have discussed the ways in which Facebook is a space of surveillance, especially between parents and children which can be as positive as parents sharing expertise to ensure safe social media use and use the site as a source of protection, but also negative if used as a tracking device to 'keep an eye' on children to the extent that it compromises their independence. In such circumstances, young people operationalise different disclosure practices for different audiences or take their discussions with friends and peers onto different platforms away from family on Facebook.

In the following chapter we turn our attention to the documentation and performance of leisure on Facebook as one of the key arenas of life that is shared on social media. Leisure is of course linked to family, but as our fourth and final arena of 'growing up', also operates as a site for growing independent, risk-taking, and world-building.

References

boyd, d. (2008). *Taken out of context: American teen sociality in networked publics*. University of California, Berkeley.

Duffy, B. E., & Chan, N. K. (2019). You never really know who's looking": Imagined surveillance across social media platforms. *New Media & Society*, 21(1), 119–138.

Goffman, E. (1959). *The presentation of self in everyday life*. London: Penguin.

Greenhow, S. (2015). Chatting online with my other mother: Adoptive family views and experiences of the use of traditional and technological forms of post-adoption contact. PhD, Durham University, Durham.

Leaver, T. (2017). Intimate surveillance: Normalizing parental monitoring and mediation of infants online. *Social Media+ Society*, 3(2), 1–10, 2056305117707192.

Leaver, T., & Highfield, T. (2018). Visualising the ends of identity: Pre-birth and post-death on Instagram. *Information, Communication & Society*, 21(1), 30–45.

Light, B., & Cassidy, E. (2014). Strategies for the suspension and prevention of connection: Rendering disconnection as socioeconomic lubricant with Facebook. *New Media & Society*, *16*(7), 1169–1184.

Lincoln, S. (2015). 'My Bedroom is Me': Young people, private space, consumption and the family home. In E. Casey & Y. Taylor (Eds.), *Intimacies, critical consumption and diverse economies*. London: Palgrave Macmillan.

Lincoln, S., & Robards, B. (2016). For the first generation to grow up on Facebook, online identities hold both promise and pitfall. *The Conversation*. https://theconversation.com/for-the-first-generation-to-grow-up-on-facebook-online-identities-hold-both-promise-and-pitfall-67876. Accessed April 24, 2019.

Marwick, A., & boyd, d. (2014). 'It's just drama': Teen perspectives on conflict and aggression in a networked era. *Journal of Youth Studies*, *17*(9), 1187–1204. http://doi.org/10.1080/13676261.2014.901493.

Perrin, A., & Anderson, M. (2019). Share of U.S. adults using social media, including Facebook, is mostly unchanged since 2018. *Pew Research*, retrieved 2/5/19 from https://www.pewresearch.org/fact-tank/2019/04/10/share-of-u-s-adults-using-social-media-including-facebook-is-mostly-unchanged-since-2018/

Phillips, S. (2007). A brief history of Facebook. *The Guardian*. https://www.theguardian.com/technology/2007/jul/25/media.newmedia. Accessed April 30, 2019.

Robards, B. (2014). Digital traces of the persona through ten years of Facebook. *M/C Journal*, *17*(3): http://www.journal.media-culture.org.au/index.php/mcjournal/article/view/818

Shamberg, S. (2012). Facebook's commercial: No, THIS is why Facebook is like a chair. *Huffington Post*. http://www.huffingtonpost.com/scott-shamberg/facebook-commercial_b_1942400.html. Accessed April 30, 2019.

Yellow. (2018). Yellow social media report. https://www.yellow.com.au/social-media-report/. Accessed August 27, 2019.

Zhang, D., & Livingstone, S. (2019). Inequalities in how parents support their children's development with digital technologies. Parenting for a Digital Future: Survey Report 4. Department of Media and Communications, LSE. http://www.lse.ac.uk/media-and-communications/assets/documents/research/preparing-for-a-digital-future/P4DF-Report-4.pdf. Accessed April 30, 2019.

CHAPTER EIGHT

Documenting Leisure: Partying, Travel, Music, and Hanging Out

'Drinking never stops', Mary (27) remarked as we were scrolling back through her Facebook Timeline. 'It's a common theme' she announced jokingly with a wry smile as we skimmed over another photo of her with her friends, a drink in hand. Looking back over the interview transcript with Mary—a finance worker in Tasmania, Australia—there were a lot of references to drinking: 'More drinking … an awful lot of drinking back then … more drinking … drunken night'. Mary acknowledged that a lot of her social activities revolved around or at least included the consumption of alcohol, and it made sense that these activities and events were the ones that came to be posted on Facebook. These were times spent with friends, relaxing, having fun, when people were likely to take photos and share them.

The documentation and 'performance' of leisure time is central to the spectacle of social media. In one reading, this might distort our view of the people around us, making it seem like the people we follow on social media are always out, having fun, drinking, travelling, but of course these are the times people are most likely to document and make visible in networked publics. There's an aspect of the presentation of Goffman's (1959) idealised self here (see Chapter Three), but there is also a process of recording the good times as set apart from the mundane and everyday. In this sense, recording and later reflecting on leisure time (sometimes privately, other times socially through tags and comment threads) becomes 'protective' against the banality of the everyday.

In this chapter, the fourth and final 'arena' of life we now turn to is leisure, encompassing travel, hobbies, sport, shopping, watching movies, playing video games, hanging out in schools, cafes, and movie theatres, and a range of cultural pursuits like attending music festivals. As with education and employment (Chapter Five), romantic lives (Chapter Six), and family (Chapter Seven), Facebook serves as a crucial site for organising, recording, and later reflecting on a wide range of leisure pursuits. Indeed, leisure is also an arena of life in which narratives of growing up are forged, where boundaries independent of school and family are tested, where identities are exercised and experimented with, and where friendships can be made.

We divide this chapter into three parts, focusing on just three aspects of leisure that were most common in our scroll back interviews: first, we continue with the theme of alcohol consumption, considering how the performance and documentation of drunken sociality intertwines with what Brown and Gregg (2012) described as 'pedagogies of regret'; second, we examine the mediation of experiences of travel on Facebook, where independent travel is framed both as a key rite of passage for many young people, and also a site for the creation of new networks of friends; and third, we turn to the role of Facebook in mediating experiences of music and music festivals. Throughout this chapter, our goal is to highlight the ways in which Facebook has become an archive of down-time, relaxation, leisure, and everyday interactions that constitute friendship.

Drinking Cultures

In many societies and cultures, 'chemical cultures'—and especially the consumption of alcohol—are deeply embedded into national identities, and rendered an important rite of passage for many young people (Alley et al. 2016; Measham & Brain 2005; Szmigin et al. 2008; White, Wyn & Robards 2017: 355). In Australia and in the UK, turning 18 and being able to buy alcohol, and drink in bars, pubs, at sporting events, and music festivals is both an introduction into adult spaces and practices, but also a test of responsibility and control. At the same time, young people's participation in these drinking cultures has also been the subject of various health campaigns and moral panics about underage drinking, youthful excess, and 'unruly behaviour' (Atkinson 2018; Jayne et al. 2008; White et al. 2017: 355). Thus, young people are often caught in a double bind, where drinking is both expected of them socially and culturally (and often through peer and even family expectations as well as social media (Burgess, Miller & Moore 2018)) but also heavily moderated, where they may receive health, educational, and police messaging about the harms and risks of alcohol consumption (McCreanor et al. 2012). The messaging on the risks of alcohol consumption are also often highly gendered (Atkinson & Sumnall 2019), where young women are often framed as both the victims of and responsible for sexual harassment in chemical cultures (Brown & Gregg 2012: 357; Hutton 2006).

There is a growing body of literature that considers the ways in which drinking cultures are presented by young people across different social media platforms, and the significance of displaying drinking-related activities on social media in networked publics. As Goodwin et al. (2014) note, 'while such [heavy] drinking cultures have traditionally been locally bounded, they are now increasingly mediated through online social networking practices' with the sharing of drinking stories now commonplace on social network sites (1). While the practice of drinking itself remains primarily locally bound (in our research, participants would talk about drinking in bars, clubs, at home, at friends' houses, on the beach), at least in the early teenage years it becomes globally shared through social network sites meaning that young people need to negotiate 'forms of social connection and precarious popularity online in an active effort to navigate the risks and opportunities associated with drinking as a site of pleasure, leisure and self-display' (1).

In their article that examines why young people engage so actively with alcohol-related content on Facebook, Goodwin et al. highlight the prevalence of alcohol-related content on social network sites in the existing literature, especially research situated within the realm of public health. For example, Buellens and Schepers (2013) found that positive references to drinking alcohol correlated to stronger peer ties demonstrating the high visibility of such references. In addition, to use Light and Cassidy's (2014) phrase, alcohol is used (literally and metaphorically) as 'social lubricant' in maintaining peer relationships and upping the popularity steaks online. Goodwin et al. (2014) engage their focus more on the question of why young people engage with alcohol-related content in such intense ways, exploring the qualitative description of young people's drinking stories online. Moreover, their analyses are framed within the context of neo-liberalism and precariarity whereby young people's narratives of sharing alcohol-related content highlights the risks and opportunities as well as the contradictions and deliberations of being young and the emergence of selfhood that determines or impacts upon those sharing practices.

Christine Griffin and colleagues have conducted in-depth, longitudinal research on the relationship between youth drinking cultures and media, that also considers the role of alcohol marketing online in perpetuating those cultures. In their report 'Would you 'like' a drink? Youth drinking cultures, social media alcohol marketing' (2013) they concluded that 'a strong pro-alcohol profile on Facebook was taken for granted and generally seen as a good thing' (1) among their participants (aged 18–25 years) with drinking framed as primarily about 'fun, pleasure, socialising and bonding' (1). Excerpts from their interviews reinforce the role of Facebook as a memory prompt in the event of getting so drunk one cannot remember what happened until a photo 'trigger[s] your memory'. In addition, looking back at images of drunken nights out sparks feelings of nostalgia and reminiscing about the good times with friends.

Given the centrality of alcohol consumption in experiences of growing up, it is no surprise that mediating experiences of drinking on Facebook was a common theme in our research. To return to Mary's observation from the beginning of this chapter, where she herself remarked that drinking was a recurrent theme in her own Facebook Timeline, it is also true that processes of visibilising alcohol consumption on social media are increasingly fraught. For example, in Chapter Five we discussed the ways in which some of our participants actively embarked on 'cleaning up' their profiles—erasing drunken photos, for instance—in order to prepare themselves for employment futures, and present themselves as ideal employees. Brown and Gregg (2012) have explained how documenting a night out on the town is complicated by what they call 'pedagogies of regret' as young people are taught to reflect critically on how images and stories involving alcohol and other drugs might compromise future 'professional identities'.

In their work, Brown and Gregg (2012) seek to speak back to discourses concerning alcohol consumption that centre regret in government health advertising. Instead, they set out to attend to the pleasures of drinking, especially as they are mediated through Facebook. Afterall, by eliding pleasure, health messaging on alcohol consumption—around the risks of binge drinking, underage drinking, and the relationship between drinking, violence, and harassment—ignores the key motivations around 'getting drunk'.

In building a case around the pleasures of drinking, Brown and Gregg point to an ethnography by Waitt, Jessop and Gorman-Murray (2011) involving working-class women in Wollongong, a regional centre on Australia's south-east coast. Waitt et al. found that for the young women in their study, a night out was about bonding with friends, dressing up, and being sexually assertive and confident. Pubs, they explained, were simultaneously 'dangerous and pleasurable, public and private, as well as offering possibilities where both subjectivities are both found and lost' (Waitt et al. 2011: 272). In this sense, there are broader parallels with social media and the various moral panics that have framed young people's internet use more generally. Waitt et al. further explain that for their participants, a sense of self in the context of going out and drinking was 'always co-constituted through the interplay within the social networks underpinning people, places and politics'

(Waitt et al. 2011: 272). This interplay, within the context of a 'night out', is a perfect example of a broader set of leisure practices we are concerned with here, that together constitute an arena of life in which growing up stories are forged. While Waitt et al. do not refer to social media or the role of the internet in this co-constituted interplay (between people, places, and politics), in the years since this research was undertaken the digital mediation of chemical cultures (or the 'night out') and the associated pleasures and risks have become unavoidable. Social media operate as intermediary 'places' where other actors join in—as spectators, as potential participants, as judges, as the excluded. At the same time, social media also become semi-durable asynchronous records of nights out.

Brown and Gregg (2012) point to the 'further pleasures' of intoxication through processes of 'witnessing on sites like Facebook'. They suggest that, especially for working-class women:

> 'Drinking and online social networking provides experimentation and temporary relief from seemingly fixed selves and relationships at a time when actual opportunities may be limited. Both experiences offer a chance to escape the confines of inherited, embodied identity, and that is their pleasure' (Brown & Gregg 2012: 365).

This pleasure they describe resonates with the accounts of some of our own participants, such as Mary (27) with whom we began this chapter. We would note, however, that there are important limitations on the extent to which social media now offer opportunities of 'escape'. In some ways, as we have explored in this book, the mediation of young lives on social media have also become anchors from which young people seek escape. Key examples we have covered are in the context of employment, relationships, and family, but certainly in each of these arenas the recording and sharing of intoxication produces uneven challenges. Brown and Gregg point out that 'it is assumed young people will therefore regret their leisured use of Facebook in the *future*, i.e. once they reach the age for the job market' (Brown & Gregg 2012: 361, italics original). 'Regret' here is clearly modulated by different social structures, such as gender, class, and race. For instance, women experience heightened pressure when it comes to managing 'reputational damage' (Dobson & Ringrose 2016), especially when it relates to their sexuality (i.e. slut shaming in sexting discourses). Similarly, as we explored in Chapter Five, a young doctor may feel more surveilled on Facebook—and expected to present a professional identity on social media—compared to another worker who might see their work as a 'job' rather than a 'career'.

Goodwin, Lyons, Griffin and McCreanor (2014) also argue that the mediation of drinking cultures on social media produces both challenges and opportunities for young people. On the one hand, these practices can be empowering forms of self-expression (as in Brown & Gregg's 2012 work), but can also come to represent examples of 'the negative health implications and ties to marketing and corporate capital (Goodwin et al. 2014: 63). These more negative readings can produce 'digital iterations' of long-standing moral panics centred on young people's leisure (White et al. 2017: 242). Goodwin et al. also point out that for young people navigating complex changes—to family forms, the decline of working class communities, and the role of consumption in identity-work—documenting, reflecting on, and re-living 'good stories' like the night out through digital media can be deeply significant. Producing digital traces of the night out (photos, status updates, check-ins) figures into broader processes of self-making, engaging in reflexive processes of ordering coherent identity projects. They can also be looked back upon, the process of which conjures up nostalgia, but also more visceral re-connections as we explored with Shaima and her role as a fan of a Korean singer in the previous chapter. Goodwin et al. (2014) contend that this kind of digitally mediated identity-work, that draws in chemical cultures as an element of that identity-work, helps young people to navigate and face broader structural changes.

As we scrolled back through Facebook with Argo (25), a participant living in Launceston, Australia, like Mary (27) he commented on how many of his posts centred on drinking: 'We did a lot of drinking back then'. He also explained how drinking and partying marked out other periods of transition and change in his life as we scrolled back through his Timeline with him:

Argo: We have 2013, so this would have been just after I sold my first business and a little bit before I started the second one. So I've probably hit a bit of a gap a little but, not doing a lot until the second business because that was halfway through the year.

Int.: It's interesting to see, too, how the fluctuation of posts changes.

Argo: It's while I was working a lot I suppose a lot less because I wasn't going out and doing as many things out at night, going to bars or hanging with friends. And I probably wouldn't do as many parties because you tend to be working more and stuff.

In other words, for Argo, the visiblising of leisure time—partying, going to bars, and spending time with friends—filled in gaps between more intense periods of work. As a young entrepreneur, Argo started and subsequently sold two small business in his early twenties while also living and working for periods of time overseas. While undoubtedly intense and busy and in his own words, 'significant' parts of his life, this kind of work was mostly invisible on Facebook. Instead, it was the lulls in the more visible partying—as described above—that marked out the 'work'. Argo explained that he spent three or four hours each day on Facebook, usually in ten to fifteen minute bursts spread out across the day. So it wasn't that he wasn't using Facebook consistently, but was posting and being tagged in less.

Erin (21) also pointed out, as we were scrolling back through her Facebook Timeline, that the photos she was tagged in tended to be centred on alcohol consumption, because social events where people would take photos were likely to involve drinking alcohol. Erin hinted at the tension here in terms of impression and reputation management that we discussed earlier:

> Erin: ... free drinks for a birthday. So a lot of the photos you take are when people are drinking to be honest.
> Int.: Yeah it's true.
> Erin: Which is the time that you probably don't want people to be taking photos.
> Int.: But that's when people are together I guess.
> Erin: Well yeah, it's true.

Erin's comment is somewhat flippant here, but returns us to Brown and Gregg's (2012) unpacking of the 'pedagogies of regret' produced in government health campaigns around young people's drinking practices. As we scrolled back through Erin's Facebook Timeline, she recounted more than a dozen stories centred on alcohol and getting drunk. She had worked in a bar and also did occasional promotional work for local bands, so there was a clear blurring between work and leisure when it came to drinking cultures for Erin. Prompted by the images in her Timeline, many of the stories she told where alcohol consumption was central were about friendship and family and experiences of bonding. Despite these positive stories, Erin still—even if somewhat flippantly—remarks that it is times like these 'that you probably don't want people to be taking photos'. Have the 'pedagogies of regret' described by Brown and Gregg (2012) taken hold here, even amidst happy stories of connection and friendship?

Beyond the government 'responsible drinking' campaigning critiqued by Brown and Gregg (2012), pedagogies of regret manifest in other ways for our participants too, often in very subtle forms and instigated by key transition in 'growing up narratives'. For example around employment and professionalism that we explored in detail in Chapter Five. Cate (22) who was a final year University student in the UK recounted a social media talk given at a Careers fair. The emphasis of the talk was around career progression and using social media to gain employment, but there was also some discussion about personal profiles and having them 'potential employer ready'. This extract from our interview with Cate provides an example of how pedagogies are produced in nuanced ways, and socialised:

> We had a careers fair a couple of weeks ago and they were—there was like a social media talk and they were saying how you can use it to help you. There's so much

around now that wasn't around and you can use that to kind of find people, get an internship, things like that which in interesting. And then also the flip side of it that they can use that to look into you and how companies do that and that's actually becoming the norm to search you to look at your things.

But they said there's an element of it that *they want to see that you're having a good time*. They want to see you're a well rounded person and you've got a Facebook account and everything like that. But obviously they kind of advise us more on like language; what you were saying rather than photos of you on a night out. Apparently that's *less bad*, not that bad as writing really controversial or rude things which makes sense. Because everyone goes out and wants to have a good time but I suppose it's more of what you're actually saying.

In this training scenario, while the careers advisor is not directly suggesting that Cate should cut out stories of her partying past altogether, the advisor is certainly instilling the idea that disclosures depicting nights out, partying, and drinking may need to be revisited. The advisor is suggesting that being able to 'see you're having a good time' is important, and moreover being able to see this on social media makes people more authentic, likable, 'well rounded', and seem sociable. In this respect, having a totally sterile profile where there appears to be no evidence of 'having a good time' might be considered almost as dubious as having one that is full of drunken nights out. The sterile profile is flagged as suspicious. This raises some difficult dilemmas for a young person who finds themselves at a crux in their life where they are moving towards employment, careers and professional life, as we discuss in Chapter Five. Considering these dilemmas within the framework of 'pedagogies of regret', what is the tipping point between having too much fun and not enough? How do young people 'measure' or 'assess' the extent to which they are having a good time over having *too much* of a good time? How do they decide which posts should remain on their Timeline as positive representations of their authentic, 'well rounded' self who is able to have a good time responsibly? Clearly such practices fall within the neo-liberal framework of self governance and self care; being responsible for one's own future (Rose 1999). Such responsibility is immense, especially given the context is so subjective and fragile, varying across time, and modulated by gender, class, and race.

Travel

Our second key theme under the broad life arena of leisure is travel. Narratives about travel featured heavily in almost all of our participant's accounts of scrolling back through Facebook. Like being out with friends, travelling and sightseeing were also prime times for taking photos that would be shared on social media. So too was time spent travelling also a time when new friends were made, and Facebook was often a convenient way of staying in touch with friends made while travelling, without the costs of phone calls or text messages, and the formality of letters or emails (Wang, Park & Fesenmaier 2012: 380). As Xiang and Gretzel (2010) have found, tourists use social media as a source of local and situated knowledge, so in using social media, users are producing important information for other travellers—through reviews, sharing tips, photos of locations, posting menus, commenting on prices, tracing popular routes, logging public transport data, and so on. In this way, social media use while travelling contributes to a broader tourism economy. Importantly for our project, the sharing of travel photos, friending people met while travelling, and geo-tagging specific locations and places also serves as a process of record-keeping for personal memory-work.

Studying practices of social media self-representation of volunteer humanitarian tourists, Schwarz and Richey (2019) point to the tensions in the ethics of picturing and posting images of humanitarian work. Is it self-serving for a white person to use a photo of them 'standing near racialized children in unnamed locations recognized as the "Third World"' (Mason in Schwarz & Richey 2019: 7) as their Tinder profile picture? Is it 'virtue signalling' (the conspicuous expression of moral values) or fetishising for a wealthy tourist to post photos of themselves teaching English to a class of Cambodian children on Instagram? Or are these important practices of self-representation in social media cultures? The answer to all of these questions is probably yes, in that these processes of self-representation can be read and decoded in very different ways.

Schwarz and Richey (2019) interviewed UK-based volunteers in Kenya, to ask them how they navigated the ethics of representing their own experiences of travel and volunteer humanitarian work. They explained that while their participants appeared to be '"in on the joke"—in that they displayed a keen awareness of the prevailing critiques levied at international volunteering—they seemed unsure how to proceed when reflecting on and representing these experiences to a public audience'. (Schwarz & Richey 2019: 13). One of their participants talked about only posting photos of 'fun things' (rather than feeding into stereotypes of impoverishment) and another chose photos that were 'the best ones, the most interesting ones and then ones that are politically correct' (Schwarz & Richey 2019: 14). These examples point to a much wider set of practices and conventions that shape what and how and to which platforms people make social media disclosures, not just in the context of humanitarian tourism or travel in general, but also broader practices of self-representation on social media that this book documents.

Much of the tension in the ethics of picturing and posting around 'volunteerism' or 'digilantism' is about capital, and various forms of capital if we follow Bourdieu's (1986[2011]) theorisation. Travel is an expensive leisure pursuit, especially when it involves airfares, accommodation, eating out, visas, and taking time away from work, and thus the sharing of travel experiences on social media is a performance of *economic* capital. Images of and check-ins at specific landmarks, adjusting to local customs, language, and conventions might also be read as performances of *cultural* capital. Making new friends while travelling, and friending them on Facebook or following them on Instagram, and then including images of them in travel photos, could further be read as a performance of *social* capital. Similarly, travelling with a close friend or with family signals a closeness, as travel can be a bonding experience. For our own participants, sharing experiences of travel on social media was significant in a range of ways, including as part of the performance of various forms of capital, but also in more nuanced ways, involving self-discovery, personal reflection, and the strengthening of familial ties.

Cate (22), whose story we will return to later in this chapter, explained that sharing images of travel on Facebook were important so that her parents could be involved in her trip, to see where she was going:

> My Dad got Facebook when I went away and he never was interested before. My Mum I think had it but he said it was really useful when I was away because you see I was posting photos and I was really doing it for them and also for me but not because like all my friends were going to see them and stuff. Like I was uploading a lot because I knew they'd sit down every night and have a look. So that was important. But yeah it was useful in keeping in contact, sharing photos, things like that.

There is a practical element to Cate sharing travel photos on Facebook, in keeping her parents in the loop and letting them know she was safe and having a good time. There is also something more nuanced here in terms of Facebook's role in mediating this significant rite of passage—travel—for Cate, as she imagined her parents 'sit[ting] down every night and hav[ing] a look'. While she was also aware of her friends seeing her photos, and the value of the images for her own reflection and memory-work, she explained that one of her key motivations was really 'doing it for them', her parents.

When it came to the cost of travel, Lena (24) pointed out a family trip from Launceston in Tasmania to Melbourne as we scrolled back through her Facebook Timeline:

> **Lena:** I went to Melbourne with my family—
> **Int.:** Oh cool. Do you travel a lot?
> **Lena:** Not lately unless mum and dad pay.

For many young people, the cost of travel is prohibitively expensive. In Australia, a highly geographically dispersed and otherwise isolated country, travel between major cities usually involves air travel. Leaving Tasmania, Australia's southern island state, where Lena lives, is only possible by flight or an eleven hour ferry ride. Partly because of this, for many young Australians, international travel is a privileged and often hard-fought rite of passage. Mark (22) explained that his trip to the US, UK, and Europe was a 'defining moment', partly because he paid for it himself, but also because it was a time for self-discovery and re-invention as he came out as trans:

> I came out—so the summer between 2011 and the beginning of 2012, so it was like November to February, I was overseas for the first time by myself. I did like a big round the world trip. I went to the States, the UK and then Europe. That was probably one of the most defining moments in my life in the sense of like it wasn't the same as like coming out on YouTube. That is obviously a defining moment but that was one of those things that I think I'm going to remember as the crucial moment in my life, I guess like a growth period type of thing like that, doing that all by myself—organising it, saving, working literally four jobs for 12 months to have the money for it. Then standing in New York City and being like "I could literally be whoever I wanted to be and no-one would look twice". It was kind of like the start of the process of figuring out who I really was.

Mark's story—first introduced in Chapter Six—is an impressive and remarkable one. He had a knack for coming through with many 'quotable quotes' in our interview, and there are clearly many salient points in this quote, but we want to dwell on two. First, to stay with our point from above, the cost of travel is clear. Mark points out that he worked multiple jobs to pay for the trip over a 12 month period, and this heightened the experience of achievement for him. Travel was a goal that he worked towards independently, and achieved independently. The second key point here is the real potential for travel to be transformational. The scene he describes—standing in New York City—conjures imagery from film of a young person, perhaps in Times Square, amidst the hustle and bustle of the big smoke on a journey of new discoveries and self-learning. Being away from friends, family, and familiarity can prompt a unique kind of self-reflection. This was all taking place during a time of personal change for Mark as he came out as trans.

As we scrolled back through Mark's Facebook timeline, he explained how he had restarted a fresh Facebook profile around the time of his transition in order to distance himself from a dysphoric past. It was images of time spent travelling, however, that Mark cherished, and he downloaded these from his old profile (which was under his birth name) and re-uploaded them to his new profile. The photos of travel—landmarks, friends met along the way—were 'salvaged' as critical traces of his experience of growing up. Their (re)inscription on his new Facebook profile became not only important traces of the past, but also performances of hard-fought capital and personal achievement.

As we scrolled through images of a trip Evelyn (26) made to Sydney, she also described how travel was important for developing a sense of independence but could also present challenges to her 'adulthood':

> Well, I had actually never been to Sydney before so it was significant for me in that respect, I'd never been and we were only there for a couple of days so we didn't get to do much and I had [daughter] with me. We actually stayed in this little hotel, it was so funny, the guy was crazy, as high as a kite the whole time. And I've always looked quite young for my age apparently and I was only 23 when we were there and he looks at me and he's like "are you here by yourself?" I'm like "are you kidding, I'm a grown up, damn it!".

Evelyn's story—as a single mother travelling with a young daughter—points to the ways in which travel can be structured. While it was a significant trip for her, with new experiences, she clearly took the hotel operator's question as a question about her independence. Her reaction, asserting her adulthood, reminds us of the liminal status of 'young people' (or perhaps younger appearing, in Evelyn's case) operating in ostensibly 'adult' environments. For both Mark and Evelyn, independent travel was a site of 'adulthood', or at least bound up in processes of marking out independence. Images of travel shared on Facebook might not have explicitly documented these specific moments or processes—the 'defining moment' for Mark 'figuring out who [he] really was', or defiantly asserting 'I'm a grown up, damn it!' to a hotelier for Evelyn—but they evoked them.

Cate (22) recounts her experiences of a 'round the world' trip during her gap year between finishing 6th form and going to university in the UK. Looking back over her Facebook Timeline during this period prompted rather stoic reflections from Cate, reflections that were bound up in narratives of growing up in the first instance, as well as narratives of regret. This was not regret in the sense that she felt that the trip had been a mistake but in the sense that, looking back, perhaps she had been too young and naive and lacking the necessary experience to take on such a trip. Her 'round the world' trip took her to India, Thailand, Cambodia, Vietnam, New Zealand, Australia and Hong Kong and while Cate is clear that she doesn't 'regret that at all. I can't regret that' there are clearly narratives of regret running through her assessment of what she could have done differently. These narratives of regret start with Cate's reflection that: 'I felt like we were really young like looking back, I think I was quite young to go away'. Cate was 19 years old at the time.

In her interview Cate was very clear about the fact that she had be presented with a lifetime opportunity to travel the world. She talked about how this had been a long term goal for her and her friend throughout school, and while she did not say this explicitly it was understood that her parents had paid for the trip, or at least a large chunk of it. Yet while Cate acknowledges this, and does repeatedly say what an amazing opportunity it had been, she also repeatedly used the word 'regret' in her retelling of that experience. While scrolling back photos of the trip document exotic locations and what appear to be enviable experiences, yet in her repeated use of the word 'regret' there seems effort on Cate's part to convince herself that she does not, should not feel this given the opportunities she had. She'd talked about some of the difficulties encountered while away, running out of money, spending too long in one place that she presented as clear signs of her perhaps being too young to take such a trip on, being too naive to navigate such a journey with just her friend. As Cate's story reveals, the expectation does not always match the experience:

> I didn't want to go straight to university and I don't regret that at all. I can't regret that. When I look back on that gap year and when I was away a lot went wrong, a lot happened to me. A lot of things I would probably change but at the same time there's no point regretting it because that's just the way it panned out.

Her statement that she 'doesn't regret, she can't regret' encapsulates the tensions she still feels about the experience. While she did not elaborate in her interview on 'what went wrong' on the trip, she is clear that the trip did not turn out the way she had expected. We learn that there had been a lack of planning and at times she had run out of money. The repetition of the word regret enables her to emphasise how grateful she was to be in a position where she could go on such a trip, but also how her lack of life experience had impacted on this.
As Cate says:

> I just think yeah I did it and I was young and there were a lot of mistakes and I just think if I went back again I would know how to do it differently, how to have a different outlook on everything. So yeah, there's no point regretting it. It was obviously amazing.

This trip represented a critical moment in Cate's life, a moment that represented the ultimate opportunity to gain independence as well as a one-off chance of a lifetime trip. At the time of our interview, Cate was beginning to think about the next phase of her life as she approached the end of her university studies. She notes earlier how careers advisors had already got her thinking about the state of her social media profiles and thinking about how her life has been represented on sites like Facebook thus far.

This trip represented a critical moment in Cate's life, a moment that represented the ultimate opportunity to gain independence as well as a one-off chance of a life time trip. She notes earlier that careers advisors had already got her reflecting upon her social media use and thinking about how her life has been represented on sites like Facebook thus far.

Here lies a potential tension for Cate who had a profile that captured her experiences of travelling with her friend as well as other holidays with her family indicating a 'worldliness' that would undoubtedly be appealing to an employer. Yet, there were clearly aspects of her round the world trip that she still felt regretful about, her philosophical insights representing this. As an archive that she may look back on as a memory store of her teenage years and her youth, Cate is potentially faced with some interesting dilemmas that compromise her 'authentic' self over the ideal version she should consider as she moves into her professional life. Arguably the photos of nights out with friends at university capture her truly enjoying life and being happy while images of travelling the world, while ideal markers of the 'well rounded', experienced person, have not necessarily captured the pure enjoyment of being young that Cate will soon move away from. As we learn more about the role social media plays in the hiring of young people as an addition to the tradition CV, this scenario alerts us to the personal tensions that may rise when faced with the prospect of curating the 'well rounded' self online over preserving the young and free, or in this case 'student' self. It also highlights the importance of context provided through the interview method and significance of the back story to the images and disclosures shared on the site that are not revealed by the disclosures alone.

Music

Music plays a significant role in the leisure narratives of young people growing up on Facebook. Going to a gig for the first time, or attending a music festival with friends was often identified as a critical moment in our interviews, with such events being framed in the context of independence and freedom as well as changing musical tastes and interests. In addition to text-based disclosures and geo-location check-ins, these events were also captured through video clips and photos which often made for a more nuanced representation of a particular music-related disclosure or story. What was evident in the findings of our project was that disclosure practices changed over time, particularly in relation to the quantity of disclosures with our participants posting less on the site as they got older (or, perhaps, as the site itself 'grew up' as we discussed in Chapter Two). In terms of the quality, more recent disclosures tended to be less personal, more generic and more discerning than posts made in their early teens. This shift was particularly reflected in disclosures about music, for example in the early years of Facebook use some participants would disclose personal thoughts and opinions on particular songs, bands, or artists while more recent music-related disclosures would be made in other ways such as by sharing an article or a YouTube video. In the context of growing up, young people's use of Facebook changed for a variety of reasons (for example, they no longer use the site as often, they prefer other platforms, and they have become more conscious about data sharing). However, drawing on Giddens' (1991) concept of the 'project of self' as enrolled earlier in the book (see Chapter Three), changes in use also served as markers for a more established identity; one that no longer required the level of interaction that applied in the teenage years when music tastes operated as a more direct 'marking out' of identity. Participation in music-related culture had either disappeared from their Timelines altogether, or their musical interests were served through sharing existing information such as articles or reviews.

Music-related narratives emerged in a variety of different ways on Facebook capturing the significance of music as an important leisure related activity for young people. For example, our participants spoke about going to a gig for the first time, attending music festivals with friends, engaging in practices of fandom, playing in bands, writing for the music press, sharing reviews, video clips, articles and so on.

Music has long been associated with youth culture, as a resource through which to articulate experiences of growing up. The Birmingham Centre for Contemporary Cultural Studies (CCCS), for example, recognised the crucial role of music in youth subcultures (Hall & Jefferson 1975), particularly in relation to 'style' (Hebdige 2012[1979]). Angela McRobbie and Jenny Garber noted in their work 'Girls and Subcultures' (2002[1975]) that music provided an important resource for teenage girls whose lives primarily revolved around the domestic sphere. Music enabled them to engage in 'bedroom culture' through listening to music and reading about their favourite pop idols in magazines alone or together with a small group of friends. Later work by Reed Larson (1995) stresses how the relationship between young people and music changes as they move into their teenage years. He argues that music starts to take on new meanings for young people as they begin to experience emotional and psychological changes, as well as changes in their relationships with family, friends and peers. Larson also argues that spaces such as bedrooms also begin to take on a new significance as the main 'private' space in which teenagers listen to music.

Musical tastes and interests can also be documented on bedroom walls, outwardly expressing fandom or being 'in the know' about latest artists (Lincoln 2012). Lincoln's work on 'bedroom culture' assesses the connections that young people make between their bedrooms and virtual online spaces using music as a way to engage in bedroom culture beyond the physical space, engaging in online fan communities or using practices associated with bedroom culture such as personalising an online space in line with musical tastes and interests (see also Hodkinson & Lincoln 2008; Lincoln & Robards 2014).

One of our research participants, Shaima, who we introduced in Chapter Four, engaged in what might be described as a form of bedroom culture when using her Facebook profile for fangirling moments with a K-pop band (K-pop is a genre of popular music originating in South Korea). Shaima's passion for the music made by this artist came to represent her identity on the site as she interacted with other fans, shared images, commented, liked, and made posts. As we described in Chapter Four, Shaima was a reluctant Facebook user who's use was very low despite her desire to be more prolific on the site. She described a short 'crazy' period in her life when she was a fan of a K-pop singer, who she had been able to meet when he visited her home country. During our interview, the 'buzz' associated with that time re-emerged as Shaima scrolled back through this period of time, marked out by posts on Facebook that re-ignited the joyful feelings she had at that time. Later, Shaima became a fan of K-drama and in her interview she recounted the excitement of sharing posts about favourite actors. However, as is quite typical in youth culture, this was another phase of a frenzied fandom that was at first exciting, but as Shaima notes 'as you get older, you are like embarrassed'. She goes on to say 'and now at this age, this stage, you are more keeping it to yourself. So you still like him, you still like this kind of scene but you don't have to expose it.'

The sphere of leisure was not always limited to these more fleeting and momentary fads and phases, and on a number of occasions we heard how leisure transcends other arenas of life such as work and employment. We heard, for example about the ways in which a Facebook profile can be used as a professional music profile (despite being set up as a personal—not business—page). Louis (20), for instance, used Facebook as a professional, promotional platform for his own music as well as for leisure related activities such as going to gigs and sharing his musical interests.

Louis (20) was a final year university student living in the UK. Music played an essential role in many aspects of his life including his studies, playing in a band, writing reviews for magazines and DJing for the university radio station. For Louis, Facebook was a key portal through which he discovered new music especially in his teenage years as well as an essential space in which he now nurtured his professional music career:

> I also started, it must have been in the first two years or so [of using Facebook], my tastes of music developed and I sort of used Facebook as a space to visit the different bands' Facebook pages and interact with what they were doing, and things like that, and then as time passed I started doing my own music and I used Facebook as a sort of commercial space as well. So I created a Facebook page for a number of bands I've been in, released music on there, posted music videos and things like that. So we also used it to get concerts, which is a, kind of odd way of doing it but promoters sort of contacted us via Facebook so, yeah.

> ... For me, playing music is such a central part of my life, I wanted to share it with as many people as I can. So on the first level I use it to sort of show my friends, oh this is what I'm doing, give it a listen and come to my shows, and stuff like that, but on the second level obviously, I use the Facebook page rather than the profile as a means of presenting myself in sort of a formal way essentially. So I want the page to look good. I want it to represent how seriously I want to take music as a profession, in a way.

Louis's articulate reflections above capture the essence of Facebook as a space that transcends the personal and professional aspects of music cultures, as well as the growing up narratives of a user who has joined the site in their early teens and now finds themselves on a trajectory into a more professional life as they near the end of their university studies.

In the early years of his use, Facebook gave Louis the opportunities to connect with his favourite artists, learn more about them, find out about their latest projects and—importantly—interact with what they were doing. Louis's interests would be shared among his Facebook friends, a number of which had similar interests, forging small Facebook communities that thrived on genuine mutual appreciation. As a user who had grown up on the site, and seeing the ways in which his favourite bands and artists used their professional pages, when Louis started to play his own music and perform in different bands, a Facebook presence as a musician seemed the most obvious thing to have. Louis emphasises the importance of the site for getting the music 'out there', using it as a promotional tool through which to get gigs and nurture a fan base. Significantly, he uses narratives of identity to explain his uses of Facebook over time, recognising his own transitions from music fan to 'serious' musician: from a teenage 'muso' to professional adult musician. The curation of a professional identity takes time, labour, and effort, affecting a narrative of 'how serious I take my music'. The process is an ongoing 'project of self' (Giddens 1991) and for Louis is clear that a social media presence needs to be maintained and curated as it paves the way for future success.

As we were scrolling back through her profile, music was a regular feature on Erin's (21) Facebook Timeline too. Introduced in Chapter Five and earlier in this chapter, much of Erin's life revolved around music as she worked in a bar doing promotional work for bands, spent a lot of time with musicians, and saw music as an important part of her identity. In one post, Erin recalls lamenting the decline of live music in her town in Australia:

> Yeah. Because it's obviously affected my friends' income. But also my friends that weren't musicians, they're not going out and stuff.

In this one segment, Erin points to the complex interrelationships between economic, social, and cultural worlds. As we scrolled back, she also pointed out photos of her at a music festival—the Big Day Out, where Erin and her friends travelled to Melbourne for the festival. She also pointed out other festivals, including Soundscape in Hobart and Breath of Life in Launceston. These were significant events for Erin, and marked out points in the year for her.

Like a night out on the town or travel, attending music festivals and seeing live music gigs are also important 'sites' in the transition towards adulthood. These spaces are often dominated by young people, but also function as liminal spaces for growing independence, engaging in various forms of controlled excess (with paramedics, security, and police nearby), and asserting forms of 'subcultural style' (Hodkinson 2002). Peterson and Bennett describe music festivals as 'large multiday events that periodically bring together scene devotees from far and wide in one place, where they can enjoy their kind of music and briefly live the lifestyle associated with it with little concern for the expectations of others' (2004: 9–10). In Australia, archetypal youth music festivals were events like the Big Day Out—mentioned by Erin—or more recently Splendour in the Grass and Falls Festival. In the UK, prime examples are Glastonbury and Reading Festival. Equivalents in the US would be Coachella, Lollapalooza, and South by South West. Each operates on different scales and 'scenes', but all operate as liminal spaces of youth culture and sites of 'growing up'. When coupled with the 'calculated hedonism' (Szmigin et al. 2008) of binge drinking, being with friends, and being away from the rhythms and pressures of everyday lives of study and work, music festivals can be significant moments of leisure. The planning, anticipation, recording, and later reflecting on of these events through Facebook is a prime example of the interplay between digital and physical spaces.

Conclusion

In this chapter we have mapped out three broad areas of the life arena of leisure, all of which overlap and intersect—participation in drinking cultures, travel, and music. There are of course many more aspects of leisure—such as simply hanging out with friends, playing sport, watching movies, and so on. We chose to focus on drinking, travel, and music as three inter-linking examples of leisure as they were the most prominent in our interviews.

Beginning with the 'night out', we linked participation in drinking cultures to discourses of both pleasure and regret, when it comes to reflection and documentation in enduring networked publics. Our participants talked about the centrality of drinking in their social lives, and thus why images of alcohol consumption featured so prominently in their social media histories (Mary, Erin), and how digital traces of 'nights out' contoured and shadowed things happening in their lives not named explicitly (Argo, Cate). Turning to travel, we examined the transformative potential of travel (Mark) and the ways in which travel is a marker in stories about transition towards adulthood (Evelyn). Crucially here, we reflected on how the sharing of travel photos and the use of social media while travelling mapped onto various forms of capital—social, cultural, and economic. Photos of travel posted to social media work to provide a connection to family back home (Cate), but also serve as a potent aid in personal reflection and memory-work (Mark). We ended with a consideration of the enduring centrality of music in the 'growing up story' as mediated on Facebook, from personal entrepreneurship (Lois) to work and music festivals (Erin). All three examples of leisure are contested and uneven, accessible to some young people but not others, while also often being bound up in moral panics about excess, control, and independence.

The lines between leisure and (paid) labour are blurry in the age of social media, as many of the examples from our research indicate. Gregg (2011) has pointed to the ways in which technology brings work into the domestic arena, distracting parents from their kids, extending office hours, and making employees seem always available to employers. Carah and Dobson (2016) have also pointed out the ways in which 'hot bodies' are harnessed in drawing people into nightclubs and drinking cultures, algorithmically amplified through social media. They **explain how** young promotional workers are 'entangled' in a web of both '*commercial* and *self*-branding' (p. 3, italics original, 2016) on social media as they go about their promotional work. In this chapter, Erin's example of how her work as a venue promoter mapped onto the ebb and flow of live music in her town, and also her entanglement in alcohol cultures, is an example of this.

In the next and final chapter, we bring the threads of the book together to consider what is absent in our social media scroll back interviews with our participants, especially around processes of disconnection, political discourses, and discussions of mental health. We also begin to look forward and outward at the challenges of networked publics, especially for young people, in an era of declining public trust in companies like Facebook.

References

Alley, K. A., Lovatt, M., Meier, A. B., & Holmes, J. (2016). Developing a social practice-based typology of British drinking culture in 2009–2011: Implications for alcohol policy analysis. *Addiction, 111*(9), 1568–1579.

Atkinson, A. M. (2018). The role of the media in shaping young people's drinking cultures, practices and related identity making: Studies of multiple media platforms, Liverpool John Moores University, Liverpool, UK.

Atkinson, A. M., & Sumnall, H. (2019) 'Isn't it mostly girls that do pre-drinks really?' Young men and women's accounts of pre-loading in the UK. *Drugs: Education, Prevention and Policy, 26*(1), 60–69.

Beullens, K., & Schepers, A. (2013). Display of alcohol use on Facebook: A content analysis. *Cyberpsychology, Behavior, and Social Networking, 16*(7), 497–503.

Bourdieu, P. (1986[2011]). The forms of capital. In M. Granovetter & R. Swedberg (Eds.), *The sociology of economic life* (3rd ed., chapter 5), London: Routledge.

Brown, R., & Gregg, M. (2012). The pedagogy of regret: Facebook, binge drinking and young women. *Continuum, 26*(3), 357–369.

Burgess, A., Miller, V., & Moore, S. (2018). Prestige, performance and social pressure in viral challenge memes: Neknomination, the Ice-Bucket challenge and SmearForSmear as imitative encounters. *Sociology, 52*(5), 1035–1051.

Carah, N., & Dobson, A. (2016). Algorithmic hotness: Young women's "promotion" and "reconnaissance" work via social media body images. *Social Media + Society, 2*(4), 2056305116672885.

Dobson, A. S., & Ringrose, J. (2016). Sext education: Pedagogies of sex, gender and shame in the schoolyards of tagged and exposed. *Sex Education, 16*(1), 8–21.

Giddens, A. (1991). *Modernity and self identity: Self and society in the late modern age.* Cambridge: Polity Press.

Goffman, E. (1959). *The presentation of self in everyday life.* London: Penguin.

Goodwin, I., Lyons, A., Griffin, C., & McCreanor, T. (2014). Ending up online: Interrogating mediated youth drinking cultures. In A. Bennett & B. Robards (Eds.), *Mediated youth cultures* (pp. 59–74). London: Palgrave Macmillan.

Gregg, M. (2011). *Work's intimacy.* New Jersey: John Wiley & Sons.

Griffin, C., Lyons, A., McCreanor, T., Goodwin, I., Hutton, F., Moewaka Barnes, H., & Vroman, K. (2013). Would you 'like' a drink? Youth drinking cultures, social media and alcohol marketing online. Institute for Policy Research, University of Bath.

Hall, S., & Jefferson, T. (Eds.). (1975). *Resistance through rituals: Youth subcultures in post war Britain.* London: Hutchinson and Co.

Hebdige, D. (2012). *Subculture: The meaning of style.* London: Routledge.

Hodkinson, P. (2002). *Goth. Identity, style and subculture.* Oxford: Berg Publishers.

Hodkinson, P., & Lincoln, S. (2008). Online journals as virtual bedrooms? *Young People, Identity and Personal Space, 16*(1), 27–46.

Hutton, F. (2006). *Risky pleasures? Club cultures and feminine identities*. Aldershot: Ashgate Publishers Limited.

Jayne, M., Valentine, G., & Holloway, S. L. (2008). Fluid boundaries—British binge drinking and European civility: Alcohol and the production and consumption of public space. *Space and Polity 12*(1), 81–100.

Larson, R. (1995). Secrets in the bedroom: Adolescents' private use of media. *Journal of Youth and Adolescence, 24*(5), 535–550.

Light, B., & Cassidy, E. (2014). Strategies for the suspension and prevention of connection: Rendering disconnection as socio-economic lubricant with Facebook. *New Media & Society, 16*(7), 1169–1184.

Lincoln, S. (2012). *Youth culture and private space*. Basingstoke: Palgrave Macmillan.

Lincoln, S., & Robards, B. (2014). Being strategic and taking control: Bedrooms, social network sites and the narratives of growing up. *New Media & Society 18*(6), 927–943.

Measham, F., & Brain, K. (2005). 'Binge' drinking, British alcohol policy and the new culture of intoxication. *Crime, Media, Culture, 1*(3), 262–283.

McCreanor, T., Lyons, A., Griffin, C., Goodwin, I., Barnes, H. M., & Hutton, F. (2012) Youth drinking cultures, social networking and alcohol marketing: Implications for public health. *Critical Public Health, 23*(1), 110–120.

McRobbie, A., & Garber, J. (2002). Girls and subcultures: An exploration. In S. Hall & T. Jefferson (Eds.), *Resistance through rituals* (pp. 209–222). Routledge.

Peterson, R. A., & Bennett, A. (2004). Introducing music scenes. In A. Bennett & R. A. Peterson (Eds.), *Music Scenes: Local, Translocal, and Virtual* (pp. 1–16). Nashville: Vanderbilt University Press.

Rose, N. (1999). *Governing the soul: The shaping of the private self*. London: Free Associations Books.

Schwarz, K. C., & Richey, L. A. (2019). Humanitarian humor, digilantism, and the dilemmas of representing volunteer tourism on social media. *New Media & Society, 21*(9): 1928–1946.

Szmigin, I., Griffin, C., Mistral, W., Bengry-Howell, A., Weale, L., & Hackley, C. (2008). Re-framing 'binge drinking' as calculated hedonism: Empirical evidence from the UK. *International Journal of Drug Policy, 19*(5), 359–366.

Waitt, G., Jessop, L., & Gorman-Murray, A. (2011). 'The guys in there just expect to be laid': Embodied and gendered socio-spatial practices of a 'night out' in Wollongong, Australia. *Gender, Place and Culture, 18*(02), 255–275.

Wang, D., Park, S., & Fesenmaier, D. R. (2012). The role of smartphones in mediating the touristic experience. *Journal of Travel Research, 51*(4), 371–387.

White, R., Wyn, J., & Robards, B. (2017). *Youth and society* (3rd ed.). Melbourne: Oxford University Press.

Xiang, Z., & Gretzel, U. (2010). Role of social media in online travel information search. *Tourism Management, 31*(2), 179–188.

CHAPTER NINE

Disconnections, Absences, Conclusions

In this book we set out to provide an account of how young people mediate and reflect on their experiences of 'growing up' on Facebook, and also how Facebook itself—as a platform, and a set of socio-cultural practices—has 'grown up' and evolved over time. We have put 'growing up' in quotation marks because of course growing up is never really finished for people. Throughout this book we have drawn on Giddens' (1991) notion of the reflexive project of the self to capture a self always in motion, always learning, always 'in process' (although we acknowledge this idea has a much longer lineage). Alongside our cohort of 41 twenty-somethings, Facebook as a company has continued to evolve, acquiring new platforms (Instagram, WhatsApp, Oculus, and many others), enduring through controversies around privacy breaches, government sanctions, and declining public trust. For both young people using Facebook and Facebook itself (along with the broader social media landscape), the last decade and a half has seen significant change, and we hope this book will go some way to documenting that.

This final chapter is divided into three sections. First, fittingly we think for a conclusion chapter, we engage with the debates around disconnecting from Facebook. Here, we consider how disconnection and absences as strategic practices of managing content are undertaken by young people. In the context of 'growing up' what is *not* said on the site is just as, if not more important, than what is. Second, we turn to three substantive areas that the book has not attended to closely, but which are important and warrant some attention as areas for ongoing and future work—political engagement, mental health or 'wellbeing', and the issue of public trust in Facebook. In the preceding chapters we have mapped four arenas of life in which young people's experiences of growing up occur: education/employment, love/relationships, family, and leisure. In these chapters, discussions of political engagement and mental health/wellbeing were rarely explicit but existed often between the lines. So in this chapter, we seek to make some of that material explicit, and point to these as areas of ongoing work in understanding how young people 'grow up' in networked publics. Third and finally, we consider the issue of public trust in Facebook. If, as we have suggested in this book, social media platforms like Facebook have become personal archives of memory, what are the implications of declining public trust in these 'guardians' of personal histories? What other future challenges are on the horizon for Facebook?

Absences and Disconnections

Since its launch in 2004, Facebook has promoted an ethos of sharing and connecting with friends. From Facebook's motto to 'connect and share with people in your life' to its 'Friendaversary' feature that invited users to celebrate friendships alongside Facebook's thirteenth birthday, the site operates on a logic of sharing (van Dijck 2013; Kennedy 2016). However, there is also an important and multidimensional notion of 'absence' that plays out on Facebook: obvious gaps, disclosures that are erased, and significant events (deaths, breakups, failures) deemed inappropriate for the site. In Chapter Five (Education and Employment), we described the ways in which digital traces of lives on Facebook were edited, pruned, or erased in the context of employment futures—such as tidying up profiles to remove hedonistic, alcohol-fuelled nights out to present a better face for a future as a professional worker. In Chapter Six (Love and Relationships), we made use of Light and Cassidy's (2014) attention to 'disconnection' on social media as a kind of 'social lubricant', to talk about how past love and relationships are erased to diminish painful memories, but also to appease new partners. In Chapter Eight (Leisure), we drew on Brown and Gregg's (2012) work on 'pedagogies of regret' to think about how nights out and drinking cultures were inscribed and then revisited (and sometimes erased) on Facebook. In this way, we have attended to absences and disconnections throughout this book, but this process of and practice of disconnection deserves deeper analysis here.

Our scroll back method—putting participants in dialogue with their own Facebook Timelines—works to reveal what was happening in lives, through periods of transition, that never made it to Facebook, or that would never have been appropriate for Facebook: experiences of depression, loss, even periods of intense work. Consider, for instance, Mary's (27) story—detailed in Chapter Seven (Family)—where unrelated images reminded her of a difficult time in her life where she had separated from a partner and was staying temporarily with her father. The images we scrolled back through were not sad images per se, but they evoked a specific time in Mary's life that she recounted for us, prompted by Facebook but also explicitly absent from it.

For Light (2014), *dis*-connection on social network sites is not solely about 'non-use'; it is underpinned, practiced and understood through the lens of connection. Our own research has revealed that alongside their emerging social media literacies mapped in this book, our young participants engage in a complex set of practices around 'absences' on Facebook: erasing, hiding, de-friending, blocking, muting, and filtering out. All of these practices are disconnective, but they are also about facilitating connection in other ways. These disconnective practices also afford processes of highlighting, revealing, curating friends, teaching the algorithm about what you do want to see, and filtering *in* people you want to connect with. Similarly, absence is not as straightforward as 'not being present' and that 'not being present' on the site can be performed, managed, and mediated in a number of ways, such as not posting, but actively scrolling; or muting someone from a newsfeed, but intermittently manually visiting their profile.

Light argues that 'scholars in the area ... have been clear to articulate that while social network sites, and the networked publics they are commonly associated with, might encourage a particular line of appropriation (boyd 2008), or attempt to set the tone for use (Papacharissi 2009), users may not experience them as the designer envisioned' (1170). This kind of 'off-label' use—using a social media platform in a way that wasn't intended, or imagined (Albury & Byron 2016)—was common in many of our interviews. Claudia (20), for instance, described how she did not use the main algorithmically generated Facebook newsfeed, nor did she use the app on her smartphone. Instead, when she accessed Facebook, she did so through a web browsing app on her phone, bookmarked to take her to her own profile first. From there, she manually searched for friends she wanted to see. She explained her avoidance of the central newsfeed in these terms:

> a lot of things on there [the newsfeed] are just ridiculous ... sometimes like people are complaining that their boyfriend broke up with them; all these things I don't want to see—and if I want to actually see how my friends are going, I go to their profiles.

This bypassing of the algorithmically generated newsfeed gave Claudia control, and created a sense of 'visiting' specific friends directly rather than incidentally seeing their posts surface occasionally in the newsfeed. Certainly this can be understood as an off-label practice, but it also has disconnective properties—disconnecting from the newsfeed, and the smartphone app itself, but still connecting in deliberate and—for Claudia—productive ways to friends through Facebook.

Disconnection also manifested in more direct and explicit ways in our research. Ali's (23) experiences led him to 'de-friend' his ex-girlfriend and to promise that he would not use Facebook to communicate with a romantic partner again. Unlike becoming friends with someone on the site, the act of 'de-friending' does not appear as an event on the Facebook Timeline. Undoubtedly this is a deliberate design feature that furthers Facebook's 'mission' to connect with people, not to promote friends falling out. However, 'de-friending' is complex and political, subject to what Karppi (2011) describes as 'shades of disconnection' that is, the fading out of connective practices. We refer to this in Chapter Six (Love & Relationships; also see Robards & Lincoln 2016) when processes of de-friending are done in very subtle ways to avoid drama or confrontation. For our participants, 'fading out' a relationship using the functions of the site (i.e. being able to be 'in a relationship' but not necessarily tagged to another person) also becomes an important disconnective practice as we saw with interim statuses before being 'officially single' on the site (for example, see Tina in Chapter Six (Love & Relationships)). Light's (2014) attention to the practices of disconnection shifts paradigms in how we think about social network site use, and argues that such practices can be understood as 'a social lubricant' because it ensures that social relationships off Facebook can still potentially be maintained. We saw this too with Mary's (27) de-friending of her father in Chapter Seven (Family) to avoid the 'emotional stuff' he would post that would 'ruin [her] whole day'. By disconnecting on Facebook, she explained how she was actually protecting their relationship.

Such practices around disconnection and absence can differ depending on which audience they are performed for and the ethical responsibilities the user feels they have for that audience. In this respect, we consider the 'backstage' work (Goffman 1959) as part of the decision-making that helps to determine what will and won't be disclosed on the site. An event such as the death of a grandparent might be a key critical moment in the life narrative of a young person, but posting about this on Facebook may be deemed inappropriate, perhaps because it disrupts the presentation of an idealised self, or because it might be read as 'attention seeking', or otherwise does not fit the performative conventions of the space for that user. Similarly, some participants chose to keep posts about romantic relationships off the site because they consider this to be something deeply personal or their relationships might be at odds with religious and/or cultural expectations (see Chapter Six Love & Relationships).

In the following two sub-sections, we further explore practices and processes of disconnection, disuse, deactivation, and intentional absences. Fittingly, for our conclusion chapter, we want to dwell on some of these practices that cut across many of the themes in the previous chapters, but also point to explicit instances of pushing back against a dominant logic of sharing in networked publics. These practices also neatly resist discourses that frame young people as hapless dupes, sharing everything in the era of social media, re-casting the stereotype of the naive kid unconcerned with issues of privacy and data protection.

Abstinence, Restraint, and Deactivation

As part of the interview process, we sought to learn more about different types of Facebook use among our participants, including abstaining from having a Facebook profile—this could involve periods where they 'held out' from adopting Facebook when others started using the platform, or times when they would deactivate their accounts. However, this did not always mean non-use of the site. On a number of occasions participants spoke about 'abstainers' among their friends and peers: those who had never had a Facebook profile, or adopted Facebook later. When probed to tell us more about why they thought those people had made the decision to abstain, some insightful comments emerged that further contribute to the arguments we began to set out in Chapter Two on the declining (or perhaps non-existent) 'cool factor' of Facebook. Justification for not having a Facebook profile was sometimes presented as a kind of 'badge of honour' or an impressive act of restraint that made a person stand out from their peers as Nena (20) explains.

> She was very ... she was extremely intelligent, quite a ... she'd always be doing her work and she was really popular as well. She was head girl and all through college and all through high school she still didn't have an account because she didn't like pictures of herself being on and having tagged and stuff but also, I think it was just to stand out from the crowd maybe? She was one of those people who wanted to be different.

However, the extent to which this absence is absolute was challenged by Nena. While her rationale for the girl not having a Facebook profile is about her wanting to stand out from the crowd and be different, Nena undercuts this with her follow up comment below:

> Maybe it's just to do with ... I don't know. She just never ... yeah maybe just wanted to be different or not wanting to follow ... I know for a fact she went on her sister's account to look at everyone.

There may be some hints of envy here on Nena's part, of this girl's ability to refrain given the drama and tension that can play out through the site (Marwick & boyd 2014). However, Nena's comments point to a disruption of the girl's 'front stage' performance of abstinence when she explains that 'I know for a fact' that she uses her sister's account to 'look at everyone'. This leads us to think that privately, this girl is unable to resist the temptation of using the site to look at others. However, an alternative reading suggests that the girl had made some sensible decisions and had given due consideration to the fundamental uses of the site that would potentially invade, undermine, or challenge her privacy or focus which as a 'extremely intelligent', seemingly hard-working, and 'really popular' girl, may already be tested. Nena's explanation also suggests that 'looking in' through someone else's profile is something negative, like a form of spying done in secret or a form of cheating when the girl had been so vocal about not having a profile but again this 'looking in' may be openly done with the sister's approval.

As she reflects back, another participant—Cate (20)—offers a more sympathetic rationale for a similar situation encountered at her own school:

> I remember there was one girl who I was friends with at school who never got it and she was very adamant that she wasn't going to get it. And at the time we all thought that was really silly of her. We wouldn't be horrible but we just couldn't really understand it. I remember we were trying to get her to get it and she was very like strong minded about it. She was just like no and now I look back and think she was so mature the fact that she could make that decision and actually … And I know she's got it now.

There are three key aspects to this interview extract. First, is the point that Cate remembers not understanding why a friend of hers at school might not want Facebook; it was ubiquitous and any downsides to participating seemed either negligible or nonexistent entirely. Second, is the later-realisation, and apparent respect of the friend's 'maturity' in not adopting Facebook. This ties in to our earlier discussions of narratives of regret around social media use, related to employment futures (Chapter Five) or the visibilisation of drinking cultures (Chapter Eight), for instance. That Cate reflected back on her friend's avoidance of Facebook with respect is significant, because it points to the development of discourses of ambivalence, declining trust, and growing notions of unease and discomfort with Facebook. This shift is neatly summed up in the movement from not being able to understand why a friend would not want to have Facebook, to respecting them for resisting it. This is tempered in the twist in the third act of the quote, however, when Cate undermines her largely flattering comments by revealing that the girl who abstained at school did at some point get a Facebook account, presenting it in such a way that feels it like a weakness, as if Cate's friend had finally succumbed to a movement that Cate now perhaps at least partly regrets.

The technique of using Facebook use or non-use as a marker of status continues in the context of the 'Facebook vacation', that is, taking short or medium term breaks away from the platform. For our participants, these breaks often coincided with key transitions such as studying for exams but could also be taken for other reasons such as relationship problems or personal traumas or changes. Robert (25), for instance, talked about temporarily deactivating his account to study for exams.

> Int.: How did that go?
> Robert: I managed to stay off it for a good several weeks. A friend of mine had the password to unlock it ... I think in terms of study, I'll know I need to do it and I'll do it.

Robert not only deactivated his account, but also had a friend be responsible for changing the password so he could not reactivate it himself. That Robert felt he needed this extra level of accountability to manage distraction around exams reveals how embedded and habitual Facebook use was for him, but there's also a level of intimacy and trust in the sharing of passwords with his friend here that serves a social function in itself.

Facebook was repeatedly discussed as a source of distraction, with full withdrawal from the site often cited as the only way to disconnect from the dramas of everyday life. This was framed as being a mature and responsible step; a sentiment that represents the internalisation of discourses that situate Facebook and social media more generally as a vacuous distraction, where the individual is responsible for managing that distraction. However, there was also a clear sense that this deactivation would be temporary and that once exams are over (for Robert, for instance) or a particular drama has 'died down', then the profile is reactivated. Ali (23) experienced a combination of events which provoked him to deactivate and as we note in Chapter Six (Love & Relationships) he was involved in a difficult and challenging long term and long distance relationship. The drama of this relationship played out substantially through the site, so for him deactivating his profile during that time was to 'mute' that drama and disconnect him from the relationship. However, despite the stress around the relationship, Ali admits his Facebook abstinence was short-term and lasted less than two weeks:

> I think it was around my exams sort of and that sounds like it was a really responsible decision. I think it was to do with the girl I mentioned before, she was in Australia and we basically broke up for our last time and it was just an added stress that I didn't need. So I think there came a point where I was just like I deactivated it. And I think it only lasted a week or two. You know maximum two weeks before I reactivated it again.

Deactivating for a short period was also a technique used as a way of letting dramas play out and pass by. As Essa (20) explains below, having Facebook is such an essential part of everyday life and so much of life plays out on the site that not logging in enables you to avoid real drama:

> Int.: Why did you decide to reactivate? Was there not a point where you thought actually I could live without it?
>
> Essa: No, I think as soon as the stress sort of subsided I was just like straight back on. I don't think there was actually much thought process in it. I think it became just a natural instinct; having Facebook is just what you do. So I don't think I really even thought about it that much. It was just you know I'll deactivate it now because it's a source of a problem and as soon as that problem disappeared just get back on.

Importantly, Essa's decision to temporarily disconnect from the site meant she was also disconnecting from—and absenting—stress from her life, such is the significance of the site as a platform on which problems are mobilised. Her pragmatic and unemotional approach to deactivating underlines a strong sense of agency where we see Essa deactivating as she 'opts to miss out' on drama but with all intentions of reactivating once that drama has passed because 'Facebook is what you do'.

"My aunt kind of lost it …": Absences and the Imagined Audience

This theme of 'Facebook is what you do' continues into practices of absence and absenting on the site with how Facebook was used as a way to keep 'peripheral friends'—with whom you may no longer share meaningful connections or talk to frequently—available, accessible, and visible on Facebook. As Vanessa (20) explained 'there are a lot of people that I know that because we've disconnected, I know they don't check my stuff and I don't check their stuff. They're just like invisible. A sleeping friend.' This notion of the 'sleeping friend'—sleeping only from the perspective of Vanessa—is worth dwelling on, as Facebook in this sense becomes a kind of storage system of contacts that Vanessa might want to reconnect with in the future. The 'sleeping friend' retains a possibility, an imagined potential for reconnection. We have discussed the role of Facebook in creating imagined ties in other contexts such as the breakup of a relationship (Chapter Six Love & Relationships). In this example, while a person may no longer be significant, Facebook operates as a 'holding space' that keeps some form of a tie, be it very distant and functional making that friend 'invisible' to use Vanessa's word, but still available. Other participants described similar forms of absenting as keeping old acquaintances 'on file' should there be a reason to reconnect, such as an old school friend or travelling companion. These friends become a by-product of the intended Facebook audience, part of a list of hundreds of weak ties.

Absenting is not only the practice of being on or off the site or a strategy used to maintain different levels of connection, absenting is practised with content too. In Chapter Seven (Family) we discussed the strategies used by young people to share information with different groups of Facebook friends with family being one of the more challenging groups to deal with. In this respect, what is not disclosed on the site can be as significant as what is disclosed, with nondisclosures leaving gaps that our participants interpreted for us as being critical moments and transitions. Take Essa (20) for example who grew up in Dubai before coming to the UK to study. When scrolling back through her Timeline, Essa was puzzled to find practically a whole year (2011) where no disclosures had been made. She tried different ways to find them, thinking she must have hidden the content, or deleted it although she had no memory of doing this. She then remembers:

> Do you know what? I think that in 2011 was the first time that I actually went out without a chaperone with permission from my mum.

This important marker of independence was represented on the site through non-disclosure. As she began to go out without a chaperone and with her friends she also took part in activities that she could not share on the site because of the repercussions with her family (and besides, she was out with her friends now so had less need to use Facebook to hang out with them). The significance of the absences on Facebook were further substantiated when Essa described how the privilege of going out without a chaperone was sometimes exploited and that she would sometimes lie to her parents about where she was going. For example, she would say she was going to a tuition when she was actually going to the mall to meet her friends:

> It was, it definitely was [risky]. Because if my mum sees that any how I would get into serious trouble because it would be either like I'm at someone's house or I'd gone for tuitions but instead I'm in a mall. So that would be super risky. I think I remember one time I put pillows under my blanket to pretend I was home when I went for a movie. Grandma came outside. I thought they wouldn't check my room. My Grandmother came in and called my mum. My mum's like where are you? And I'm just like ... so I got into trouble for that.

The thrill of risk-taking by young people is of course not new and Essa's example of the pillow in the bed to hide the fact that she had snuck out is an old trick. However, social media does add another layer to this risk, especially if disclosures about Essa's unpermitted activities are disclosed by another friend on the site. Visibility in this sense is not only controlled by Essa herself, but is subject to processes of recording and sharing undertaken by her friends.

Photographs of 'risky' activities were shared among Essa's group of friends using Facebook. While the disclosures were hidden from Essa's Timeline, the fact that they were uploaded in the first place opened up new risk possibilities as the photos may be 'leaked' or recontextualised outside of the intended audience through comments, tags, or shares on or off Facebook. However, like the risk of getting caught in the shopping mall when your parents think you are studying, this activity came with an added thrill as those 'risky' boundaries were pushed, in this case through capturing the events on camera, then putting them on social media. Absence in this scenario then plays out in a variety of carefully staged ways, managed through the discourse of new independence and 'growing up' as it is mediated on Facebook. Aspects of these key transitions and critical moments were being played out online through the discovery of absence, notably captured through Essa's realisation that practically a whole year of disclosures were absent from her Timeline.

Another dimension to Essa's absenting practices was clearly informed my her cultural background. As Muslims, Essa's family were what she described as typically 'reserved', particularly when it came to her social life and relationships, and this reservedness was also evident on Facebook. As Essa explained:

> When I'm home they are always like 'you can't put that in a post and pictures and everything'. And I think as well they're a bit reserved. My brother posted pictures of him and his girlfriend at the time. My aunt kind of lost it ... got really mad and made him take it down. So I think especially when we were in high school they were just a bit reserved about what we posted especially ... you're not supposed to. And even though we stayed in Dubai we still had family back in India so it was more like if you have a picture with a boy it's kind of like 'who is that?' In my culture it's a bit reserved.

The decision to leave things unsaid on Facebook is made within quite complicated contexts for Essa as she considers what is appropriate to say 'in front of' family on the site. She described off-site discussions that took place between family members, about keeping a 'clean' image on social media, and not being seen to do things that potentially challenge or harm the more traditional approaches of older family members and respecting one's ancestry. In short, for Essa, absence in this particular scenario spoke much louder than what was visible, and using her Facebook Timeline as a prompt enabled her to articulate the significance of what she had left unsaid on the site which beforehand did not seem such a significant part of her life story but in fact revealed a critical part of it.

Leaving practices of disconnection and absenting aside, we turn now in the final sections of this chapter and the book, to a two substantial areas we have not yet touched upon in detail, but that we feel deserve some mention here: political engagement, mental health and wellbeing, and public trust in Facebook.

Political Engagement

An important area of young people's lives that we have not touched on in this book is around political engagement. While we did not probe for things like participation in political parties, attending rallies, or even look at examples of civic participation in the form of meme sharing or changing a profile picture to support a cause (see, for instance, Bashky 2013; Robards & Buttigieg 2016), there were instances of everyday politics in action. For example, after the election of conservative Prime Minister Tony Abbott in Australia in 2013, Evelyn (26) posted an 'uplifting message for everyone' to Facebook, as she and her friends were largely disappointed with the outcome. She narrated the post in our scroll back interview (partly paraphrased and truncated here):

> To my Facebook friends in light of recent events I can completely understand your temptation to leave the country, but here is why that's not a good plan. Australia needs people like you to spread the love, show compassion and be open minded ... In spite of public policy, you can make a difference just by living what you believe. If you believe in equality then treat others as equals, regardless of race, religion or sexuality ...

Evelyn's post was a direct and hopeful response to Abbott's election platform of fear and division, especially his 'turn back the boats' agenda to stop the irregular maritime arrival of asylum seekers in Australia. Abbott would also later go on (unsuccessfully) to be a leading opponent of the same sex marriage movement in Australia, and Evelyn's post hinted at the multiple implications of his election in 2013.

In 12 focus groups with young people across the US, UK, and Australia, Vromen, Xenos and Loader (2015) found that Facebook played an important role in the organisational maintenance of political groups for young people, such as organising events and broadcasting information, and served as a vehicle for 'everyday political talk' (Vromen et al. 2015: 5). Certainly Evelyn's status update could be understood as a form of 'everyday political talk'. Some of Vromen et al.'s participants raised concerns about the 'quality of information shared or broadcast via social media and pointed to the limitations of online political debate and collective action' (Vromen et al. 2015: 16). Indeed, concerns about the flow and reliability of political news and discourse on social media continue to dominate today, from Trump's insertion of 'fake news' firmly into the vernacular, through to the revelations in the Cambridge Analytica scandal (Cadwalladr & Graham-Harrison 2018)—which we will explore further below—around how political messaging and manipulation on social media was employed in Trump's election and in the Brexit movement in the UK.

Beyond 'Party Politics', it is also clear that for many of our own participants, their very lives were political in an everyday sense. For our LGBTIQ+ participants, for instance, as discussed in earlier chapters, visibility on social media—as in any public or quasi-public space—was political. A queer couple holding hands, being intimate, or otherwise celebrating a relationship, carries serious risks that range from discouraging looks and verbal harassment through to physical assault, losing a job, or being excluded from a family, even in progressive Western democracies like Australia (Leonard et al. 2012) and the UK (Hudson-Sharp & Metcalf 2016). Similarly, trans or non-binary people's very existence in public space can be enough to generate aggression. These risks are magnified and further complicated on social media. For example, recall Robert's (25) strategy to never post images of or allude to relationships with boyfriends on Facebook, to avoid his conservative family in Hong Kong seeing them, or Mark's (22) girlfriend not being willing to be tagged in photos with him on Facebook, in case her family found out she was in a relationship with a trans man (See Chapter Six Love & Relationships). At the same time, Mark found being out as a trans man on YouTube to be empowering, supporting other young trans men in their journeys and by being visible, working to assure them they were not alone.

Mental Health and Wellbeing

Another area that we have not touched on explicitly in this book, but which is a topic of important research on experiences of growing up in the social media age, is mental health and wellbeing (for example see Barry et al. 2017; Frost & Rickwood 2017; Gunnell et al. 2018; Salmela-Aro et al. 2016). Many of the narratives that young people shared about themselves pointed towards mental health and wellbeing imperatives such as self help and self care. Take Tina (20) for example (Chapter Six Love & Relationships) who's technique of 'fading out' her relationship status gave her the time and space to come to terms with the end of a long term relationship. Alice (20) stumbled across an image related to a night of a 'traumatic event' that she still found hard to deal with. However, seeing an image from that night that was still on Facebook enabled her to reflect on how far she had come, and the extent to which she had been able to deal with it since. When talking about the end of a relationship, Alice stated: 'I think Facebook is … in relationships I think it really can be a big part of like letting go, like to unfriend or to block, like that's me, officially letting go because otherwise you're still in my life.' For Alice, the formality of this disconnection is liberating and empowering, offering a sense of finality in what have otherwise may have felt like a vague or ambiguous end to a relationship.

Earlier in this chapter, we discussed the deactivation practices of a number of our participants, for example Essa who 'opts out' of Facebook when dramas seem to be emerging, Ali who sees the deactivation of his profile as a way to 'deactivate' his relationship, and Robert who takes a Facebook vacation as he studies for exams. All of these examples can be understood as strategies undertaken to maintain 'good' mental health, focus, and to find balance with other priorities, because disconnection helps to manage distraction and drama. However, these strategies also evidence the extent to which Facebook can be a source of 'poor' mental health, as for these young people the dramas that play out on the site can become magnified and deeply intense.

In both popular discourse and in various academic literature, there are a range of growing concerns about the ways in which social media figure into unhealthy body image comparison (Fardouly 2015; Chua & Chang 2016), poor sleep quality (Woods & Scott 2016), and experiences of anxiety and depression (Primack et al. 2017). While these topics are beyond the scope of this book, they are important to flag here and to acknowledge that significant work is being undertaken in these areas. However, we would also flag our skepticism about the extent to which social media are solely to blame for these issues, amidst much broader structural challenges such as uncertain and precarious employment futures (Chesters & Cuervo 2019; Chesters et al. 2019), heightened standards around body image for young women and increasingly for young men (Hatton & Trautner 2011), existential anxiety related to climate change, and short-term policy-making from political leaders. Clearly there are a range of competing factors here, and social media must be understood as part of a wider socio-cultural assemblage when it comes to mental health and wellbeing.

As we reflect on the Facebook Timelines project, particularly our methodological approach of scrolling back with participants as co-analysts of their own longitudinal digital traces, it is evident that for at least some of our participants, the process was partly therapeutic. We often ended our interviews by asking the question: how did you find that? The sheer amount of data held in a Facebook Timeline makes scrolling back through an entire social media history an almost impossible task. At best, scrolling back would be something they might sporadically do as Phil said 'just more or less during procrastination sort of you have a wee scroll back.' In this respect, the scroll back method we employed enabled participants to go back into their own digital archives in a deliberate way, giving the process real life use for them outside of our research. Our participants responded positively to the scroll back with comments such as:

> I found that really, really useful. Because we are talking about [my] everyday life (Shaima, 29)

> I've never really like consciously gone back to 2008. So I'll definitely go back and probably delete some stuff. (Ali, 23)

> I've found posts that I forgot I even had. But I don't feel like I'd go back and change it because—I said I did but I don't think I will ... but I think what I care about is all these pictures and stuff. Like I feel like my Facebook isn't really representing who I am now. It represents like a 16 year old me and I've forgot that you know—it's been on my mind for a while [to scroll back] because I remembered that I'm adding people right now in my life and they're looking at who I used to be. (Essa, 20)

This quote from our interview with Essa particularly captures the past, present, and future significance of Facebook in Essa's life. Scrolling back has enabled her to revisit content she had forgotten about, which connects us to an argument for Facebook as a site of memory-work that we developed in Chapter Four (Scrolling Back). The interview gave her the opportunity to talk through the disclosures that constitute her Facebook Timeline, thus enabling her to rationalise its existence and be okay with it remaining there. As the quote above reveals, where she talks about changing her mind about going back and changing or deleting certain posts, this process also enabled Essa to reflect on what her profile says about her, and what version of her it projects to others and those she will add in the future. For Essa, scrolling back was about assessing her life from multiple perspectives, with Facebook firmly remaining in her future.

Revisiting a younger self can often be hard and certainly scrolling back to those early Facebook days provoked a range of responses for our participants as we discuss in Chapter Four (Scrolling Back) and throughout the book. Nena (20), for example, said: 'There's a lot of stuff on here which I wouldn't want other people [to see] like it's just embarrassing stuff. Just stuff that makes you go "ooh God I actually said that; I actually typed like that?"' Despite these awkward moments of encountering younger selves, the process did enable our participants to critically reflect on their experiences of being on social media over five, ten, fifteen years, and the development of their media literacies pinpointing the appropriateness of language, topics, images, and so on as markers of their emerging more 'adult' selves.

Our research has also highlighted how social media are used as platforms for *projecting* wellbeing: that life is good, relationships are solid, friendships are strong, work is going well. Sometimes this may actually be the case, other times not. As we have argued in Chapter Six (Love & Relationships) the platform is also used as a place to validate relationships, to make a relationship 'Facebook Official'. Wellbeing means different things at different times to different people. The biographical narratives of 'growing up' that we have captured through the Facebook Timelines project help us to understand the contextual and temporal aspects of what makes people happy, worried, sad, anxious, as well as how these expressions are shared in networked publics.

So what is the future for Facebook? If Facebook has become—as we have evidenced through this book—a record of personal histories, archives of people's lives, to what standards should we hold it as a platform and a corporation? Do we distinguish between the important social and cultural processes that take place on Facebook—in arenas such as education, employment, family, and intimate relationships marked out in this book—on the one hand, and the corporate governance of the platform, with associated issues around exploitation of data produced by individuals on the other?

The Future of Public Trust in the Personal Archive

Under capitalism, it would be naive to think that we could access and participate in a global social network like Facebook with an enormous operating cost, for free, but what price are we willing to pay? Do we trade institutional privacy for the ability to easily connect with grandparents on the other side of the world? Do we accept targeted advertisements based on our web searches and browsing habits in exchange for the ability to bring together friends, to organise a rally, to share photos of newborn babies? Do we surrender aspects of personal privacy to gain access to our own personal histories, inscribed in algorithmically generated videos that celebrate friendships and critical moments in our lives?

In many countries, like the US, the UK, and Australia, for the majority the answer is yes, but for many others the answer is no and the price is too high. There have been myriad scandals about user privacy breaches and how information provided to or via Facebook by users is used, but perhaps the most damaging and revelatory was the 2018 Cambridge Analytica scandal (Cadwalladr & Graham-Harrison 2018), which saw public trust in Facebook decline rapidly:

> Cambridge Analytica—a company owned by the hedge fund billionaire Robert Mercer, and headed at the time by Trump's key adviser Steve Bannon—used personal

information taken without authorisation in early 2014 to build a system that could profile individual US voters, in order to target them with personalised political advertisements.

Christopher Wylie, who worked with a Cambridge University academic to obtain the data, told the Observer: "We exploited Facebook to harvest millions of people's profiles. And built models to exploit what we knew about them and target their inner demons. That was the basis the entire company was built on" (Cadwalladr & Graham-Harrison 2018).

In the weeks following the scandal, there was a 66% drop in people who agreed with the statement 'Facebook is committed to protecting the privacy of my personal information'. The people who agreed with this statement dropped from 79% of respondents in 2017, to 27% after the scandal made headlines (Weisbaum 2018). Given Facebook's secrecy in how they report user participation in their platform, it is difficult to ascertain what impact this has had on use more generally. To return to the discussion in Chapter Two of this book, however, Facebook still appears to be very much central to the wider social media landscape, and the economic implications of the scandal remain unclear.

As Rigby (2019) reports, Facebook was fined five billion US dollars after the scandal, 'the largest approved by the FTC [US Federal Trade Commission] against a technology company, and the largest against any company for a privacy violation'. At the same time, as Rigby (2019) also points out, US$5bn is a 'mere fraction of Facebook's 2018 revenue of US$55.838bn, and the platform's share prices have actually increased in the wake of the FTC decision' (Rigby 2019). In this sense, we could argue that the penalties for such enormous breaches in public trust are largely inconsequential, and the will for greater regulation and oversight of social media companies seems absent.

We acknowledge that this line of argument represents a speculative opening out of the implications of the book, without providing any certainty or neat conclusions. We have endeavoured to centre the voices of our own participants who let us into their longitudinal social media histories, and effectively narrated them for us: reflecting, analysing, explaining. Through this process we came to understand the significance of these digital traces of lives, and it seems important that we end this book by drawing attention to the very complex challenges here around public trust in platforms (Facebook in particular), data privacy, and the future of how this kind of personal data is used. This takes us to a cross-roads, where we want to champion and highlight the complex, significant, and reflexive ways in which young people are using social media, at the same time as we must—as sociologists and media studies scholars—be critical of the ways social media platforms are using the data of their users.

The participants whose stories have given this book life and shape are amongst the first group of people to have grown up using Facebook and other social media platforms that have cropped up around it. In using social media—to post status updates, images, share links, friend people they meet (or want to meet), organise events, form group chats, like and react to posts made by their friends, and participate in comment threads—they have inscribed a longitudinal record of a version of their lives on the platforms they are using. In many ways, as we have discussed, these personal histories are of course only partial, incomplete, and modulated through evolving processes of impression management. In our social media scroll back interviews, however, these partial traces of life have often been enough to provide a scaffold for memory-work, reflection, and co-analysis that sketch out wider and richer life histories, where participants fill in the blanks and explain the subtext. This kind of research scenario would have been difficult for researchers of the past to imagine. Treating these personal histories with respect and care is important for us as researchers, but it is also critical that we exert pressure on platforms themselves to extend this kind of care too. Some might suggest the battle here is already long lost, but as scandals around user data and privacy that we have alluded to here indicate, many are still surprised to learn about the way their data—their lives—are being used. Why is this still the case when such stories abound? Is it because people think they don't affect them? Is it because they still trust social media? Is it because they feel that they can navigate these issues with confidence? We cannot tell you the answer to that with absolute certainty but we do hope that *Growing up on Facebook* will enable readers and researchers to seek the answer themselves.

References

Albury, K., & Byron, P. (2016). Safe on my phone? Same-sex attracted young people's negotiations of intimacy, visibility, and risk on digital hook-up apps. *Social Media+ Society*, *2*(4), 2056305116672887.

Barry, C. T., Sidoti, C. L., Briggs, S. M., Reiter, S. R., & Lindsey, R. A. (2017). Adolescent social media use and mental health from adolescent and parent perspectives. *Journal of Adolescence*, *61*, 1–11.

Bashky, E. (2013). Showing support for marriage equality on Facebook, *Facebook*, https://www.facebook.com/notes/facebook-data-science/showing-support-for-marriage-equality-on-facebook/10151430548593859/. Accessed July 11, 2019.

boyd, d. (2008). Taken out of context: American teen sociality in networked publics. PhD thesis. University of California, Berkeley.

Brown, R., & Gregg, M. (2012). The pedagogy of regret: Facebook, binge drinking and young women. *Continuum*, *26*(3), 357–369.

Cadwalladr, C., & Graham-Harrison, E. (2018) Revealed: 50 million Facebook profiles harvested for Cambridge Analytica in major data breach. https://www.theguardian.com/news/2018/mar/17/cambridge-analytica-facebook-influence-us-election. Accessed July 15, 2019.

Chesters, J., & Cuervo, H. (2019). Adjusting to new employment landscapes: Consequences of precarious employment for young Australians. *The Economic and Labour Relations Review*, *30*(2), 222–240.

Chesters, J., Smith, J., Cuervo, H., Laughland-Booÿ, J., Wyn, J., Skrbiš, Z., & Woodman, D. (2019). Young adulthood in uncertain times: The association between sense of personal control and employment, education, personal relationships and health. *Journal of Sociology*, *55*(2), 389–408.

Chua, T. H. H., & Chang, L. (2016). Follow me and like my beautiful selfies: Singapore teenage girls' engagement in self-presentation and peer comparison on social media. *Computers in Human Behavior*, *55*, 190–197.

Fardouly, J., Diedrichs, P. C., Vartanian, L. R., & Halliwell, E. (2015). Social comparisons on social media: The impact of Facebook on young women's body image concerns and mood. *Body Image*, *13*, 38–45.

Frost, R. L., & Rickwood, D. J. (2017). A systematic review of the mental health outcomes associated with Facebook use. *Journal of Adolescence*, *76*, 576–600.

Giddens, A. (1991). *Modernity and self identity: Self and society in the late modern age*. Cambridge: Polity Press.

Goffman, E. (1959). *The presentation of self in everyday life*. London: Penguin.

Gunnell, D., Kidger, J., & Elvidge, H. (2018). Adolescent mental health in crisis. *BMJ*. https://doi.org/10.1136/bmj.k2608. Accessed June 16, 2018.

Hatton, E., & Trautner, M. N. (2011). Equal opportunity objectification? The sexualization of men and women on the cover of rolling stone. *Sexuality & Culture*, *15*(3), 256–278.

Hudson-Sharp, N., & Metcalf, H. (2016). Inequality among lesbian, gay bisexual and transgender groups in the UK: A review of evidence. Report for the National Institute of Economic and Social Research, https://assets.publishing.service.gov.uk/government/uploads/system/uploads/attachment_data/file/539682/160719_REPORT_LGBT_evidence_review_NIESR_FINALPDF.pdf. Accessed July 18, 2019.

Karppi, T. (2011). Digital suicide and the biopolitics of leaving Facebook. *Transformations*, *20*, 14443775.

Kennedy, J. (2016). Conceptual boundaries of sharing. *Information, Communication & Society*, *19*(4), 461–474.

Leonard, W., Pitts., M., Mitchell, A., Lyons, A., & Smith, A. (2012). Private lives 2: The second national survey of the health and wellbeing of GLBT Australians. https://www.glhv.org.au/report/private-lives-2-report. Accessed July 18, 2019.

Light, B. (2014). *Disconnecting with social networking sites*. Basingstoke: Palgrave Macmillan.

Light, B., & Cassidy, E. (2014). Strategies for the suspension and prevention of connection: Rendering disconnection as socioeconomic lubricant with Facebook. *New Media & Society*, *16*(7), 1169–1184.

Marwick, A. E., & boyd, d. (2014). "It's just drama": Teen perspectives on conflict and aggression in a networked era. *Journal of Youth Studies, 17*(9), 1187–1204.

Papacharissi, Z. (2009). The virtual geographies of social networks: a comparative analysis of Facebook, LinkedIn and ASmallWorld. *New Media & Society, 11*(1–2), 199–220.

Primack, B. A., Shensa, A., Escobar-Viera, C. G., Barrett, E. L., Sidani, J. E., Colditz, J. B., & James, A. E. (2017). Use of multiple social media platforms and symptoms of depression and anxiety: A nationally-representative study among US young adults. *Computers in Human Behavior, 69*, 1–9.

Rigby, B. (2019). NEWSFacebook 'fined $5bn' over Cambridge Analytica privacy violations. https://mumbrella.com.au/facebook-reportedly-fined-us5bn-over-cambridge-analytica-privacy-violations-588831. Accessed July 15, 2019.

Robards, B., & Buttigieg, B. (2016). Case study: Marriage equality, Facebook profile pictures, and civic participation. In E. Gordon & P. Mihailidis (Eds.), *Civic media: Technology, design, practice* (pp. 131–136). Cambridge MA: MIT Press.

Salmela-Aro, K., Upadyaya, K., Hakkaraininen, K., Lonka, K., & Alho, K. (2016). The dark side of Internet use: Tow longitudinal studies of excessive Internet use, depressive symptoms, school burnout and engagement amongst finnish early and late adolescents. *Journal of Youth and Adolescence, 46*(2), 343–357.

van Dijck, J. (2013). "You have one identity": Performing the self on Facebook and LinkedIn. *Media, Culture & Society, 35*(2), 199–215. http://doi.org/10.1177/0163443712468605.

Vromen, A., Xenos, M. A., & Loader, B. (2015). Young people, social media and connective action: From organisational maintenance to everyday political talk. *Journal of Youth Studies, 18*(1), 80–100.

Weisbaum, H. (2018). Trust in Facebook has dropped by 66 percent since the Cambridge Analytica scandal. NBC News, https://www.nbcnews.com/business/consumer/trust-facebook-has-dropped-51-percent-cambridge-analytica-scandal-n867011. Accessed August 26, 2019.

Woods, H. C., & Scott, H. (2016). # Sleepyteens: Social media use in adolescence is associated with poor sleep quality, anxiety, depression and low self-esteem. *Journal of Adolescence, 51*, 41–49.

About the Authors

Brady Robards has a PhD in sociology from Griffith University, Australia. He is a Senior Lecturer in Sociology at Monash University. Brady's work is published in journals such as *New Media & Society*, *Qualitative Research*, *Sociology*, and the *Journal of Youth Studies*. Recent books include *Digital Intimate Publics & Social Media* and *Youth & Society*.

Siân Lincoln has a PhD in sociology from Manchester Metropolitan University, United Kingdom. She is an independent scholar. Her monograph *Youth Culture and Private Space* was published in 2012. She has also published widely in a range of journals and anthologies. She is co-editor of two book series: Cinema & Youth Cultures and Palgrave Studies in the History of Subcultures and Popular Music.

Index

A

absence(s) 73, 166, 170, 172, 176, 178
   absenting 176
   as content management 169
   challenges to 173
   practices of 171, 177
   See also disconnect(ion)
abstinence 10, 173
   abstainers 173
   short-term 175–176
   See also disconnect(ion)
acquisition(s) 14, 18
active use 68–71
   in- 68
activity log 68
addiction 32
adulthood 31, 69, 73, 79, 87, 87, 144, 148, 158, 164, 165
   See also identity/ies
agency 32, 44, 45, 83, 142, 176
alcohol 10, 86, 91, 92, 94, 129, 147–148, 165, 166, 170
   marketing 149
   positive references to 149
   visibility of 150
   See also drinking culture(s); leisure
algorithm(ically) 51, 86
   amalgamated posts 86
   cruelty 65
   decision-making 36
   generated 2, 65, 127, 171, 183
   prediction 22
   sorted 61, 143
   teaching the 171
ambiguity 17, 38, 73, 91, 110, 181
   See also context(s); disclosure(s)
analogue
   diary 67
   journal 67
   photo album(s) 141
   scrapbook(s) 4
announcement(s). *See* disclosure(s); post(s/ing)
anonymity 72, 113
   See also confidentiality, methodology

appropriation 171
archive/ing. *See* document(ing)
argument(s). *See* confront(ing/ation)
artefacts of self 41–43
audience(s) 18, 40, 78, 86, 137, 141, 144, 145, 155, 172, 178
   engaged 106
   (in)visible 116
   managing 82, 96, 121
   multiple 92, 96
   new 101, 135
   responsibility to 172
   segregation 90, 112
   See also Goffman, Erving
authentic(ity) 22, 35, 37, 46, 69, 154, 160
   See also self
autobiography 15

B

backstage 39
   role 96
   work 172
   See also Goffman, Erving
Bandaru, Krish 4
banter 16
belonging 30, 79
   systems of 30, 31
Bebo 21, 27, 52, 127, 130–131, 132
behaviour 84
   (un)acceptable 89
   aggression 102, 106, 180
   -al boundaries 92
   delinquency 102
   in/appropriate 88, 89, 135, 138, 148
   management 88
   normative 57
   individual responsibility for 91, 92, 97, 148
   secretive 113
behind the scenes 109, 143
binary opposition(s) 72
Birmingham Centre for Contemporary Cultural Studies 162

bisexual 114
   See also LGBTQ
Black, Mhairi 80
block(ing) 171, 181
blog(s) 67, 96
blurring
   of digital and physical 27–47
   of personal and professional 90, 91, 93, 94, 153
   of public and private 72, 105, 140, 150
   See also boundary/ies
body image 181
boundary/ies 24, 40, 69, 72, 106, 118, 119, 120, 140, 141
   absence of 140
   failure of 116
   fragile 95
   breaking of 81, 128, 136
   institutional 132
   management of 78, 86, 91, 93, 94, 96, 97, 111, 112, 114, 137
   (re-)inscription of 16, 116
   respecting 82, 142, 174
   testing 148, 178
boundary work 18, 114, 137
boyd, danah 3, 6, 8, 15–17, 28, 30, 39, 52, 72, 103, 105–106, 110, 125, 137, 143, 171, 174
bully(ing) 89

C

calculated
   amateurism 96
   hedonism 165
Cambridge Analytica 180, 183
Cannarella, John 13
capital 156
   corporate 152
   cultural 156, 165
   economic 156, 165
   performance(s) of 158
   social 21, 84, 156, 165
capitalism 183

career(s)
  See employment
caution 58, 66, 90, 94, 106, 112, 118, 134, 143, 161
  See also disclosure; post(ing)
celebrity/ies 80, 91, 103
  internet 29
  micro- 29, 96
Chan, Priscilla 126
  See also Zuckerberg, Mark
change 53
  See also transition(s)
changing orientations 69, 71
chat room 84
check-ins 161
  See also tagging
choice
  See agency
Christensen, George 80
class 32, 44, 150 - 151, 162
  See also identity/ies
collaboration
  tool for 52
come/ing out 114, 118, 129, 157
  See also LGBTQ
community 15, 19, 21, 45, 52, 56
  See also network(s/ed)
complaint 88, 171
  See also vent(ing)
computer-mediated communication (CMC) 84
conflict 106, 118, 129
  See also confront(ing/ation)
confidentiality 72, 81
confront(ing/ation) 1, 6, 54, 63, 65, 66, 68, 69, 90, 91, 106, 118, 135, 172
connect(-ion/ivity) 20, 21
  cross-platform 18
  connective link 94, 176
  levels of 177
  See also network(s/ed)
consent 58, 59, 142
  See also methodology
consequences 80–81, 86, 88, 177
  emotional 18, 101

fine(s) 80
social 18
  See also employment; family; relationship(s)
context(s) 54, 59, 62, 69, 78, 117, 132, 143, 154
  clash of 24
  cross-platform 18
  cultural 133
  economic 133
  multiple 83
  out of 7, 59, 137
  professional 81, 160
  recontextualise(d) 29, 88, 93, 177
  social 84, 133
  wider 15
context collapse 18, 19, 72, 125
control 94, 105, 139, 148, 166, 171, 178
  -led excess 164
  strategies of 143
  of self-presentation 36
cool 13–24, 30, 68, 69, 94, 127, 173
  hierarchies of 68
  un- 13–24, 173
cover photo 109
crisis of identity 32
  See also Hall, Stuart
cultural/es
  background 178
  chemical 151
  expectations 148, 172
  landscape 80
  marker(s) 101
  messages 17
  narrative(s) 103
  practice(s) 109
  pursuits 148
  world(s) 129
curation/ing 141
  by Facebook 85 (*see also under* algorithm(ically))
  by user 45, 61, 78, 96, 101, 144, 148, 164, 171
CV (curriculum vitae) 83, 84, 85, 160
curriculum vitae 83, 84, 85, 160

D

data
  excess of 70
  exploitation 183
  flow of 143
  harvesting 184
  presentation of 73
  research 59, 97
  sharing 161
  storage 36
  use 84
  See also privacy
Davies, Caitlin 80–81
Davies, Cassini 5
deactivation 43, 125, 173, 175, 181
  reactivation 175
  See also disconnect(ion)
decode/ing 110.
delete/ion
  by Facebook 36
  by user 42, 45, 62, 63, 65, 72, 108, 115, 117, 142
  pressure to 115, 116, 118
depersonalise(d) 113
digging 4
  See also scroll(ing)
digilantism 156
digital
  age 128
  communication 32
  expression 45
  inequalities 133
  inscriptions 120
  interaction(s) 39
  manifestation 9, 85
  media 29, 152
  social spaces 41, 51, 79
digital dualism(s) 28–29
digitally mediated 29, 84, 151, 152
  challenges 29
  connection(s) 28
  narratives 107
  opportunities 29

digital traces 18, 29, 42, 51, 51, 53, 56, 59, 62, 72, 77, 85, 86, 87, 115, 116, 120, 152, 165, 170, 184
  as co-constituted 58
  historical 63
  longitudinal 121, 181
  long term 132
  modify 95
disability 133
disable. *See* disconnect(ion)
discussion forum(s) 39
disclosure(s) 54, 56, 58, 59, 62, 72, 85, 86, 88, 91, 93, 107, 127, 135, 143, 182
  absence of 102, 118, 134, 144, 152
  and exclusion 38, 62, 68, 85 (*see also* self-editing)
  as exposure 110
  as temporal 106
  changing over time 104, 161
  erased 102, 118, 170, 177
  filtering 129, 137, 171
  hidden 177
  implied 102, 109
  management of 105, 143, 133, 182
  modes of 110
  narratives of 69
  non- 73, 107, 113, 125, 177
  of intimacy 119
  of personal information 105
  over- 70
  overt 102, 108, 117
  partial 73
  positive 120
  practices 68, 69, 107, 110, 125, 130, 131, 134, 145, 154, 155, 161
  public 109
  reducing 70, 71
  relationship 21, 102, 104, 107, 111, 113, 117
  revised 102, 118
  shadowed/ing 107, 109, 110, 113, 120
  text-based 161
  unease with 63
  (in)visible 152

disconnect(ion) 90, 116, 119, 144, 166, 169–179
   as empowering 181
   practices of 169, 170, 171, 172, 176
   -ive properties 172
   through Facebook 114, 119
discrimination 81, 90
disuse. *See* disconnect(ion)
distraction 175
   management 175, 181
document(ing) 9, 54, 143, 147–166
   good times 147
dramaturgical framework 30, 38–42, 116, 137
   limitations 39–41
   See also Goffman, Erving
drinking culture(s) 147, 148–154, 165, 166, 170, 174
   activities 149
   binge 150
   challenges of 151
   drinking stories 129
   excessive 147
   locally bound 149
   pleasures of 150, 165
   underage 148
drugs 91
   See also leisure

E

economy/ic
   implications 184
   landscape 79
   life 107
education 21, 52, 77, 102, 106, 129, 148
   higher 44, 56, 79
   secondary 77
   special educational needs (SENS) 133
   tertiary 77
emotion(s/al) 54, 62, 102, 172
   ambivalence 19, 120, 174
   amusement 138

anger 178
anxiety 62, 63, 65, 107, 181
awkward(ness) 40, 112, 115, 120, 132
changes 162
close(ness) 156
comfort 58
confidence 150
depression 171, 181
despair 103
distress 52
elation 107
embarrassment 36, 40, 54, 63, 68, 105, 113
empowerment 151
envy 174
excitement 163
fear(s) 90, 179
fondness 2
frustration 17, 118, 136
grief 29, 65
guilt 65
happiness 20, 102, 109, 120, 160
heartbreak 29
hope 179
humour 68, 106, 147
hurt 106
irritation 138
jealousy 116
joy 29, 66, 118, 162
loss 171
love 97, 101–121
-ly driven 127
nostalgia 66, 150
offended 143
panic 65
passion 102, 162
pleasure(s) 150, 165
regret 66, 151, 165, 175
sadness 171
satisfaction 107
shame/ing 54, 68, 150
stress 175
surveilled 24, 78, 151
tension 159, 160, 174

ties 118
trauma 130, 132, 180
un- 176
unwanted 52
upset 52, 142
well-rounded 154, 160
employment 21, 44, 45, 52, 63, 77, 84, 101, 102, 129, 148, 153, 157, 163, 165
    advancement 77
    advice 154, 159
    ambitions 91
    anxieties 78
    application(s) 77
    aspirations 56, 66
    creative 29, 83
    employers 82, 90
    employer responsibility 82, 92
    first job 77
    future(s) 73, 82, 86, 92, 150, 170, 174, 181
    history 84
    loss of 82
    opportunity 84
    precarity 79, 88, 181
    recruitment 78, 81, 82, 86, 90, 160
    trajectory 92
    seeking 78, 81, 83
    un- 79
    vetting 81
    working life 73, 87, 140
    workplaces 21, 78, 94
epidemiological model of social networks 13
    See also Canarella, John; Spechler, Joshua A
ephemeral(ity) 17/
erase. See delete/ion
ethnicity 133
events. See leisure
everyday
    activities 6
    banal 53, 67, 130, 136, 147
    embedded in 19, 20, 125, 126, 128, 132, 133, 141, 175
    experiences 6, 7, 42
    interactions 43, 71, 148
    life/lives 51, 55, 67, 72, 84, 95–96, 119, 165, 175–176, 182
    stories 103
    understandings 14

F

Facebook
    'about' section 103
    adoption of 19, 23, 56, 60, 88, 89, 125, 126, 145, 173
    advertising of 127–128
    advertising on 183
    app 171, 172
    as archive 53, 55, 61, 63, 65, 66, 70, 104, 132, 141, 148, 160, 182, 183
    as assemblage 118
    as bridge 104
    as communication tool 71, 142, 164
    as contact list 70, 71, 176
    as dead 14, 15, 16
    as freeing 127
    as normative 57
    as personal record 62, 155
    as prompt 67, 150
    as public 91
    as restrictive 127
    as resurfacing tool 127
    as source of problems 116, 176
    as temptation 174
    as travel log 113
    as trivial 29
    as validation 66
    comments on 109, 113, 147
    controversies 169
    conventions of 17
    corporate governance 183
    cost of 183
    cull(ing) 101
    development(s) of 14, 22, 61, 64, 68, 84, 126, 127, 169
    'doing' 135, 176
    domestication of 128
    Facemash 126

fines 184
flight from 13, 20, 126, 129
Free 116
functions of 19, 172
functionality 45, 126
future of 64, 151, 183
history of 18, 19, 21, 64, 126, 127, 170
introduction to 55
likes 61, 109
management of 127, 135, 143
marketing of 4, 19, 127
Messenger 22, 45, 54, 106, 129 (*see also* messaging)
News Feed(s) 86, 171
not being on 94–95, 104, 139, 173
participation narratives 68
philosophies of 90, 91, 126, 127, 128, 170
policy 136
popularity of 20, 21, 23
positive experience of 125
practices of 169
profile 103, 157
profile as text(s) 71
public page 90, 91
reporting by 184
revenue 184
routines 60
secrecy 184
sign-up 21, 132
stalk(ing) 112, 134, 139
status(es) 113, 116, 184
stories 42
ten years of 52
The Facebook 19
Timeline(s) 18, 19, 22, 51, 54, 64, 72, 85, 104, 114, 115, 127, 142, 147, 157, 158, 172
ubiquity 128, 174
use(s) of 14, 18, 20 - 23, 58, 68, 101, 126, 127, 137, 141, 163, 173
vacations 14, 175, 181 (*see also* disconnect(ion))
Wall(s) 21
Workplace 84, 85, 91

Facebook Official 101–121
  as contested 101, 104
  as confidence 117
  as performative 119
  as public 120
  as site of drama 101, 119
  as a test 109
  significance of 107, 183
  See also romantic relationship(s)
Facebook Timelines project 23, 47, 52, 54–56, 130, 181, 183
face-to-face 29, 94, 95, 106, 118, 140, 141
fad(s) 22, 163
fade out 115, 117, 119, 172, 180
  See also romantic relationship(s)
fake news 180
family 54, 59, 96, 102, 103, 121, 125–145
  affair 127, 131
  as filter 134–137
  as complex 125, 139
  beginning a 79
  bereavement 130, 170, 172
  biological 132
  challenges 133
  close(ness) 143
  composition 133, 152
  connection(s) 18, 104, 144
  (co-)construction 140, 141
  dispersed 142
  doing 127
  drama 129, 136, 137, 143, 145
  dynamics 55, 125, 135
  events 143
  expectations 148
  extended 142
  foster 132
  gossip 136
  guidance from 125, 131, 132
  history/ies 125, 141
  holiday(s) 130
  home 130
  identity 144
  influence 136, 139
  interference 144
  life 125–145

life on Facebook 130, 125–145
 management of 129
 narratives 140, 141
 negotiating 132, 135, 140, 141
 networks 127
 performance for 90
 performance of 128
 rebellion against 135
 significance of 130, 142
 support 145
 tensions 18, 125, 129, 132, 141, 145
 ties 130, 156
 traditions 134
 trauma 125, 130, 132
 See also parents; relationship(s)
fandom 22, 66, 67, 84, 152, 161, 162
fashion 38. *See also* leisure
fields of visibility 86
first generation 73, 140
follow(ing) 18, 29, 95, 96, 147, 156
 un- 114
foster care 132
free time, *See* leisure
friend(s/ing) 59, 61, 116, 130, 141
 connection with 104, 117
 de- 109, 114, 115, 119, 142, 171, 172, 181
 finding 127
 (in)visible 176
 peripheral 176
 practices 58, 93–94
 process 111
 requests 107
 sleeping 176
 strategies 111
 with researchers 56
 un- (*see under* friend(s/ing))
 university 144
 visiting 171
Friends Day 22
Friendster 21, 52
friendship 57, 103, 107
 management of 91
 networks 132

staying connected 155, 156
 work 93
Friendversary 19, 127, 170. *See also* prompts
front
 of house 16
 stage 39, 174
 See also Goffman, Erving
future(s) 24, 64, 79, 88
 challenges 10, 170
 research 10
 responsibility for 80
 See also employment
futurity 96, 97

G

Gallen, Paul 80
gap year 158–159
gay 114, 118
 See also LGBTQ
gender(ed) 37, 38, 44, 45, 70, 133, 149, 150–151, 158, 162
 display 43
 dynamics 118
 conduct 119
 labour 92
 (in)equality 29, 92, 151
 ownership 119
 responsibility 119
generation(al)
 cross- 129, 133, 145
 gap 142
 inter- 18, 79, 125, 127
 older 127, 178
 use 128
Generation Y 79
Giddens, Anthony 43, 44–47, 78, 82–86, 101, 103, 106, 107, 161, 169
GIFs 22, 103
glass bedroom 39, 40
Goffman, Erving 18, 30–43, 84, 90, 116, 137, 147, 172

Google 78, 79, 87.
graduation(s) 52
  between platforms 19, 21
  life-course 19
Greenhow, Sarah 140–141
Grindr 18, 28, 106
group(s)
  chat 28, 185
  closed 18, 45
  study 45, 71
growing up 21, 23, 27, 32, 52, 54, 68, 69, 70, 79, 102, 104, 106, 108, 137, 145, 158, 165, 169, 178, 180
  independence 130, 134, 144, 145, 148, 157–159, 161, 164, 166, 177, 178
  naivety 139, 158, 159
  narratives 30, 55, 60, 62, 73, 78, 90, 120, 134, 149, 153, 158, 163, 165, 183
  responsibilities 77, 88, 101, 175
  See also confront(ing/ation); relationship(s)

H

Hall, Stuart 31–32, 162
hanging-out 147, 177
  See also leisure
harassment 150, 180
  sexual 139
hashtags 43, 111
health 102
  campaigns 148–150, 152–153
  displays of 43
  See also mental health
hiding 114
history/ical
  figures 103
  perspective 18 (*see also* longitudinal)
  personal 51, 62, 78, 92, 183, 185
hobbies 52, 59, 117, 148, 165
  See also leisure
homophobia 91, 180
  See also discrimination

hyper
  -link(ed) 118
  -text 45

I

ICG 21
  See also precursor(s)
ideal(ised) self 35, 36, 37, 43, 147, 160, 172
  performance 36
  presentation 36
  revisions to 36
  -typical 106
identity/ies
  archived 116, 132
  as assembled 32
  as co-constructed 28, 125
  as co-performed 113
  as constructed 28, 43, 79
  as curated 96, 160
  as difference 31
  as fragmented 32
  as in-progress 43, 70, 101
  as messy 32
  as multifarious 46
  as private 111
  as projected 31
  as reflexive 43
  as sameness 31
  collective 43
  compromised 142
  costumes 37
  defining 31
  discourses of 82
  established 161
  exhibition(s) 41, 116
  experimentation with 148
  formation of 32, 140
  framework(s) 30
  late-modern 32
  management of 29, 79, 82, 144
  mediation/mediated 30
  modern 83

multiple 90
national 148
navigation of 31
performance 28, 30, 31, 36, 38, 40, 77–97, 121
personal 9
play 46, 129
postmodern 32
practices 30
presentation of 29
professional 9, 29, 63, 77–97, 151
projects 152
reconstitution 32
representation of 162
sense of 141
situated 30
spaces 54
tradition(s) 32
understanding 72
youth 31
See also self
identity devices 38
identity theft 32
identity-work 27, 44, 47, 92, 93, 152
online 30
reflexive 46
illness 129, 130
imagined
audience 18, 125, 176
commonalities 103
ties 176
impression management 29, 30, 41, 78, 81, 87, 89, 91, 92, 94, 97, 104–105, 112, 129, 135, 137, 153, 185
individual
experience 103
-ised 82
solutions 96
influencer(s) 95–96
information
journey(s) 32
packets 32
injury 129
Instagram 18, 29, 43, 46, 53, 68, 80, 83, 97, 106, 142, 155, 169

professional use 29
stories 18, 41, 42
integrity 35, 37, 90
See also authentic(ity)
intentionality 57, 62
internet use 150
intimacy 175
electronic 106
hierarchy 105
initiation to 105
layered 106
turn 105
See also relationship(s)

L

labour
division of 107
emotional 65–68, 144
online 96, 144
physical 65
See also employment
late-modern society 44, 45, 106
legitimate
See authentic(ity)
leisure 18, 21, 129, 134, 143, 145, 147–166
as contested 165
narratives 161
performance of 147, 148, 152
practice(s) 151
LGBTQ 17, 46, 56, 90, 180
activist/m 111
equal marriage 107, 179 (*see also* politic(s/al))
trans and non-binary 38, 56, 111, 157, 180
(in)visibility 112, 114
life
event(s) 61, 170 (*see also* growing up)
erasure of 115
narrative(s) 63, 102, 107, 108, 144, 172
progress 109, 159
likes
See Facebook

LinkedIn 82, 83
literacy
    media 133, 182
    social 70
    social media 69, 71, 104, 125, 137, 171
Live Journal 132
Livingstone, Sonia 133.
longitudinal
    narrative(s) 18, 53
    record 185
    text(s) 51
    use 22, 54, 127
Look Back Video 19, 22, 127
    See also nostalgia; prompts

M

mapping 60–61
Madinou, Mirca 18
    See also polymedia
Malaysia 66, 67, 90
Marwick, Alice E. 3, 8, 15, 16, 17, 28, 52, 72, 103, 106, 110, 119, 125, 137, 143, 174
mature/ing 21, 62, 68, 70, 101, 104, 105, 117, 130, 137, 174, 175
    See also growing up
McCollum, Andrew 2
meaning(ful) 20, 110, 114, 176
    as multi-layered 52
    -less 114
    making 28, 32, 62, 85, 162
mediated/ion 45, 53, 169
    by Facebook 96, 104, 106, 110, 114, 115, 116, 125, 130, 140–142, 145, 150, 156, 178
    by family 133
    by technology 32
    by social media 150
    communication 40
    practices 133
    technologies of 43
    See also digitally mediated
meme(s) 36, 103, 179
memorialising 46

memory/ies 42, 60, 66, 78, 118, 129, 150, 170
    absent memories 66, 177
memory-work 53, 67, 154, 156, 165, 182, 185
Mendelson, Andrew L 36
mental health 10, 166, 170, 180–183
messaging 18, 21
    See also well-being
methodology 51–73, 181
    chronology 61, 71
    co-analysis/ists 51, 59, 72, 85, 181, 185
    feminist 57
    interviews/ing 55, 57–64, 72, 107, 117, 140, 173
    longitudinal approach 69, 149
    participants 58, 68, 77, 85, 96, 106, 130, 154, 162
    qualitative 72, 117
    research ethics 57–60, 71–72
    research sample 55–56
    scroll-back 56–73, 117, 170, 182
    timeline narration 61
    timelining 72
Millennial(s) 79
    See also Generation Y
milestone(s) 85
    birthday(s) 130
    educational 77
    life 84, 140
Miller, Daniel 13, 18
    See also polymedia
MMOs (Massively Multiplayer Online Role Playing Games) 42
moment(s)
    defining 158
    fateful 60
    critical 60, 109, 120, 129, 130, 131, 157, 159, 160, 161, 172, 178, 183
    crucial 105, 157
monogamy 9, 102, 103, 108
    See also romantic relationship(s)
mono-media 18
moral panic 29, 79, 148, 150, 152, 166
Moskovitz, Dustin 2

motherhood 158
motivation(s) 21, 55, 85, 117
MSN 21, 54
  See also precursors
music 108, 129, 147, 161–165
  as a profession 108, 153, 163, 165
  festivals 10, 16, 36, 41, 73, 129, 148, 161, 164
  live 96, 148, 161
  tastes 161
  See also leisure
muting 171, 175
Myspace 19, 21–23, 27, 30, 52, 127, 132

N

name(s)
  changes 87, 94
  common 94
  real 22
  un-searchable 136
narrative(s)
  of regret 66, 67, 90, 158–159, 174
  of the private 141
neo-liberal(ism) 78, 80, 87, 88, 97, 149, 154
network(s/ed)
  existing 21
  new 148
  professional 29 (*see also* employment)
  public(s) 54, 72, 105, 119, 131, 132, 147, 149, 165, 166, 170, 171, 183
nights out 62, 63, 86, 129, 131, 151, 160, 165, 170
  See also leisure
nostalgia 22, 64, 127, 152
  See also emotion(s/al)

O

occupation(s)
  See employment
Oculus 169

off-label
  practice 172
  use 171
off-site 106, 117, 118, 177, 178
offline 28, 69
  communication 32
  relationships 142
  See also off-site
online 28, 69
  being 18
  harms 133
  mistakes 140
  safety 130, 133, 134
  See also risk(s)
online/offline distinction 28
  See also digital dualism(s)
On This Day / Memory 64, 65
  as profile maintenance 65
  See also prompts
ordering
  See curation/ing.
organising
  See leisure

P

paradigm shift 17
paradox(ical) 15
parent(s) 23, 37, 130, 137, 142, 156
  role of 133, 159
  supervision of 130
  use of Facebook 137, 172
  See also family
partying 112, 114, 129, 147, 152
  See also leisure
Papacharissi, Zizi 36
performance of connection 107
performance of the personal 70
performative/ity 107
  act 109
  context 16
  cues 39
pedagogies of regret 10, 148, 150, 153, 154, 170

perception(s)
  of/by others 30, 66, 86, 92, 93
  of self 30, 70, 86, 92, 108, 138
personal
  trajectory 130
  website(s) 44
Pew
  Internet Research 13, 14
  Research Centre 126
Pinch, Trevor 40–41
place(s) 8, 42, 111, 151
  intermediary 151
  trusted 89
plan(ning)
  See leisure
platform(s)
  multiple 18, 97
poke/ing 21
  See also Facebook
politic(s/al) 151, 172
  belief(s) 2, 80, 114
  discourses 166
  engagement 170, 179–180
  -ians 80
  limitations 179
  manipulation 180
  participation 79, 179
  Party 179, 180
  policy 46, 107, 179, 181
  policymakers 27
  sanctions 169
  talk 179
popular culture 103, 120
popularity
  decline in 13
  precarious 149
  See also Facebook
polymedia 18, 19, 68, 106
post(s/ing) 45, 59, 70, 87, 106
  access to 17, 119
  (in)appropriate 142, 170, 172, 178
  commenting 37
  cross- 18
  erased 118
  frequency 85, 153

images 104
practices 62, 66, 68, 70, 71, 96, 104, 105,
  113, 118, 138, 139, 141, 143, 153, 156
popularity of 65
re-circulation of 103
salvaging 157
shadow 113
unacceptable 80–81
See also disclosure(s)
power dynamics 118
predict(ion) 22
  See also algorithm(ically)
presence 41, 61, 114
  co- 28, 40, 41 59
  non- 171
  See also, Goffman, Erving
privacy 23, 59, 68, 70, 71, 72, 78, 79, 81,
  82, 89, 91, 112, 118, 131, 133, 144,
  174, 183
  breaches 169, 183
  management of 17, 70
  of data 14, 184, 185
  practices of 58, 136, 144
  settings 17, 62, 63, 70, 88, 94, 95, 105,
    111, 132, 135
  strategies 110
professional
  athletes 80
  life 113
  -ism 78
  sports people 96, 113
  standards 89
profile picture(s) 61, 108, 130, 131,
  138, 179
prompts 59, 105, 129.
protection 94, 118, 132, 145, 147
psychic reorganisation 44
  See also Giddens, Anthony
public
  culture 102
  physical 96
  See also network(s/ed)
public/private divide 39
public trust 89, 166, 169, 170, 174, 183–185
  breaches in 184

Q

queer(ness) 112, 117, 180
    See also LGBTQ; romantic relationship(s)

R

race 151
    racialized 155
    racism/t 91
    See also ethnicity; discrimination
reaction
    See confrontat(ing/ation)
record(ing)
    See document(ing)
Reddit 18
reflecting/ion 56, 65, 147, 150, 152, 156, 165, 180, 182, 185
    public 147
    social 147
reflexive project of the self 44-46, 54, 77, 82–86, 101, 103, 161, 169
    See also Giddens, Anthony
regions 37, 44
    standards in 37, 44
    See also Goffman, Erving
relatable value 103
relationship(s) 45, 84, 162
    contemporary 104, 119, 120
    friendship(s) 27, 145, 147
    history 105
    intimacy 42, 96, 105, 106
    late modern 107
    maintenance of 104, 178
    management of 95, 97
    marriage 79, 106
    messy 9, 107
    narrative(s) 104
    negotiating 24
    normative 102, 119, 120
    parental 69, 114, 138
    peer 27, 54, 69, 93, 111, 145, 149
    performance(s) 112, 117, 120
    pure 106
    semi-professional 71
    sibling(s) 55, 130, 131
    status 101, 102, 103, 107, 108, 110, 111, 112, 135
    validation of 97, 183
    See also family, romantic relationship(s)
relationship trace(s) 102, 108, 117
    absence of 112, 113, 114
    erasure of 113, 115
    practices 102, 112
    -work 120
relevance 135
religion 66, 90, 129, 135, 144, 172, 178
remembering 62, 140
    mis- 60
    See also memory/ies, prompts.
repercussion(s)
    See consequences
representation(s)
    circulation of 103
    of children 142
    of love 102
    of family 126
reputation 29, 96, 135, 151, 153, 178
respectability 87, 92, 178
restraint 90, 173
    See also disconnect(ion) caution
resumé
    See CV (curriculum vitae)
review(s)
    product 18
    service 18
risk(s) 29, 69, 70, 83, 87, 90, 132, 133, 149, 177–178, 180
    -taking 145, 177
    See also consequences
rite(s) of passage 53, 77, 79, 102, 120, 129, 148, 156, 157, 161, 164, 172
    See also growing up
romantic relationship(s) 97, 101–121, 129, 141, 148, 172
    as available 105

as linear 102
as central to identity 108
as complex 102, 109, 120
as extension of self 118
as part of identity 108
as private 102
as source of well-being 102
avoidance of 120
boyfriend 115, 144
breakup(s) 103, 111, 114, 115, 142, 171, 176
building 104
dating 102, 104
dating apps 18, 106
dating ritual(s) 104
decision-making 117
drama 101, 106, 107, 109, 120, 172, 175
early 102
ending 97, 101, 110, 111, 114, 116, 118, 119, 120, 181
erasure 114, 119
exes 103, 110, 115, 116, 117, 119, 141, 172
formalisation of 109, 120
girlfriend 108, 109
hook-up apps 18
(in)visibility 102, 103, 107, 111, 113, 114, 117, 120
long distance 113, 116, 175
low quality 102
management of 111
naming a 101, 117, 119, 120
narratives of 105, 118, 120
negotiating 118
new 101, 109, 118, 119, 170
on Facebook 103–107
performance of 107
phase out 118
pressure in 109
progression 101
projection of 110
real 111
revision 114
romance 102

sexual intimacy 102
shadow(ed) 104, 114, 117
suspension of 110
tension in 113, 120
validation of 109, 116

S

Saverin, Eduado 2
Schmidt, Eric 79
school
   See education
screenshot 88, 112
  -able 29
  -ted 37
  -ting 42
scroll(ing) back 51–73, 92, 115, 147, 152, 157
  automated 65
  therapeutic 181
  See also methodology
scroll(ing) 5, 171
scrutiny
  by others 86, 87
  of public figures 80–81
  professional 80, 81
Second Life 38
security 112, 132
  See also privacy
self
  adult 53, 182
  as ephemeral 42
  as an object 45
  as co-constituted 150
  as co-constructed 85
  as co-produced 37
  awareness 142
  branding 166
  -care 143, 154, 180 (*see also* well-being)
  -censorship 110
  -communication 82, 83
  construction of the 27, 44
  continuity 44

-discovery 156, 157
-editing 9, 38, 87, 101, 136
-esteem 102, 120
-expression 82, 152
fake 37
-governance 154
-help 180
-hood 149
-image 21
-learning 157
maintenance 135
-making 45
narrative(s) 38, 45, 63, 83, 143
 negotiation 44
performance of 39, 41
postmodern 46
presentation 27, 29, 30, 43, 54, 78, 84, 93, 113
professional 84
-projection 143
-promotion 82, 96, 108, 117, 163
reconstruction 44
-reflection 113, 157
-regulation 43
re-invention 14, 157
-representation 92, 154, 155, 182
restriction 66, 90
-selection 56
sense of 39, 44
visually displayed 43
-work 82
selfie(s) 96, 112
sexism 81, 102
sexting 29, 151
 See also risk(s)
sexuality 21, 45, 56, 150–151
 hetero- 108
 heteronormative 119
 See also LGBTQ; romantic relationship(s)
sharing 85, 97, 135, 163, 165
 by others 37, 178
 ethics of 155
 filters 134

granularity of 16
logic of 104, 170
not 118
practices 149, 155, 177
re-sharing 73
See also disclosure(s)
sign-equipment 37, 38
 clothing as 37
Skype 28
slut-shaming 29
 See also gender(ed); risk(s)
SMS messaging 28
Snapchat 18, 28, 42, 46, 53, 88, 97, 106
sport 113
 See also leisure
social
 actions 40–41
 activities 147
 actors 27, 150
 bonds/ing 104, 150, 153, 156
 change 69
 collisions 93
 connection 149
 constructs 43
 curiosity 127
 environment 46
 events 153
 exchanges 45
 expectations 148
 function 175
 interaction 32
 lives 21, 107, 135, 165, 178
 lubricant 119, 149, 170, 172
 marker(s) 101
 mobility 35
 order 103
 participation 45
 practices 30
 privacy 82
 structures 30, 43
socialising 131, 150
socialisation 36, 133
sociality 28, 30, 89
 drunken 148

social media
  access 55
  adoption of 126
  as co-constructed 54, 72, 88
  as escape 151
  as mandatory 45
  as normalised 132
  as paid work 78
  as professional tool 45, 164
  as site of knowledge 155
  as work 95, 96
  as work-adjacent 96
  at work 93
  challenges 151
  cultures 155
  ecology 18
  editing 45, 62, 63, 110, 170
  faux pas 80
  history/ies 19, 30, 165, 181, 184
  information quality 179
  joint profiles 131
  landscape 18, 21, 169, 184
  lives 55
  logistics of 84
  management of 71, 96, 127, 129, 134
  manager 96, 113
  movement between 106
  multi-layering of 54
  multiple profiles 89–93, 113, 136, 137
  non-use 171
  opportunity 151
  patterns 60
  practices 54, 136
  profiles 45, 127
  profile tidying 64, 65, 72, 78, 86, 92, 135, 150, 170
  regulation of 184
  role of 160
  spectacle of 147
  ubiquity 28
  use 30, 51, 56, 69, 133, 134, 137, 161, 184
  user content 60, 62, 118
  user control 82, 86
  worlds 138

social network(s)
  as space of rebellion 136
  expanding 84
  -ing sites 27, 30, 39, 45, 46, 52, 68, 84, 104, 118, 132
  See also social media
social steganography 17, 30, 110
socio
  -cultural assemblage 181
  -economic status 133
sociology of doors 40
  See also Goffman, Erving
space(s)
  adult 148
  commercial 163
  desirable 23
  digital 28, 29, 30, 39, 46, 47, 78, 89, 117, 118, 137, 142, 162
  domestic 128, 162
  ephemeral 105
  Facebook as 125
  family 125
  holding 64, 176
  hybrid 42
  liminal 164, 165
  personal 55, 138
  physical 28, 89, 137, 162
  public 89, 180
  private 21, 88, 105, 162
  quasi-public 103, 106, 180
  semi-public 101
  share(d/ing) 52, 88
  social 138
  virtual 141, 162
Spechler, Joshua A. 13
stable individual 44, 82
  See also Giddens, Anthony
story-telling 83
stranger(s) 27, 58, 104
structural
  challenges 181
  changes 79
  conditions 79
student(s) 66

surveillance 24, 78, 130, 137–140, 145
  by employers 80, 92
  by family members 130, 137
  by friends 139, 174
  discipline 136
  institutional 88
  intimate 142
  looking in 174
  See also emotion(s/al)
survival strategy 114, 118
symbolic
  control 30
  equipment 37
  interactionism 39, 44

T

tagging 36, 37, 45, 59, 61, 111, 113, 120, 147, 153, 172
  geo- 155, 161
  re- 113
  un- 36, 96, 113
technology/ies
  developments 21
  in everyday life 40, 166
  knowledge of 139
  new forms 105
  old 40
  shaping by 86
teenage(rs) 19, 23, 62, 101, 105, 106
  (in)experience 53, 69, 73, 129, 130, 134, 136, 144, 159, 160
  bedroom 21, 54, 55, 64, 89, 162, (*see also* space(s))
TikTok 8
time
  investment of 16
Timehop 64
Timeline
  See Facebook
Tinder 18, 97, 106, 155
  See also romantic relationship(s)
transition(s)
  between platforms 21
  critical 129
  formalise(d) 129
  from education to employment 77–97
  in life 19, 84, 153, 165, 175, 178
  narratives 44, 63
  See also graduation(s)
transition texts 85
transparent/cy
  See trust
travel 29, 111, 113, 147, 148, 154–161
  as transformational 157, 165
  cost of 156–157, 159
  humanitarian tourism 155
  tourism economy 155
  See also leisure
trend(s) 22
  See also fad(s)
trust 58, 174, 175
  building 104
Tumblr 18, 53, 68
Twitter 18, 68, 106
  (re)tweet 96
  subtweet 110

U

uploading
  See post(s/ing)

V

vague-booking 110
vanguard 19, 30
vent(ing) 16
violent/ce 80, 150, 180
  See also behaviour
virtue signalling 155
Vitak, Jessica 8, 16–17, 28, 72, 105
volunteerism 156
votes/ing 80
vulnerability 90

W

Watts, Andrew 14, 16
    See also blog(s)
well-being 102, 117, 118, 120, 170, 180–183
    protecting 183
Whatsapp 2, 14, 18, 169
work
    See employment
world(s)
    -building 145
    cultural 164
    economic 164
    -liness 160
    social 129, 164

Y

Year in Review 22, 86
    See also under Facebook, *see also* nostalgia, prompts

youth
    culture 52, 54, 162
    disowning 79
    erasure of 87, 96
    -ful excess 148, 166
    experienes of 31, 96, 177
    language of 105
    representation(s) of 105
    status of 158
    subcultures 162, 164
    young love 102
youthful construction of the self 27
    See also self
YouTube 111, 157, 161, 180

Z

Zuckerberg, Mark 2, 5, 20, 22, 23, 90, 91, 126

General Editor: *Steve Jones*

Digital Formations is the best source for critical, well-written books about digital technologies and modern life. Books in the series break new ground by emphasizing multiple methodological and theoretical approaches to deeply probe the formation and reformation of lived experience as it is refracted through digital interaction. Each volume in **Digital Formations** pushes forward our understanding of the intersections, and corresponding implications, between digital technologies and everyday life. The series examines broad issues in realms such as digital culture, electronic commerce, law, politics and governance, gender, the Internet, race, art, health and medicine, and education. The series emphasizes critical studies in the context of emergent and existing digital technologies.

Other titles include:

Felicia Wu Song
   Virtual Communities: Bowling Alone, Online Together

Edited by Sharon Kleinman
   The Culture of Efficiency: Technology in Everyday Life

Edward Lee Lamoureux, Steven L. Baron, & Claire Stewart
   Intellectual Property Law and Interactive Media: Free for a Fee

Edited by Adrienne Russell & Nabil Echchaibi
   International Blogging: Identity, Politics and Networked Publics

Edited by Don Heider
   Living Virtually: Researching New Worlds

Edited by Judith Burnett, Peter Senker & Kathy Walker
   The Myths of Technology: Innovation and Inequality

Edited by Knut Lundby
   Digital Storytelling, Mediatized Stories: Self-representations in New Media

Theresa M. Senft
   Camgirls: Celebrity and Community in the Age of Social Networks

Edited by Chris Paterson & David Domingo
   Making Online News: The Ethnography of New Media Production

To order other books in this series please contact our Customer Service Department:

peterlang@presswarehouse.com (within the U.S.)
orders@peterlang.com (outside the U.S.)

To find out more about the series or browse a full list of titles, please visit our website:

WWW.PETERLANG.COM